Universal Prostitution and Modernist Abstraction

Universal Prostitution and Modernist Abstraction

A COUNTERHISTORY

JALEH MANSOOR

Duke University Press
Durham and London 2025

Printed in the United States of America on acid-free paper ∞
Project Editor: Ihsan Taylor
Designed by Dave Rainey
Typeset in Minion Pro and Trade Gothic
by Westchester Publishing Services

Library of Congress Cataloging-in-Publication Data
Names: Mansoor, Jaleh, [date] author.
Title: Universal prostitution and modernist abstraction : a counterhistory / Jaleh Mansoor.
Description: Durham : Duke University Press, 2025. | Includes bibliographical references and index.
Identifiers: LCCN 2024041585 (print)
LCCN 2024041586 (ebook)
ISBN 9781478031758 (paperback)
ISBN 9781478028529 (hardcover)
ISBN 9781478060734 (ebook)
Subjects: LCSH: Art, Modern—20th century. | Labor in art. | Work in art. | Philosophy, Marxist. | Abstraction. | Communism and art. | Labor theory of value.
Classification: LCC N6494.M64 M357 2025 (print) | LCC N6494.M64 (ebook) | DDC 709.04/052—dc23/eng/20250121
LC record available at https://lccn.loc.gov/2024041585
LC ebook record available at https://lccn.loc.gov/2024041586

Cover art: Francis Picabia, *Universal Prostitution* (detail), 1916–17.

To the Young-Girl of whatever gender: Rise up! Know your values!
And for M, singular in your art of creating freedom.

CONTENTS

PREFACE

Ordinarily, the objects in front of one's perception and the field in which they appear, "things as they are," are understood to be concrete. That which is concretely tangible is real. This field and its apperceived objects are taken for reality.

What we see before us in everyday life is as natural as flowers. *Bouquet II*, a bouquet of flowers in a glass vase on a pedestal, is one such object. It was arranged by Dutch artists Willem de Rooij and Jeroen de Rijke in 2003 to summon nature itself and to out-speed the mimetic verisimilitude expected of Dutch still-life painting, which had been historically linked to memento mori, an allegorical reminder of death's imminence in everyday life. By presenting live flowers as an apparently unmediated thing in itself, the work seems to make a bold claim to the field of the real—commonly understood as empirically present objects. But after a moment of luxuriating in the flowers' fragrance and vital color, the viewer might realize the degree to which a strange reversal takes place. The bouquet flips metaphysical categories around to stand them on their feet in the space of another reality.

The artists' choice of blooms summons a living history of flowers in analogy to European cycles of accumulation, mustering the way in which tulips were extracted from western Asia and initially functioned as a form of currency acceptable for payment, so invested was their immediate material value. The bouquet joins tulips, bred through centuries to generate new subspecies such as "French tulips," with other genera culled from Dutch-occupied lands, such as orchids and certain rose varieties. The flowers act as symbol of sensuous accumulation as such. All are equally seductive and fragile. Part of the tension of the piece derives from the recognition that this sensuous composition invokes the ponderous historicity of colonial dispossession in capital's second major cycle of accumulation, the Dutch cycle of the seventeenth century, but are ephemeral and short-lived in the fact of their current embodiment.[1] Conjugating transient natural resources with fluid finance, sensual opulence expressed as currency might be identified as the work's primary referent.

Flowers wither and decay, their brief life set in contrast to the persisting capacity of capital itself. Yet in the grand scheme of historical time, so do cycles of accumulation, leaving bewilderment on the part of social relations abandoned by capital flight.

And while material fragility attendant on economic crisis once signaled a sea change in the geopolitics of accumulation and in the civil sector built to mediate it, now, in the fifth century of the Anthropocene, it suggests the precarity of global life itself, and of the delicate interdependence of the natural world in which we as a species are embedded. We, the viewer, are suddenly set into identification with the piece for reasons other than the consciousness of natural death evoked by traditional memento mori. That we are currently, collectively, as biopolitically contingent as flora suddenly strikes through thinking the piece as silently yet effectively as the bouquet's material fragrance. Produced by the same forms of wealth that are historically and socially generated, and yet just as "natural," we are equally determined by a man-made climate that make species death quite possible in capital's race to the bottom of resource extraction. We are as tenuously contingent on our own conjugation with value extraction as the flowers, accelerating and ratcheting our mortal contingency on time itself. The memory of flowers as a historical vehicle for financial exchange precipitates the self-reflexive recognition that we too are nodes in similar circuits, that much of our time is spent organizing ourselves as vehicles for material exchanges that enable our own brief lives. As workers earning a living and consumers who consume resources to stay alive, we are conduits in material paths of exchange, selling our labor time and purchasing that which keeps us vital.

Bouquet II rallies not just the memory of cultural symbolizations of the concrete reality of death in traditional Dutch painting, or the actual circulation and accumulation of currency for which the flowers historically acted as vehicle, but also that other language of flowers drawn from the domain of eros. "It is to flowers in general, and not to any specific flower, that one is tempted to attribute the strange privilege of revealing the presence of love," as surrealist Georges Bataille noted in "The Language of Flowers."[2] Bataille is quick to toss these flowers-as-metaphorical-eros into an equally metaphorical "puddle of liquid manure" in order to perform the operation for which he is best known, attacking idealism by locating the base and low within the symbolism of beauty.[3] At heart is the transposition from low to high, and equally of high to low, in which meaning switches places as though gliding through a semiotic fluidity in which transpositions move like a gentle tide against fixed reference.

But this "multiplicity of reference" set into play by *Bouquet II* as a kind of instant art history lesson and reminder of polysemy signals yet another perceptual economy, one foundational to and yet occluded by modernism: the anonymous and abstract labor-time that by the second decade of the twentieth century made traditional representation impossible by changing the very fabric of the reality to be represented, and at a faster pace than mimetic correlation could ever hope to keep pace with. Lived experience no longer afforded a grasp of the social field necessary to the most basic encounters and exchanges. A new metabolic of everyday life required a new means of articulation. Received representational forms lost any referential capacity in the face of seismic social change wrought by an accelerating economic metabolic known as real or concrete abstraction, the elaboration of second nature by labor-power. That which we have come to know as "aesthetic abstraction" or nonrepresentational art in the culture sector is one indicator of a crisis in representation.

I offer two paths into the forms of articulation that the entwinement of concrete and aesthetic abstraction begins to generate, and of which the contemporary Dutch artists' *Bouquet* is but one allegory.

This book is about that which is everywhere and therefore nowhere, like the very air in a room, an element containing every other facet of life and yet impossible to finally contain and objectify, much less symbolize: abstract social relations. What could the rarefied place of art, of aesthetic abstraction, tell us about everyday social abstraction? I wrote this book in conversation with Rosalind Krauss's *The Optical Unconscious* on the one hand and T. J. Clark's *Farewell to an Idea* on the other. Both of those art history classics are about abstract art. Both books try to address what it is that abstract art mediates in the absence of fixed reference after late nineteenth-century Impressionist painting. Both are about invisibility in relation to consciousness. *The Optical Unconscious* locates an invisible and opaque field under the modernist episteme of self-reflexivity. Krauss characterizes this field as an all but impenetrable place that nonetheless motivates instance after instance of artistic breakthrough from the work of Marcel Duchamp to that of Eva Hesse. That hidden place of motivation for Krauss is desire, which erupts into the pictorial field through any number of indexes. By contrast, Clark set the same discursive parameters, that around modernism, into a reflection of modern social dynamics reticulated through the question of collective subjectivity. Clark sees as epochal (Modernism) a time where social relations became increasingly determined by invisible class dynamics. Here, the figure of the prostitute is the very signal of modernity's social structure. Both books looked to aesthetic practices across the period known as modernism to trace their understanding of social modernity at large.

How, if at all, did these books forge a conversation? Their intersection meets in the artwork they both address, if not in their respective arguments. A conversation surfaces, vividly to me, around the question they hold in common and yet both defer. How could we locate a place where unconscious compulsions and social determinations meet, insofar as this question binds Marxism and psychoanalysis across any number of fields? That intersection strikes me as thematized in the artworks they both privilege again and again. For one, it might describe any hundreds if not thousands of paintings either thematizing prostitution or idealizing the working model in the form of the classical nude; it might also describe the Duchampian ready-made central to psychoanalytic accounts of modernism. But it marks a blindsighted intersection in the discourse.

One term for this problem, the embodied mediation between labor, capital and desire, prostitution, often serves as metaphor or allegory in the humanities. But it qualifies modernity in a specific way: it begins to signal an ontology emergent in lived, historical time for a range of activities that do not, strictly speaking, involve sex. The term *prostitution* ceases to be literal but at the same time is anything but allegorical. Flickering between a description and a metaphor, this term almost stands in for a form of mediation that has gone unseen, an open secret of Modernism.

Within the space of modernist culture, prostitution comes to stand as a kind of shorthand for real abstraction in social space across any number of contexts. Real abstraction is everywhere and nowhere, invisibly mediating social relations in the interests of value accumulation, organizing human lives in the service of surplus, through the sale of labor-power. Modern art signals an unconscious forged in the perceptual mediation of a more fundamental and unrepresentable transformation, that of concrete individual labor-become-abstract value.

The two paths I advance by way of introduction answer both Clark's and Krauss's books. The first introduction takes abstraction as a problem for epistemology and therefore for aesthetic knowledge. Looking at struggles to articulate the way that capital had made the world itself abstract, I locate those writers and artists, beginning with Karl Marx, who have tried to describe an emergent second nature. While *Bouquet II*'s presentation of flowers and Bataille's writing on flowers both circumscribe a *seeming* nature that in fact operates as a vehicle for everything from erotic reverie to industry and cash, an emergent discourse tries to locate abstraction in everyday life at the intersection of embodiment and impersonal economic forces.

In the constellation of meanings reopened by Rooij and Rijke's *Bouquet II*, a polyvalence made all the more playful and frustrating by sly deference to a "real," as though the flower's metonymy for "nature" could establish any final grounding, one stable question inheres: Why is eros in any form of symbolization permeable to the question of currency? Money is, after all, anything but embodied and specific. Why are the artists' choice of flowers not just any flowers, which for Bataille are indiscriminately erotic, but specific to the historical memory of early modern Dutch money? From metaphors of sexual pleasure to conduits of capital, the flowers accompany the voyage of inexplicable and seemingly alchemical transformations across imaginary and material terrain. But how does one referential destination merge with its antonym so swiftly? If money is the representation of value—and value the representation of labor, as Diane Elson and other theorists of the value-form have noted—how does desire, affiliated with the pleasure principle and therefore anathema to the discipline of productive exertion measured by time, come to enter the set of variables conjugable in the circuit of references opened by the flowers?[4] How does the representation of labor yield so easily to the symbolization of erotic attraction? Why would a vehicle for value work a double shift as the image of free drives and inclinations, above all an erotic orientation? Why does art become a way of probing the connection between sex and work, held in tense relation and at once sublimated and heightened in a still common cultural mystification of sex which lends itself to bourgeois morals that are ultimately indifferent to anything outside the property relation and yet which offer continual titillation?

Marxist philosopher Jason Read notes that "money becomes the general equivalent of desire."[5] Reading Spinoza, who "considers money as primarily indexed to desire" with Marx in order to probe the connection between the symbolic and material understanding of work, Read's explanation is immediately material. Money is "indexed to desire" because it can procure any embodied joy or pleasure. It is a vehicle that affords transport in a material dimension. What dimension do the flowers take us on a metaphorical ride toward, symbolic or real? And why are these material and metaphorical registers so structurally entwined as to seem indivisible?

Universal prostitution, the hybrid term introduced by Marx in 1844, as much as the eponymous artwork from 1916–17 by Dada artist Francis Picabia that lends this book its title, and finally this book itself, are all three a query into the "general equivalent of desire." If money, born of labor, is the index of desire, how does it crosses registers so fluidly? How does anonymous labor-time, valorized in transaction and fetishized in beautiful yet troubling objects, come to be confused with sensual life itself? If the value-form circulates through changing forms, how does money come to be the general equivalent of desire as much as of value? To what extent are classical metaphors of eros, from flowers to bodies, subsumed under the logic of the transaction rather than the lure of sex, of pleasure, of bodies or anything external to the tautology of the value-form?

As I argue in the introductions to follow, art had prefigured the way in which abstract labor—anonymous, commodified, and yet coursing in its myriad forms throughout capital's network of circulation—had rewritten nature itself. From Georges Seurat's painting to de Rooij's postconceptualism, the problem of figuring the new metabolic, of everyday life referred to as modernity, demanded new forms of articulation, new media, new concepts. This book tries to probe that metaphysic.

ACKNOWLEDGMENTS

This book is inspired by tremendous gratitude to those who have offered me friendship, support, and intellectual shelter. I would like to thank above all Kenneth Wissoker at Duke University Press for his faith and patience; Terry Enslin, whose professional expertise reminded me not only of my sanity but my capacity to explore its limits; to Trevor Stark for stoking my intellectual wonder and being a true friend; to Maya Andrea Gonzalez, Fulvia Carnevale, James Thornhill, Rosalind Krauss, Benjamin Buchloh, Giovanna Zapperi, Hannah Black, Robert Hurley, and Isabelle Graw for being my muses and carrying my consciousness aloft but also for demonstrating strength and compassion against all odds and when I needed to summon those capacities most.

I'm immensely thankful for and to comrades and colleagues who have invited me to test parts of this book's argument: Kersten Stakemeier, Philip Wolstetter, Sean Landis and the Red May crew, Gean Moreno, Angela Hartunianian, Samir Gandesha, Cinzia Aruzza, Kristen Romberg, Rafaelle Bedereida, Rosalia Pasqualino di Marineo, Lucca Bochioni, Edwin Adnan, Jenifer Paparero, Amanda Beech, Matilda Guidello Guidi, Zach Hicks, Nicolas Anderman, Conrad Bongard Hamilton, and Lily Woodruff, many of you with whom a glass of wine and conversation proved equally healing and mind bending, and just as many at a distance during pandemic lockdown. I'm beyond thankful to Ina Blom, Dina Al-Kassim, Nizan Shaked, Judith Rodenbeck, Arlen Austen, Judith Grant, Hilda Fernandez, and Adam Lerner. You sustain me.

I'd like to thank my colleagues in the Department of Art History, Visual Art and Theory at the University of British Columbia, on Musqueam ancestral land in so-called Canada. Special shout-out to my comrade Gareth James, whose art shines like a bright bulb in the long PNW winter, reminding me of Francis Picabia's *Lampe*.

Thanks also to Yates McKee, Sabine Bitter, Jeff Derksen, Vanessa Parent, Tatiana Mellema, Jacopo Galimberti, Teresa Kittler, Connor Crable, Katherine Jackson, Robin Simpson, Shane Wu, Ophelia Yingqiu, Ido Radon, Beth Hinderliter, and Emily Katrencik. I'm enormously grateful to Brandon Leung, Andrew Ascherl, Yasmin Amaratunga, and Ryan Kendall.

Finally, I am grateful to my late father, Mohammad Mansoor, and mother, Donna Mansoor, for their awkward, eccentric brilliance and shy beauty.

Introduction 1

Toward a Materialist Formalism

It is no controversy that the term *abstraction* summons the memory of abstract painting and any number of aesthetic experiments across media at the turn of the last century. *Abstraction* recalls the once urgent and tacitly politicized exploration of nonreferential mediations of new and often estranging sense perception generated by modernity and a newly emergent social ecology of material survival. At their origins, variations on this exploration of aesthetic abstraction—from Stéphane Mallarmé, James Joyce, Theodor Adorno, and Walter Benjamin to Virginia Woolf, Gertrude Stein, and Clement Greenberg, among many others—were attuned to facture and material process as a degree zero from which to constitute an artwork appropriately attentive to modernity, and therefore historicist in its sensitivity to contemporary materials and methods. In this implicitly political and leftist constellation of aesthetic thinking at its most current, the work's material articulation would of necessity *index*, if not represent, the dynamism of the material transformation of everyday life at an ontological level under capital.[1] This is to say that aesthetic abstraction seemed to signal a major shift in the way culture incorporated and in turn inscribed social reality: we might describe this transformation as one from a regime of representation to one of abstraction. It was as though the capacity of representation had dissolved under the increasing abstraction—estrangement, displacement, anonymity, and fragmentation—of everyday life, as though representation were historically foreclosed after seismic rupture at the molecular level of daily life sparked by a new metabolic of production and consumption.

This kind of sensitivity to history at the level of *form*, of an impressionability and articulation susceptible to new modalities of perception and apperception, preoccupied writers who acknowledged that history introduces not just new objects and technological inventions but ways of seeing, sensing, and knowing. These relationships internalized and responded to changes in the social field. As Rosalind Krauss writes, "Cultural production [is] the impossible attempt to construct an imaginary space with which to work out unbearable contradictions produced within the real field of history."[2] Earlier, Adorno had argued for the inevitable social kernel at the heart of even the most abstract cultural mediations: "There is no material content, no formal category of artistic creation, however mysteriously changed and unknown to itself, which did not originate from the empirical reality from which it breaks," reminding us that so-called autonomy is not only always provisional but also nested in a "totality," against a social and historical horizon.[3] If autonomy ever meant anything, it was art's ability to turn away not from social entanglements but instead from an all-consuming market. At stake was the horizon itself—that shifting and contingent "totality"—or at least a way to somehow figure it, however much the cultural work might remain irreducible or opaque to it. As Adorno noted, the "mysterious transmission" that the artist or culture worker generates may not be transparent or legible to that producer themselves but nonetheless remains part of an empirical reality, however seemingly ineffable. For his part, Greenberg openly avowed the umbilical cord of gold that tethered artists to the social system via the patron and the institution.[4] Key here was the way in which the work could be possible *despite*, not because of, its inscription into and fugitive escape from "gold" in the circuits of production, circulation, and reception.

And yet Piet Mondrian's resolution to the structural contradiction of flatness and depth, and of resonance against rationality in *New York City* (1942) (figure I1.1), that quintessential paradigm of painterly abstract modernism, suggests that the principle of the aesthetic mediation of impossible social contradiction, as Krauss might say, in the form of "aporetic braiding" is not recognized in the discourse as a formal allegory of a utopian collective social form. Rather, it is seen as an arrogant bid for aesthetic autonomy, a purely aesthetic sovereignty indifferent to social relations.[5] In other words, a model for progressive optical dynamics, one that accomplishes the seemingly impossible—a convincing negation of figure and ground, facture and depicted space—to disarticulate a received traditional spatial orientation to the real world is misunderstood as independent of that world. In this paradox, common to most art historical discourse, the notion of autonomy is willfully

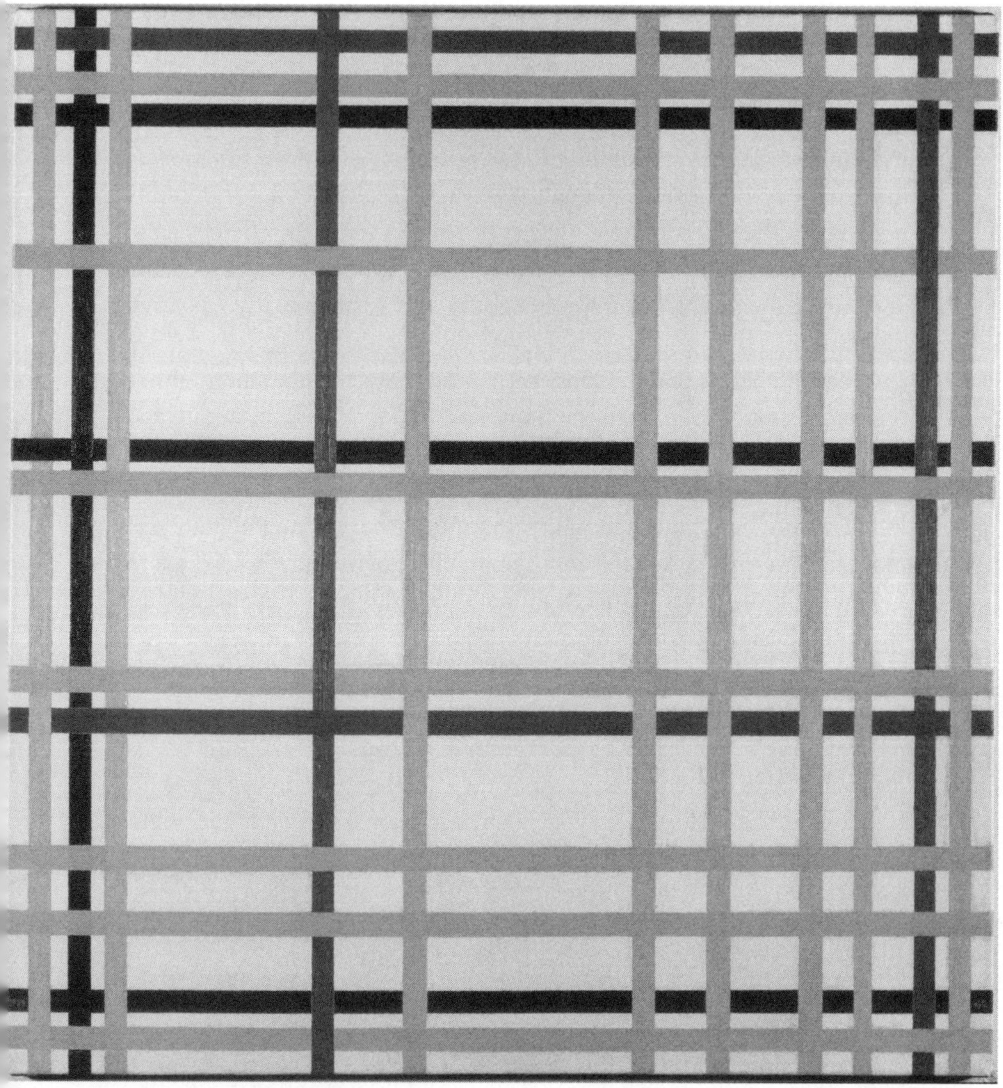

Fig. I1.1 Piet Mondrian, *New York City*, 1942. © CNAC/MNAM, Dist. RMN-Grand Palais / Art Resource, NY.

misunderstood to mean that the work is ahistorical, apolitical, and disinterested in the contradictions of the real social field through which it might offer a guide, however much open to idealist formal interpretation.

It is thereby reduced to the very logic of the fetish it wrestled against in its manifest dialectical *resistance* to the reduction of human experience to the extraction of surplus value in the everyday capitalist lifeworld. But this book is not the place to argue against travesty in the doxa whereby an artwork is either an illustration of something in this world or a self-contained alien world. Instead, another form of abstraction insinuates itself *under* that discourse.

What gets lost is that the modernists who write about aesthetic abstraction took politics to be the very framework of *any* emergent debate about art's capacities, and its relevance.[6] Taking as a given the Enlightenment imperative that aesthetics is a form of intellectual query both equal and other to science, as well as a dialectical critique of that very same Enlightenment, modernist aesthetics aspired to a kind of purposive purposelessness that functions all the more politically for being *other* to the rationalized and instrumental field of calculated rigidity.

If anything, were we to shelf the absurdism of most denunciations of the discourse of autonomy on the grounds of apoliticism, we might notice that most of these writers could be more accurately accused of explicitly bracketing their discursive query away from the complexity of an *economic* field. If they could be said to have avoided anything, it would be not the political sphere but the hidden abode of production and equally occluded market, which at once neutralizes and replicates social divisions across political ideologies. That zone was kept discreetly out of sight and mind, all the better to present it as a sublimated contradiction in culture and in art. One word that did, however, begin to probe this other economic sphere might be *reification*.

In her explanation of the socially forged cogito undergirding modern vision, Krauss points out that the problem of reification is a given, a constituted and constitutive function of perception that is contemporaneous and correlative, even causal, to capitalism's self-replication through circuits of value. But this causality or relation between reification in the world and its expression in culture does not identify itself in the space of representation. Krauss reconstructs a well-noted debate in the interwar period among Western and cultural Marxists in which the mutually enforcing relationship between politics and aesthetics is accepted as inherent but in which the specificity of a timely aesthetics *appropriate* to history becomes an object of heated contention in a search for examples.

The modernists understood that forms of seeing are themselves historically contingent. If modernity, which is to say capitalism, had made the world anew at the level of people, places, and things (proletarianization, urbanization, the commodity), how would culture remain timely and relevant to its transformative shocks, or shocking transformations? While modernists insisted on new forms to articulate new worlds, some equally leftist traditionalists thought that traditional culture provided a constant against which to measure change. Nowhere did this debate take on more acute proportions than within the Frankfurt School. Georg Lukács, who elaborated Marx's term *reification*, ironically took the traditionalist view. The modernists, Adorno and others, by contrast argued that perception itself was fundamentally changed and therefore, as a mediation for cognition fundamental to equally changing social relations, new ways of sensing must be pioneered by an avant-garde.[7]

At stake were the means, not the ends, according to Krauss.

> Georg Lukács, deploring this technologizing of the body, this need to abstract and reify each of the senses in a submission of human subjectivity to the model of positivist science, would have found nothing to argue with in such an [modernist] analysis. He would only have objected to its tone, to its assumption, which Greenberg shared with Adorno, that in the withdrawal of discipline to sensory experience . . . there was something utopian. For a utopian modernism was insisting that this sensory stratum newly understood as discrete, as self-sufficient, as autonomous—this very stratification—permitted an experience of rescue and retreat, a high ground uncontaminated by the instrumentality of labor and science, a preserve of play and thus a model of freedom.[8]

I will return to Krauss's casual definition of technology as a function of (material) abstraction that facilitates the reification of experience, but for now, Lukács's term *reification* might be read as a way to *describe* the effects of the capitalist organization of labor-power as a function of time, that which is strangely sidelined along with "science" in the quoted passage.

For Lukács, Marx's analysis in *Capital* shows that the fetishization of labor-time in the form of the final commodity hides its process of manufacture by human hands. We might add here that modern art often emphasized the phenomenology of its making as a form of *resistance*, or alterity, in relation to the commodity's tendency to conceal living labor. And for its part, while the commodity is structurally opaque to its origin, insofar as that origin is abstract, anonymous, and generalized, it is, as art historian Sven Lütticken puts it, an index nonetheless: a severed one. Unlike an indexical sign that points to its source and origin, the commodity is a "severed" index because the capitalist mode of production requires a new division and socialization of labor that renders opaque the social process of making itself—to the point of *seeming* to become almost independent of the social field in which its replication is embedded. We have heard this before. The charge of social opacity against aesthetic autonomy begins to sound like a displacement of the commodity's impenetrability, except for the way in which the latter appears instead like a fetish. As socially necessary—necessary, that is, to surplus extraction, the division and recomposition of components, including labor-power, the time spent in the process of manufacture or of delivering services is reintegrated in the interest of capital rather than at the free will of the individual or the collective worker, however free he or she may appear to be to "freely" sell that labor-time. Beyond the seemingly bounded space of work, forms of estrangement and anonymity forged in the recomposition of labor enter a winder social dynamic, which also remains oriented to work. The social field echoes the way in which value production becomes the dominant social organizing principle. In other words, the social field comes to mime and *performs* the fact of socially necessary labor-time as the very substance of modern life. It is in this sense that the commodity stands as an *index*—broken only to the extent that its conditions of emergence made possible by any number of anonymous hands and minds are impossible to trace.

Lukács "deplores" the modern dismantling of traditional form in early twentieth-century art and literature for the way in which it too seems to mimic the very nature of the commodity. It is estranging, jarring, depersonalizing. For him, the opacity of modern art is only the sad reflection of the reification of the commodity, whose mode of production through socially necessary labor-time makes it impossible to connect to time, place, hand, or intention.

By contrast, the modernists Adorno and Greenberg both saluted estranged, intensified culture as a way of remaining critical and timely *within* the fabric of a modernity that was newly and recursively recomposed at an almost molecular level by socially necessary labor-time. Key here is "labor-time" as a quantified quotient, in distinction to the laborer's subjective experience. In return for a wage, time is bought and sold on a labor market that is indifferent to the erstwhile community existence of the worker or their daily experiential life in a social totality. What matters to an abstract totality (both profit's bottom line and the everyday reproduction of the social field) is labor-power and forms of dis- and rearticulated skill. A labor market becomes the impersonal engine of society over time, overshadowing historically entrenched forms of community.[9]

For Adorno and Greenberg, the very fact that the modern estranged work demands of the viewer some exploration of its making affords the latter a space of query away from calculating self-interest, a place of suspension in a momentary apperceptive identification with the artwork itself. While modernists may have disagreed with some avant-garde forms, such as the Duchampian ready-made about which Greenberg said "anything can be reconventionalized on the spot," they understood that art was autonomous only insofar as it was not fungible or made of expropriated labor-time.[10] A last repository of purposelessness, if not traditional intention, the work of art held open a place of imagination as well as a degree zero of agency through negation.

At once summoned and warded off in the reception and production of the (art)work, the fact of socially necessary labor-time stands at the heart of modernist opacity. Lukács's theory of reification, derived from Marx's passages on the commodity fetish in which things take on the agency of subjects while subjects are refashioned as things in the blind field of capital, becomes a kind of conceptual shorthand for the strange way in which cycles of value production and circulation come to inscribe all of social life as equally reified experience, equally estranged and artificially produced. The hidden substance of this social transformation constitutive of reified experience, estranged labor-power, is the common constituent matter overwritten by the expression of any number of tropes across examples of modernist aesthetics.

For example, Mondrian's *New York City* offers a kind of visually reverberating contradiction at once clarifying contradiction while denying a false or trite closure. For Lukács, this thin line of differentiation between the abstracted artwork and the reified sense perception of daily life in relation to circuits of value would be dangerously narrow, a distinction so delicate as to simply adjust the individual to impersonal forms of exchange. For Adorno, Greenberg, and others, the only way out was through. Heightened, challenging, and dialectical perceptual experience triggered by the work was to operate as a kind of prophylactic against reified consciousness. In a sense, in the end, the artwork's broad reception brokered a deal that resulted in both reified perception and fetishized objects.

But for these modernists, the political problem with tradition in a new and modern sensory landscape was that it offered trite and immediate closure, and in this was almost indistinguishable from the immediate gratification promised by the commodity—for which a too steep price was paid through labor itself. Traditional forms of culture were no longer experientially accountable and therefore tendered more of a deferral than a real confrontation with the changing field of the real. True defiance would require a new form of mediation. Conventionalized culture failed to demand that the viewer be alert to the ultimately irreducible component parts of the work, whereby finality is held in abeyance so that dynamic processes have a chance to be set in motion, even if only at the level of consciousness. Otherwise, were cognizance not asked to sense itself sensing, it might sink into stasis and a kind of habituated and dangerously delusional representation of life against its own interest.

Rehearsing the undergirding tenets of the modernist project in aesthetic abstraction, Krauss, via literary theorist Fredric Jameson (via his reading of Louis Althusser), turns her analysis to the unconscious. Jameson's approach had influenced a generation for whom ideology critique was common to political culture in the academy from the 1970s to the 1990s, from Edward Said to Stuart Hall to Jameson himself. In this way, a deal was struck between Lukács's and Adorno's (and Benjamin's and Krauss's own) Marxism. But at what price?

The figure of the sea is one example of a modernist trope that begins to limn the open secret of labor and value and that at once denies and addresses estranged labor sold on a market. This figure recurs across modernism, from Impressionist seascapes to geometric reduction. It is presented again and again as an optically aesthetic object that also allegorizes an overwritten articulation of the totality of a world reorganized through abstraction. That is, in modernism, it indirectly articulates a world reconstituted through the sale of socially disarticulated, metricized time transposed through humans into abstract value, or currency. In the passage of substance from subject to object inherent in the commodity and therefore to a social field more broadly, the labor-time of countless lives is expressed as in the value and price of objects, as though by magic. Art here is understood to doubly raise and defer the question of value in a dialectical relation; it acts as a mimetic exacerbation, a ratcheting or reduplication of reification, while simultaneously resisting that reification by refusing any finality.

In her lucid scrutiny of Mondrian's *Pier and Ocean 5 (Sea and Starry Sky)* (1915) (which she also sees as a reworking of Claude Monet's *Impression Sunrise* [1872] [figures I1.2 and I1.3]) and, crossing media, of Joseph Conrad's *Lord Jim*, Krauss notes the way in which descriptions of the sea both dismantle and generously offer spatial plenitude. However, reduced, schematic, and almost notational in form, the modern work still delivers the gratification

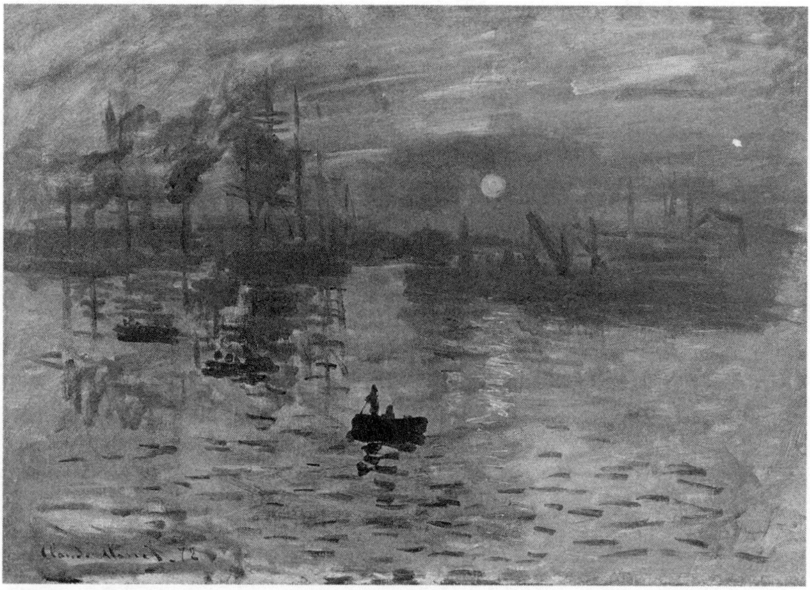

Fig. I1.2 Claude Monet, *Impression Sunrise*, 1872. HIP / Art Resource, NY.

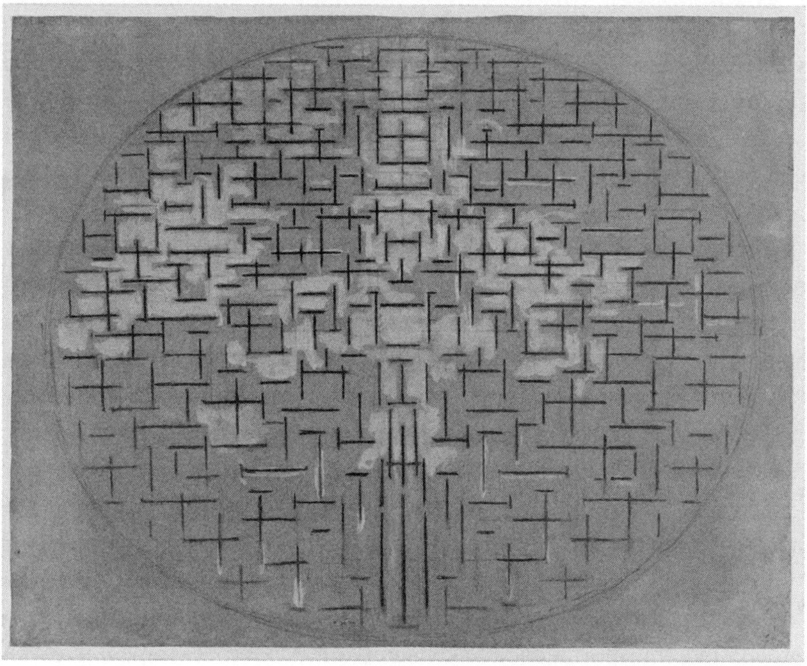

Fig. I1.3 Piet Mondrian, *Pier and Ocean 5 (Sea and Starry Sky)*, 1915 (inscribed 1914). © The Museum of Modern Art / Licensed by SCALA / Art Resource, NY.

once guaranteed by a referent: "The sea is a special kind of medium for modernism because of its perfect isolation, its detachment from the social, its sense of self enclosure and above all its opening onto a visual plenitude that is somehow heightened and pure, both a limitless expanse and a sameness."[11] Here, she notes how Jameson attends to the way that Conrad seems to reconstitute the sea at the level of language, just as Mondrian reconstitutes visual perception's component elements in an interrelated set of plusses and minuses, an aesthetic reduction that is somehow already a feature of the sea itself, and that nonetheless opens onto a pregnant fullness of depth, the way illusionism once did—but now, with any conclusive finality pulled out from under it, delivered only as a fleeting optical experience.

Bolstered by Jameson's account of the way modernists seem to abstract the sea at the level of craft and facture across media, Krauss acknowledges—in passing—that what is transposed is really the space of commerce. If Conrad's novel *Lord Jim* were to abstract anything in particular, it would be the fact of the sale of expropriated labor in the "medium" of dehumanized persons.[12] Literary analyst Sylvia Wynter, in her exploration of the significance of the sea as both the site of the Middle Passage and as a framework to grasp political economic contradiction in modern culture, argues that this trope complicates Marxism by drawing out and allegorizing three kinds of value producers: the enslaved, violently set into unremunerated production for the purposes of accumulation; the workers, who are socially coerced to set themselves into circulation for the purposes of accumulation; and the consumers, who guarantee the realization of value by purchasing the goods made by workers to keep cycles of accumulation moving.[13]

The sea is thus a "special kind of medium for modernism" on multiple entwined levels. As much a figure for emancipated optical experience as a matrix of the unconscious market whereon human time is appropriated and sold, the sea becomes a "medium" of all three forms of circulation. It were as though the abstraction of Monet's, Mondrian's, and Conrad's work were tacitly paying homage to the very conditions against which it holds a brief fugitive moment of reflection.

Pier and ocean: that non-site where what has been extracted from living labor, enslaved and freely sold, set into circulation as so much exchange value in potential waiting to be ratified on a market is summoned and deferred. This is the sea *as* circulation, as the matrix of networks that cross production, transportation, and consumption. Monet's seascape *Impression Sunrise*, which inaugurated the category "Impressionism" at the moment that its author sought financial emancipation from the academy and the state apparatus, could be said to have aestheticized the ocean and its port to the point where that aestheticized figure of a labor to capital relationship appears as an instance of "autonomy." But the smokestacks on the horizon that reconstitute the very air, or paint (they begin to feel interchangeable), of *Impression Sunrise* suggest otherwise. The place of market trade in which the ultimate commodity—labor-power itself—is both highly differentiated yet disjointed from the individuality of the labor bearer, detached from any context or place or even time, made anonymous and interchangeable and set into circulation, is, after all, the *unconsciously* privileged site of aesthetic self-reflexivity. Paradoxically, this offers the viewer an encounter of the contradiction between consciousness and its *other* unconscious: the impersonal, abstract place of transaction. The unity of the contradiction could not be more evident, held in suspension, and avoided.

In all three paradigmatic examples cited here (Monet, Mondrian, Conrad), the sea is the very matrix of the metabolic process that misreadings of autonomy accuse it of denying: the market. Krauss for her part skips right over this particular social unconscious. Instead, she takes this form of abstraction to be the figure of the cogito. The cogito, or ego founded on cognition, is also founded on the repression of its unconscious against which the repressed volcanically resurfaces as the symptom. However true this may be, she misses an altogether different unconscious: the dazzling field of market exchange, which she has already explained away through the problem of reification as Lukács understands it, and where the problem of value and its transformation in relation to human perception might be finally addressed.[14] In other words, the artwork presents itself as the crucible to decode this other scene of reification rather than to take it as a foregone conclusion. If anything, both sites (the unconscious and the market) are equally gathered *and* occluded in the abstracted presentation of the sea, or rather in the presentation of the sea *as* the very matrix of abstraction. What drives the forms of exchange mediated on so many levels by this non-place of the sea, already hidden in plain sight in the first instance?

The most honest and strident account of art making across the twentieth century as a function of the split subject, of the psyche that is driven as much by an unconscious as by the artist's own design, *The Optical Unconscious* missed only the location and *social* nature of that unconscious. *The Optical Unconscious* situated the work of modernist and avant-gardist art as at once the aesthetic space of the reified cogito *and* its reflexive unmaking through explorations of unconscious interruption. There, the artwork is shown to be forged as much by unconscious drives as by an urge to work out compositionally unresolvable contradiction from the social field in the limits of the concrete material artwork. But its argument overlooked the extent to which those two constitutive components derive from yet another *other scene*, this time other to the individual unconscious. The artwork desublimates the very masterful aesthetic abstractions to which it consciously or unconsciously aspires by reminding us of this economic register, which washes against the parameters of the frame shored up against it, like Monet's or Mondrian's or Conrad's ocean.

Iconic abstract works of art, such as those cited by Krauss, tacitly and unconsciously acknowledge that the world itself is abstract and that the work of art is painfully fragile insofar as it is "concrete." It is concrete because, standing in willful excess to the anonymous socially necessary labor-time that it indexes, it offers a momentary synthesis of a world made chaotic and seemingly arbitrary by capital.[15] In all three key examples of modernism, across media (painting, drawing, novel), labor-power itself is the structural condition of the scene against which the artist works out a momentary act of consciousness.

Wynter's reading, taken alongside Krauss's, suggests a kind of unconscious that is different from both the political unconscious posited by the analysis of ideology and the individual unconscious drives posited by psychoanalysis. If anything, the libidinal unconscious that Krauss identifies is intimately bound up with circuits of production through expropriation and exploitation as well as compulsory consumption. We might reread her privileged objects and conclude that as much as an optical unconscious, a social unconscious composed of labor scatters indices across modernism in the form of art.

So, if *The Optical Unconscious* is a response to *The Political Unconscious*, the present book is a response to both. It is about the cultural effects of an economic unconscious scattered everywhere and gathered nowhere. The most compelling and enigmatic works of the past 150 or so years mediate that other unconscious—and refuse it insofar as this might be possible for a fugitive moment in time, offering a fleeting clearing in consciousness, not where it "unveils" or "unmasks" this or that but where it can reconstitute its external field for itself, that which is mistaken for "autonomy."[16]

If anything, many artists have called out modernist abstraction on the basis that it is far from abstract, that it is in fact excessively concrete. In its emphasis on facture and assorted articulations of material and medium in relation to form, the "truth to materials" mythos that the formalists held dear, aesthetic abstraction's greatest pathos might be its concreteness. Contemporary artist Liam Gillick notes this as the *failure* of modernism, a lack rather than surfeit of abstraction.[17] Gillick's thesis might have been music to the ears of Russian formalists, those thinkers important to Stein, Pablo Picasso, and others who emphasized facture as that which is concrete on *this* side of the sign—the materiality of language or of paint, of film or of music—and who saw that facture as a place separate from and in dialectical resistance to the abstraction of value (they were thinking on the cusp of the 1917 Russian communist revolution after all, a revolution in every dimension of life and especially in the aesthetic redistribution of meaning, just before its reappropriation by the state apparatus around 1920). What emerges, then, is a kind of condition where "abstract" and "concrete" come to behave as empty signifiers insofar as both become at once opposed and interchangeable, like the famous "duck/rabbit" visual puzzle associated with modernist aesthetics.

All of this begs the question of what abstraction connotes, much less denotes, and by extension, the question of what concreteness might mean. Why must these descriptive terms generate such treacherous confusion, as though in mimicry of the opacity of the modernist artwork or worse, the opacity of the social field reflected in the commodity? It almost feels like a return to another kitschy question: which imitates which, so-called life or so-called art? What explanation might we offer for this?

In "The Open Secret of Real Abstraction," philosopher and cultural critic Alberto Toscano notes that the problem of distinguishing between abstract and concrete aspects of experience is one of perception, cognition, and formalization. Capitalist social relations restructured around the commodity and its capacity to generate surplus value exacerbate this condition. But this is trickier than it seems. Toscano sets out to demonstrate that abstraction is not that which might be clarified by Enlightenment projects of unmasking or by stripping off the putative veils of ideology. Rather, abstraction is everywhere objectively around all of us, in every moment of every day, irrespective of empirical verifiability and often impervious to local ideologies.[18] It is not that there is a hidden object but rather that abstraction is a material and historical operation that remodels the field of the real. Generated by social relations, it is the matrix of what is knowable or sayable at any given time and certainly more palpable, if diffuse, than any *thought* one could have of it. In other words, abstraction is the field of social relations that constitute the very warp and weft of human reality, against which any individual conscious thought is but a momentary fragment.

Toscano's pun, the notion of an "open secret" or of locating a secret that is in fact exposed everywhere, indicates a historical perceptual condition in which what is everywhere all at once becomes invisible if only because it becomes seemingly natural in its very hovering and ubiquitous if unnatural operation. A second nature, then, abstraction is to be discerned in the processes of capital rather than with any final "concrete truth or hidden essence that the abstractions of capital supposedly occlude."[19] Thinking on the part of individuals brackets the abstract field of the real. This is where Toscano parts ways with Althusserian theories of ideology. "To put it bluntly, abstraction precedes thought," he writes.[20] This means that for all his critical analysis of humanism and self-determination, Althusser continued to think within a framework wherein abstraction acted as a mask, veil, or misapprehension of the real via interpellation rather than as itself a form of reality.[21]

Immanent critique of ideology had it inside out, Toscano explains: objective conditions and the social reality we live within are abstract. Ideology (thought) begins on shaky ground insofar as it fails to acknowledge the conditions of its own possibility. Toscano turns to philosophy historian Roberto Finelli, who argues that insofar as abstraction is the very ontology of everyday life within capital, we are mistaken to reason by way of starting with what we find concrete and moving toward abstract thought. To have any cognitive grasp on the historical field of the real, we would do well to acknowledge abstraction itself as having recomposed the apparently concrete aspects of things. Therefore, the only way to begin to posit a social reality is to deduce it from abstractions and proceed to the concrete in relation to it. And of course, this is where the work of art gains its special relevance insofar as it bears a de-reifying function for political economist and philosopher Anita Chari and others who take the Lukácsian notion of reification as a point of entry into thinking capitalist everyday life itself.

Turning away from Althusserian notions of abstraction, Toscano points to the intervention of historian and philosopher Alfred Sohn-Rethel and, secondarily, to the Lacanian psychoanalyst Slavoj Žižek, who both argue that consciousness—thought—is but a stopgap measure against an external field of inchoate determinations. Moreover, this external field does not stand outside of human manufacture—and here both share a materialist episteme solidly rooted in Marx's analysis over and against ideology. This external field might be allegorized as the kind of social relations enacted in moments of transaction in the space of the market insofar as this is where the total circuit of appropriation, production, and consumption, the entire circuit of value itself, is synthesized. The market is the space of finality in the form of transactions. Capital can only grow in motion and through circuits wherein its forms transition from objects to money and back again; exchange is a provisional moment of absolute closure. The fully naturalized and seemingly fleeting moment of exchange ties together, invisibly, the otherwise "chaotic" atomized and anonymous social relations of everyday life. Members of social networks outside the perceivable and conceivable parameters of individual intention meet in exchange, reticulated through a market. Value reigns as sovereign, over and above any individual intention. This "real," then, is socially and historically composed yet operates outside the cultural epistemes or forms of socially oriented cognition capable of conceiving its dynamic.

A Lacanian theory of the unconscious is also at stake in relation to an economic unconscious.[22] While Jacques Lacan posits the unconscious as a repository of unconsciously internalized social codes perceived only subjectively as other and opaque, Žižek, following Sohn-Rethel, specifies a place that is *external* to the formation of the subject but which compels the subject's seemingly free or at least nominally self-conscious choices and actions.[23] And here we come full circle. For if the ultimate object of critique for both Lacan and Krauss, as well as any number of other modernist writers, had been the arrogant anthropocentric Cartesian cogito, Žižek and Toscano note the utter inability of this critique to begin to probe the nature of its object insofar as all move within a Kantian episteme that is blind to social actions outside the parameters of normative cognitive capacity. Marx implicitly posits a form of cognition capable of a political economic analysis *within* and *against* a contextual lifeworld that structurally blinds it to the sale of its own socially necessary labor on a circuit far beyond its conscious apperception.

What *constitutes* this field of social and therefore real abstraction? The circuit of value that is set into motion recursively in order to keep accumulation operative, becoming autonomous of human interest. The circuit of value breaks paths with the worker and consumer, and even with the individual capitalist, as part of a cycle of growth outside any situated human experience of it. For Žižek and Toscano, Sohn-Rethel's "real abstraction" offers a way of thinking this disconnect between capital and any specific empirical knowledge of it. This notion of "real abstraction" is drawn from but elaborated to supplement Marx's *Grundrisse* and *Capital*.

The aesthetic index offers momentary lucidity insofar as concrete value originating in labor yet untethered from its medium in any given person (or countless thereof) scatters signs of its extrahuman trail everywhere in culture.[24] We might read culture less as a sublimated and dialectically reworked political—and within the field of visual culture, optical—unconscious and more of an etiology of the gap between consciousness and the autonomy of the value-form (in a word, real abstraction) scattered everywhere in cultural practices, heightened in instances of art across the century. Art historian John Roberts has coined the phrase "a labor theory of culture," which he extracts from his reading of the Duchampian ready-made and its way of expressing anonymous socially necessary labor-time as the ontological matrix of modern life. Building on that, we might read some art forms such as the ready-made as reverse engineering alienated labor-time. Art's specific way of affording a vision into the social unconscious determined by value circulation is simultaneous with its attempt to prevent itself from collapsing into the commodity form itself.[25] Art is not a regular commodity, as Dave Beech and others have convincingly argued, but it has consistently prefigured and alerted vision to the dynamic between consciousness and its market unconscious, which draws on art's own concerns: skill in relation to value, agency in relation to a social order enacted on not only symbolic but also material terms. Art may be a model for other forms of the commodity but is not itself fungible and can de-reify as much as reify unconscious operations imposed by value's circuits of self-replication.

Marxist art historian Sven Lütticken situates Alfred Sohn-Rethel's project in the context of central European philosophical debates of the interwar period. For him, Sohn-Rethel describes money as a form that determines social relations invisibly and performatively, not unlike the way in which perspective—regardless of the particular iconography of the perspectival picture, from Perugino's *Christ Giving the Keys to St. Peter* (1481–82) to Raphael's paradigmatic *Marriage of the Virgin* (1504) to the universalizing *Last Supper* (1495–98) by Leonardo da Vinci—operates, always in the same way again and again as a formal articulation of consciousness as such, of human cognizance in reciprocity with a projected god. Irrespective of content, perspective itself sutures viewer to picture in a perceptual contract of illusionism, just as it interpolates the viewer into a Christian social contract. In other words, the form is operative in the social field, no matter what the particular iconographic content of the picture may be. This is not to diminish the latter but rather anchors it in an unconscious yet functional social context. While the visual architecture of perspective is historically derived, it comes to be constitutive of an accepted reality once it is naturalized. One rarely questions the fact that there are no straight lines in nature. Perspective, as that which falls outside the experientially or logically deducible, other to both nature and culture alike, is mathematically derived abstraction but becomes a symbolic form operating in parallel to language. Unlike language that most agree is arbitrary, it is seen as motivated by ontological certainty. This notion of form is indebted to Ernst Cassirer. More specifically yet, we owe this insight to Cassirer in a conjunctural moment in his project, just when he was elaborating his notion of "symbolic form" and about to debate Martin Heidegger on its implications for ontology.

Cassirer's central intervention was the concept of symbolic form, in which the world is structured through and by schemas that each carry a specific logic, akin to myth or science. Crossing categories of cognition, a schema derives just as easily from myth as from science, complicating any dialectic of enlightenment. Language as theorized by structural linguistics was but one such schema. The art historian Erwin Panofsky famously "applied" this theory to early modern painting—that foundational space of abstraction or metricization in picture making—to understand the illusionism made possible by central point perspective as formative of the representation of the subject itself, in symmetry with the spatial organization representative of transcendental or eternal life facing the subject. In *Perspective as Symbolic Form* (1927), this modality of pictorial organization is understood to result from engineering and mathematics but also from the crucible of the modern subject's dominant perceptual understanding of the world, the cogito. It becomes a worldview constitutive of cognition and practically renaturalized.[26] Sohn-Rethel bears a much more rooted intellectual debt to Cassirer.[27] He was in Davos in 1929 when the debates between Cassirer (with whom he studied) and Heidegger took place, solidifying the divide between the former's historicist Kantianism and the latter's theory of presence as "standing-reserve."[28] Cassirer explicitly engaged and rejected Heideggerian ontologies in his understanding of form as a socially derived determinant elaborated as a social constraint.

Sohn-Rethel theorized a cultural foundation of the subject within capitalist domination indebted to Cassirer. Epistemology grounds a form of consciousness barred from an economic social unconscious, a bulwark against nature and a "second nature."[29] This second nature is an abstraction that functions as though it were itself inevitable, "the way things are." It is not that consciousness is false, nor that "mankind"—a category that cannot in any case be universalized in any other way than historically, for example, insofar as markets mediate across borders—is "alienated." Rather, this fully renaturalized reality is also a product of the dominant means of value production and a metabolic mediating nature, however the latter is defined. Abstraction comes to saturate the field of the real and to be mistaken for it. As Sami Khatib has noted in his analysis of the value-form in relation to both aesthetics and a direly needed new theory of class, "Capitalism's physis produces its own 'naturally grown' *metaphysics*."[30]

Money is a "symbolic form" like other symbolic forms that come to ramify in the field of the real in the sense that it does not correlate to any fixed natural condition (it is an index of socially necessary labor-time calibrated by transaction, as Sohn-Rethel would come to discover and to argue), and yet the transactions that it enables come to calcify through their performance and reperformance in a social register. Above all, the logic of transaction and its indifference to either the content of that which is bought or sold, or the relationships among buyers or sellers, underlines its autonomy from the social field in which it functions and over which it comes to have immense power. This makes money as a form, a social contract from an "other" register, eerily similar to an operational "symbolic form" such as perspective.

For Lütticken, Sohn-Rethel's attentiveness to *form* as such, aside of language and immediate ideology, stands out as the key tool to understanding modernity. He takes Sohn-Rethel's *Intellectual and Manual Labour* (conceptualized intuitively in the 1920s and completed only in 1978) to be a retort to Cassirer's formalist Kantianism by way of disarticulating the formal parameters of philosophical thought from the Enlightenment notion of free will and agency. It effectively dismantles the framework determinative of liberal subjectivity by questioning the Kantian notion of self-liberation through mental faculties within the limits of individual capacity. Where for Immanuel Kant, Enlightenment is self-liberation from self-imposed external constraints, Sohn-Rethel's argument demonstrates this model of contained individual cognition and judgment to be itself already mimetically inscribed in the logic of that other abstraction: the commodity as repository of value. Sohn-Rethel thus "desublimates philosophical 'thought abstractions' by linking them generically to the 'real abstractions' of exchange and money. He thereby attempts to reveal the historically specific economic underpinnings of Kantianism."[31] And yet at the same time, this thought remains formalist—but not in the usual sense as "merely" aesthetic or even only political. What has changed is the emergence of a specifically materialist formalism, one that derives its "categories" from the real movement of the value-form in circulation, and the way that this metabolic is *remediated into thought through form*. Here, aesthetic form mediates material form. As an index (aesthetic) of an index (circulation; value as an index of labor-time), the artwork is a margin through which to sense or "see" the field of the socially mediated second nature in all its apparent abstraction.

The ultimate stakes of the Cassirer–Heidegger debate—and what is inscribed in both Panofsky's and Sohn-Rethel's debt to Cassirer—is a definition of technology and, consequently, of a worldview. While this worldview itself is historically constituted, the subject who encounters it enters into it as though into a second nature perceived as nature. No essence or ontology precedes these forms as they come to reverberate in the social field as constraints, a social framework within which the subject unconsciously moves.

Form is mistaken for essence insofar as it functions "abstractly," outside of perceived recognition, yet also "concretely," through modes of production and equally tangible and productive social relations. Both sides operate yet outside of *conscious* thought. Abstraction is a framework, an episteme and an invisible social ecology within capital, rather than an immediately manifest set of objects in an empirically verifiable place.[32] Like a functioning code or schema, it is both constituted and constitutive, not least in the way that social relations evolve within and against circuits of value that also deterritorialize and recompose the material world, driven always by markets. In sum, Sohn-Rethel attempts to do to Kantian "faculties" and modes of cognitive self-possession what Marx had accomplished in relation to Georg W. F. Hegel, namely, to set the form of thought and formal organization of process, be it the category (Kant) or the dialectic, on its feet, on solid materialist ground. This, finally, offers another perceptual and cognitive way into that other problem, one categorized under the "aesthetic" within a Kantian genealogy: the problem of the process of de-reification. The latter had been modernism 's very project from Adorno and Greenberg to Krauss and contemporary thinker of de-reification through aesthetics, Anita Chari.

Foremost here is the division between manual and intellectual labor. If René Descartes formalized the cogito, and Kant refined its many categorical capacities, this is only insofar as the collective division of labor enabled the very production of this thought, a kind of tautology in which the missing referent, the market, makes possible the products sold on it, including philosophy itself as one product among many. Far from reflecting on the material world, Sohn-Rethel reminds us that thinking too is framed for the purposes of circulation on a market. Art's so-called autonomy, a Kantian notion at its origin, only exists insofar as it is the last refuge of a form of production and consumption that isn't entirely subsumed, a momentary reprieve from the divisions managed by a market and remanaged provisionally through institutions of aesthetic judgment.

Recall Marx's infamous statement that the distribution of labor, insofar as it is mediated by a market, determines a fixed identity for he who must sell that labor:

> For as soon as the distribution of labour comes into being, each man has a particular, exclusive sphere of activity, which is forced upon him and from which he cannot escape. He is a hunter, a fisherman, a herdsman, or a critical critic, and must remain so if he does not want to lose his means of livelihood; while in communist society, where nobody has one exclusive sphere of activity but each can become accomplished in any branch he wishes, society regulates the general production and thus makes it possible for me to do one thing today and another tomorrow, to hunt in the morning, fish in the afternoon, rear cattle in the evening, criticize after dinner, just as I have a mind, without ever becoming hunter, fisherman, herdsman or critic.[33]

Reversing the common assumption that only intellectual labor, philosophy above all, transcends labor categories as violent as they are vulgar, Marx commented: "The industrialists of philosophy, who till then had lived on the exploitation of the absolute spirit, now seized upon the new combinations [enabled by the philosophy market]. Each with all possible zeal set about retailing his apportioned share."[34] Those who have been professionalized to think within the category of intellectual labor do so in such a way that unconsciously replicates the market relations that enable the material conditions for the production of formal thought as such. This circularity is lost on those who *inhabit* its circuit, a value-productive circuit not unlike the circuits on which manual labor-power and its materials inhabit. Again, far from being materially autonomous, art is "autonomous" *only* insofar as the artist need not respect the reification of production at the level of ontology. Art stands in excess to the primary division between intellectual and manual labor, capable of reflecting on labor in general. General labor is inscribed into the art's production without the work's total subsumption into a market totality. This is what passes for creation and for autonomy.

The way in which Sohn-Rethel's work dismantles epistemic categories also suggests a very different kind of "universalism" than the kind of which modernism is so frequently and perhaps rightfully accused. The materialist universalism that his analysis suggests does not preexist its formation through the networks of transactions that it in turn perpetuates. It moves where markets move. It is neither ideal nor absolute. There is no ontology or any theory of that which is revealed as "standing-reserve." Instead, transactional social relations create a form of "alienated" society that crosses identity, territory, and nation. Universalism does not originate, nor is it located, in any one geopolitical site or context—although *Intellectual and Manual Labour* privileges fifth-century Greek mercantile culture, it takes this as exemplary of generic market relations across contexts.

Sohn-Rethel's thought, as Toscano and others emphasize, returns to a basic tenet in Marxian thinking that has been all but extinguished in the bourgeois idealisms facilitated by the liberal market. This basic tenet is that to grasp anything about "real" conditions within capitalist social relations, the thinking subject must begin with the seemingly abstract and move to the concrete—not the reverse, as in bourgeois thinking. This is a basic truism in Marx's methodology as discussed in recent discourse by geographer and intellectual historian David Harvey and countless others. If anything, to begin with apparently concrete "things" and extrapolating toward generality is a sure-fire path to delusion. Marx writes:

> Hence the magic of money. Men are henceforth related to each other in their social process of production in a purely atomistic way. Their own relations of production therefore assume a material shape which is independent of their control and their conscious individual action. This situation is manifested first by the fact that the product of men's labour universally take on the form of commodities. The riddle of the money fetish is therefore the riddle of the commodity fetish, now become visible and dazzling to our eyes.[35]

In the shift from the object commodity to the abstraction of money, labor-time is no longer experienced as an object but as a screen, an immersive space as enveloping as perceived nature. As fetishized dead labor circulates in the form of commodities, the contradictions in its mode of production are both smoothed over and heightened. Labor-time is "immanent to commodities," and yet as soon as that labor-time comes to be expressed as money, it is too abstracted for its concrete immanence to be remotely visible. In the "measure of values," value as abstracted labor-time measures all the rest of life.[36] To see this "dazzling" plane of second nature requires an optics that moves from the fetish to an analysis of this socially ubiquitous yet individually irreducible totality. Art, because of its condition suspended between and among categories and discourses, and between intellectual and manual skill, offers a path through which to see real abstraction. It can afford a vision that holds open a space to not only imagine but perform and hopefully precipitate a reality other to capitalist second nature, as the historical avant-garde hoped to do. The ready-made was one such perceptual apparatus in its timely capacity to get to the core of the issue: anonymous labor-time as the *only* universal within capitalist time, a universal articulated in the commodity and expressed as money that historically displaced any form of transcendental experience of art in a Kantian register.

Other moments within the historical avant-garde have attempted to overcome the circuitry set into place by value extracted of labor, inscribed in objects and realized as money. One such instance is the Russian avant-garde in the brief moment between the Russian Revolution and the New Economic Policy (NEP) of 1921, which effectively dissolved revolutionary movement by a return to the capitalist mode of circulation and accumulation under the hollow symbolism of state communism. Any number of studies of this moment of concrete and aesthetic exceptionalism, namely, the avant-garde in the Russian context between 1905 and 1921 (revolutionary era to NEP), from those by Christina Grey and Christina Lodder to Christina Kiaer, Maria Gough, and others, have established the numerous viral exchanges among poets, artists, writers, and others in this moment. Daniel Spaulding, for one, has identified the structural intimacy between radical abstract art and an attempt to sever the relationship between everyday life and real abstraction by abolishing the value-form at the height of revolutionary capacity. Spaulding has explicitly connected this problem, namely, the necessity of overcoming the value-form, as the avant-garde's most pragmatic and fundamental aspiration across disciplines, from art to political economy. Through a reading of Sohn-Rethel's work and value-form analysis, Spaulding reads Kazimir Malevich's and others' refusal of metricization (associated with the quantified framework necessary to capital and to illusionistic representation alike) as an allegory of the entwinement of formal materialist thinking and action at that time.[37] He orients the existing scholarship on the Russian and Soviet avant-garde to the materialist underpinnings of its origins in context, by considering how value-form and aesthetic form relate in the avant-garde's most vibrant moment.

Aesthetic form probes crises in the value-form, affording anyone who looks a kind of vehicle through which to probe the coordinates of this otherwise abstract condition.[38] Crossing reified vision, art's indexicality requires the labor of reflection. This too is a problem. Consumption time is shortened to fuel the desire that lubricates production. The primary project, then, is to develop a formalism adequate to the value-form.

And yet most accounts of aesthetic form are blindsighted to the ways in which it signals social, political, and economic crisis precisely because of the way it is sensitive to other forms of circulation, above all value. One way to confront the social crises to which aesthetic form points, avant la lettre, would be to abolish the value-form altogether. But since this does not appear to be a politically viable position, the aesthetic register goes on formalizing what the conscious political field cannot: an economic unconscious inscribed by the value-form.

To overcome this blind spot, I return to the primary gambit of the avant-garde. This primary effort entailed a "transvaluation of values." The aim was to reverse the catastrophe of capital run amok and indifferent to social agents and to render possible a future in common for all individuals. This would entail abolishing the value-form and allowing socially necessary labor to be renegotiated in the interest of individuals and collectives over abstractions and corporations. For this to happen, an analytic, a new metaphysics, one that offers a "vision machine," as the collective Tiqqun would say of its personification of a commodified subject who must overcome the commodity ontology, the Young-Girl, would have to emerge and elaborate the capacity to cut through the second nature forged by surplus-value extraction.

But *how* does this complexly market-mediated relationship to time and labor determine a self? How is it foundational to a technology? But I am getting ahead of the story of the other scene. One way of thinking the entwinement—indeed, the identity—between governance and economic interest is through the question of technology, defined earlier as an organization of social time. While Adorno is quick to dismiss as "technology" that which closes the capacity for open exploration, he conjugates this understanding of technology with *abstraction*. However, he fails to qualify this abstraction as anything other than in contradistinction to intellectual experience, or what Sohn-Rethel would call "thought abstraction." Adorno writes: "As opposed to this intellectual experience, as its counterpart, everything that can be described as the so-called controlled advance of abstraction or as the mere subsumption under concepts is merely technology in the broadest sense."[39]

The objects and art practices steering the text across these pages have been chosen for the way in which the relation to labor and value carves out a medium or practice, the very form of the work: from painting in the earliest stages of the explorations of visual abstraction to the avant-garde's use of the diagram to performance, delegated performance, and beyond, spanning a century. These works function like "vision machines," not in the sense that they are literally machinelike but because of the way they hold out the possibility of de-reifying our understanding of our de- and renaturalized world in order to forge a path toward the "transvaluation of values."

Sohn-Rethel's attention to the circulation of value at a formal and structural level tracks with aesthetic and modernist formalism only insofar as it offers an account for the urgent motivation of these works. If we are to liberate persons from being tangential to their own capacity for value production and to reorganize life in the interest of preserving ecosystems that foster the lives of individuals and collectives over abstractions and corporations, we might look at what the culture sector can tell us in its own prefigurative and formal terms. For this to happen, second nature must be dismantled for a new metaphysics to emerge, one that is on sustainable terms with material resources.

Introduction 2

Modernism's Aesthetic Economy: An *Art* History of Labor's Subsumption

A striking salient feature of the internet is its proliferation of seemingly infinite ways to seek, solicit, and precipitate exchanges of an ostensibly novel kind, often in the form of reciprocal "human" connection and even in the guise of love itself. Intimacies on offer frequently lead to a type of transaction, more often than not financial. It is as though this technological medium were a prime matrix for harvesting those vestigial forms of interstitial value that might be extracted from accidental encounters with new objects and services, primarily of affect-work, or from forms of labor suspended between and among formally visible registers. It is a technology that, while certainly not inventive of the social form of the importune, accelerates the ways and means of a mode of social association already hastened by capital: that of the abstract transaction. Under the sign of any kind of content, but above all the ineffable substance of human *feeling*, the transaction hinges materially only on the form of exchange itself.

In the essay "Her Name Was Esperanza," artist Hito Steyerl tackled the myriad transactions petitioned in the guise of affective and emotional fulfillment in the era of the internet. She notes the multiplication of relationships advertised as amorous, and even and above all offers of marriage, that turn out, on points of sale, to be swindles. Clickbait flows into epistolary affect and ready-made tragedy as "the Ponzi schemes of globalized financial capitalism and its delusions are being translated into the personalized language of romance."[1] Citing scholarly research on such scams whereby under the veil of emotional connection, money is solicited in the form of the digital transfer, Steyerl notes above all the language with which these schemes, known as 419 games, are described.

Sociologist Andrew Apter "literally labels the 419 games as performance art, based on a general rise of visual deception and emptied value forms in politics as well as in an economy based on privatization and speculation."[2] Steyerl stresses the language—"performance art"—that Apter chooses to describe this peculiar synthesis of social fiction, financial reality, and intersubjective bankruptcy specific to the present.

Attending to the ubiquity of these 419 tricks, both Apter and Steyerl describe situations that allegorize much about contemporary life under capital, a condition we might call a "social factory" in which the recesses of emotion and interiority are wrested to lubricate the flow of value, generating a collective libidinal economy entwined with a real economy. Locating in this nexus a metaphor for the nature of work itself, any kind of work—the general sale of labor-time—Steyerl continues:

> The production of romance scams conjures up the idea of digital workbenches, peopled with rows of literary laborers organized within a flexibilized division of labor performing work or working in performance just like their counterparts in the "real" financial sector. The products are serial identities-on-demand which morph to accommodate every possible client fantasy. Passion-as-labor, which reverse-mirrors the idea of labor-as-passion supposed to motivate the ideal workers of the post-Fordist age.[3]

Here, Steyerl offers a portrait of the worker-subject that summons another contemporary artist's allegorical figure for capital's circuits of value. The artist collective Claire Fontaine develops "The Young-Girl" to personify the otherwise unfigurable yet pervasive "behavior" of capital itself. This character, or trope, becomes a way to grasp the subject within capital as that subject comes to be constituted through it—literally subjected to the technics of value extraction—as a ready-made self in the matrix of labor, production, circulation, and consumption. This troped persona borrows heavily from the avant-garde artists Francis Picabia's and Marcel Duchamp's figures of the worker as a diagram of a split subject divided between a socially embedded individuality and the abstract system of surplus-value creation, a machine part, and, above all, the "ready-made" itself in dialectical relation to the commodity objects in which their labor-time is ossified. Claire Fontaine takes this figure for the worker-subject and extends it to qualify the role of the artist under capitalist conditions of real subsumption, that is, the production of all social elements including subjectivity reproduced through the interests of the market. That which these artists locate already in the historical avant-garde, in any number of artistic practices across media, has now become a social type in turn motivating new expressions and media over the twentieth century and into the twenty-first, our present. The linkage between the historical avant-garde and contemporary art evidenced in the allegorical character of the Young-Girl (explored in chapter 4) resonates with Steyerl's mass worker whose labor crosses libidinal, real, and precarious economies.

The present book locates and addresses those "products [that] are serial *identities*-on-demand." Steyerl formulates the phrase "serial identities-on-demand" as a way to trace how the worker is strewn across modernism in a way that belies representation; after all, labor—especially gendered socially reproductive and affective or care labor—has proven unrepresentable. For indeed, as I will show, the co-constitutive relationship between labor and value is precipitated across much of modernism as a problem of *concrete abstraction*.

Steyerl's "products [that] are serial identities-on-demand, which morph to accommodate every possible client fantasy," are also unassimilable at the level of representation due to the contradictions they personify. There is an extent to which we might see this phenomenon as a twenty-first-century digital reiteration, a reboot, of the social nexus famously explored at the inception of Modernism by Édouard Manet's *Olympia* (figure I2.1), the 1863 depiction of a prostitute. That historical work was scandalous as much for the social reality principle it offered as for its seemingly salacious content. Above all, it presented the viewer with a stark picture of the banalization of the sale of the self by any means possible. But what struck a collective public in the 1860s was the way in which this social reality principle was articulated through a *formal reality principle* in the manifest flatness of the picture plane.

As T. J. Clark has practically proven, Manet's *Olympia*—a depiction of none other than the street-level proletarian prostitute—is the "founding monument of modern art."[4] Beyond its representational vulgarity, the painting appeared flat. Overriding his own virtuosic skill in producing volume and depth, Manet's avowal of painting's material condition was as honest an index, a term to which I will return, of modernity's new material conditions as anyone who could bear to look could possibly find in the culture. The painting's intrinsic flatness broke as much with the bourgeois delusion of three-dimensional space on a picture plane as with the fiction of social

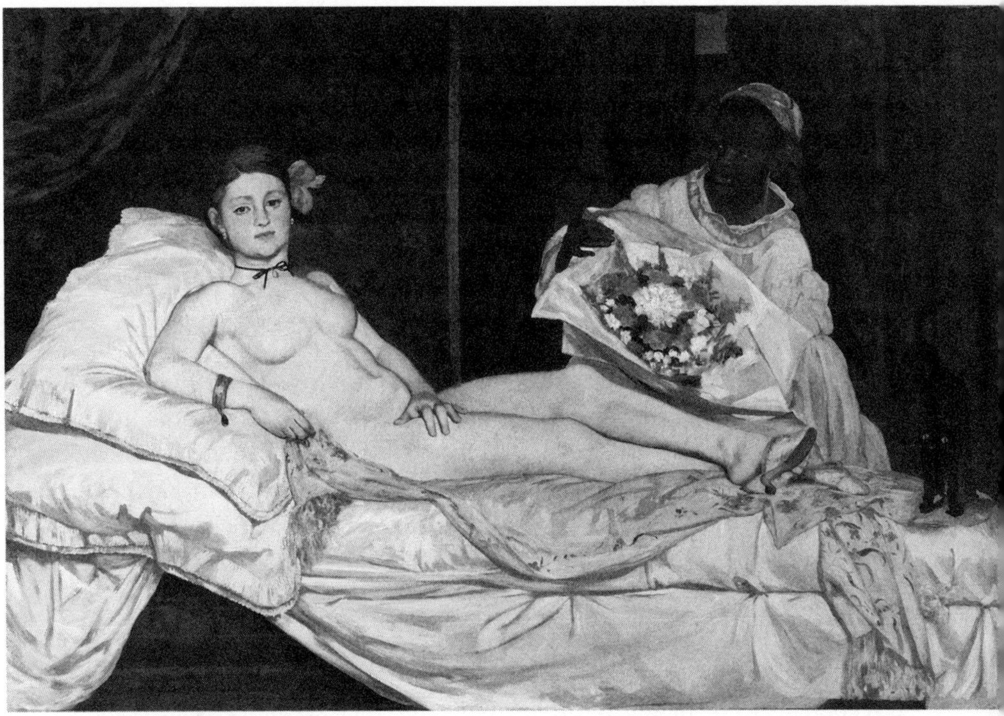

Fig. I2.1 Édouard Manet, *Olympia*, 1863. © RMN-Grand Palais / Art Resource, NY.

"morality." In that sense, the "performances" that Steyerl discusses in "Her Name Was Esperanza" might be understood dialectically in relation to Manet's *Olympia* as the foundational paradigm of Modernism. If *Olympia* had articulated a critical negativity in relation to bourgeois social norms blindsighted to the reality of class and economic relations, Steyerl's allegory of contemporaneity in "Her Name Was Esperenza" notes the opacity of a de-sublimated perceptual field in which eros and labor, artwork and work, collapse seamlessly and unconsciously into one another, the sign of a social real that has accelerated and deferred the contradictions of earlier Modernist art. After all, Apter refers to actual social relations as performance art, not performance art as an *expression* of social relations. We are not in the space of representation or illustration here. The work of art's mediation of the social field has transformed along with its media and technical support, which in turn transform to keep pace with the unfigurable in a register outside the frame. Steyerl situates the work of art as mimetically inscribed into present forms of social delusion and yet signal to those forms of delusion for those who see the artwork's capacity to probe not so much appearances as social economies hidden in plain sight.

In *Bad New Days*, an analysis of the work of artists Robert Gober, Isa Genzken, and Jon Kessler, Hal Foster defines contemporary art's primary operation as one of entering into a mimetic relationship with dominant social dynamics and heightening them. He calls this "mimetic exacerbation."[5] This maneuver intensifies the dynamics, structures, and social formations that are everywhere and yet nowhere insofar as they are impossible to represent or signify, so inchoately saturated are they into everyday life as to belie contour or concept-ready boundary. Steyerl's work and writing function by mimetic exacerbation, signaling the open secrets of social abstraction. Through mimetic exacerbation, Steyerl's work offers a dialectical expression of an otherwise inaccessible social unconscious: market operations that move beneath immediate visibility, in the social unconscious as that is synthesized in the space of transaction, on a market so totalizing it seems invisible.

What Steyerl's work suggests is that the content of this mimetic exacerbation is the social unconscious. As in Olympia, the artwork indicates an open secret so socially saturated as to be imperceptible. However, the *form* of the presentation itself has changed and this converted form offers an index of a changed social real at a particular historical moment, now as in 1863. In my use of this terminology, the "index," I lean on Sven Lütticken, who in turn mobilizes a rich corpus of thinking on the index as a peculiar kind of sign, from Charles Peirce and Rosalind Krauss to Eliseo Verón and Sohyun Ahn. "The index," Lütticken writes, "is par excellence a social sign, which cannot be relegated to a world of pure semiosis. To the extent that they indicate their origins, artifacts and fetishes are also temporary or historical signs." Art is a form of mediation different from other symbolic forms. Semiautonomous from the division of intellectual and manual labor and from immediate instrumental closure, art—as aesthetic mediation—is able to point to relationships that otherwise remain unperceived.[6]

In "Her Name Was Esperanza," Steyerl's exploration of any number of operations across a total social field takes advantage of the special affordances made possible by the medium she chooses and its technology, as in this instance where the rampant phenomenon of transactional exchange masked as personal and individual is articulated in a digital plenum, in parallel with the nature of the digital field: its capacity for volume, anonymity, et cetera. Here, intersubjective performances of authenticity slide almost imperceptibly into transactional or marketized exchanges. This slide, seemingly specific to the internet, from the intersubjective to the anonymous and abstract becomes a way to locate and figure a modality that saturates the social field in general, happening everywhere all the time in everyday life, a function of structure and circuits of value as swift and slippery as moving digital signs. For Steyerl, the performative language mobilized in the amorous and erotic fictions enabled at mass volume by the internet takes precedence over any one narrative or representation, which in any case multiply and proliferate past any given property or any one identity. Steyerl unwittingly identifies that which might have been missed the first time around, when the thematic of prostitution was made heavy-handedly transparent to a figure, an individual, or a type. Steyerl's index of transactional accumulation is too anonymized to support traditional forms of aesthetic mediation, such as narrative or figurative representation, in keeping with the accelerated attention economy of recent capital.

But if we look back past the evident *individual* figure of the sex worker in nineteenth-century painting to the social field it indexes, it becomes clear that the social relations forged in the crucible of exchange have structured and mediated the depicted visual field again and again in the history of art, in fundamental ways more structural than the representation of this or that figure. Transactional social relations crossing individuals are, for instance, thematized in Georges Seurat's capstone painting *The Models* (1888). There, rather than through figurative representation alone, remunerated labor-time comes to be reperformed in the seemingly mechanized labor-time of the pointillist *technique* itself. This inscription of rationalized labor-time is not only thematized by the depicted models but also expressed as the matrix of painting itself, prefiguring Steyerl's mobilization of the digital matrix as itself a matrix of exchange, under any particular individual transactions. Looking ahead to Steyerl, Seurat reconstitutes painting itself as the very index of anonymous, abstract labor drawn through marketized time.

The development of key strategies and tactics of the avant-garde might be recognized as a mode of coming to terms with abstract, anonymous labor-time in new techniques that confront that unseen crucible where living labor becomes fixed in the technology of production. One such example, the cornerstone of the present study, is Picabia's *Universal Prostitution*, which, I argue, inaugurated a new form appropriate to a new anthros, the worker, which became in turn a cornerstone of modernism: the diagrammatic line co-opted from "the language of industry." This query is based on the Dada exploration of the subject and its reification as an object at the point of sale and purchase of its labor-power.

And we find the very same polemic, now updated yet again, in Yves Klein's *Anthropometries*, for which the artist paid models to be "living paintbrushes," thereby making instruments of living women, as though skipping the part of reification where living labor comes to be deposited in inert, dead objects, in a rush to the full-blown thingification of the total human being. These questions have preoccupied modern and contemporary art at the level of its structural operations, even to the point of initiating new forms of practice, new media (such as delegated performance), and new genres within media (such as abstract painting). This preoccupation with the sale of the subject-rendered-thing through the almost alchemical operation of a market-compelled transaction runs like an underground stream through decade after decade of radical innovative art across the twentieth century and into the twenty-first as the very source of art practice—indeed, of the condition for the possibility of making art.

There it is again, surely enough, in the delegated performance practices of the late twentieth century, such as Santiago Sierra's, which take up the problem of time transactionally exchanged for forms of payment that defy the state apparatus, rendering the smooth movement of circuits perilous. Sierra's work mimetically exacerbates the structurally coercive conditions in which labor is compelled to suggest the naturalized cruelty of a late modern labor market that benefits from the surplus populations created by global economic restructuring and capital flight. In and of itself, this strategy might be callous spectacle. Here, however, the illegal transaction with which labor is precipitated is inscribed in the operational fabric of the work rather than exclusively at the level of figurative representation. This is to say that the anonymous transaction unconsciously structuring a social field is articulated as the very condition for the possibility of the image, the very social form that comes to be mediated by the work's support—performance and delegated performance—rather than as its immediately transparent or represented content. To reject as cruel Sierra's specific articulation is shown to be hypocritical in light of the *generalized* condition of labor which he emphasizes through the supplement of disturbing and salacious detail.

Germane to the way in which the transaction, almost alchemical in its power to reconstitute the subject through the point of sale, comes to act as the structural condition for all art making is also the way that art recognizes and performs that the artist themself is made to satisfy the compulsions of production that captures the creative *self* even more vociferously than the objectified work of art. Accordingly, the works discussed here seem to recognize more lucidly than any political economic discourse Marx's statement that "the demand for men necessarily governs the production of men, as of every other commodity."[7] Here, Marx had noted the peculiar circularity with which the production process not only relies on the labor-time of working people to churn out value-productive things treated with greater social respect than their makers; the entire value circuit in turn fabricates forms of life, people made to be ready *as* bearers of labor-power, no less relentlessly than it makes objects into commodities. This is to say that capitalist subsumption makes subjects customized to be labor-power across a wide array of forms or, rather, that this is what subsumption *is*.

This kind of manufactured subjectivity constituted in circuits of value in order to be set back into them in a new cycle of reproduction is signaled in artist Claire Fontaine's argument that the artist has become a ready-made.[8] Here, even the artist's own subject position—once thought to be exemplary and exceptional to the fray of daily life for its capacity to suspend the division between intellectual and manual work foundational to modern labor, privileged as the last custodian of historically bygone cult value, creativity and collective meaning—is itself as "produced" as any commodity.

Art making is shown to have shifted gears, exiting the quixotic domain of creation to enter the economics of production. The mystification Marx famously described wherein commodity fetishism seems to make things of people and people of things finds the source of this transposition in the crucible of transaction wherein labor, lived by the individual, is abstracted and sold as an anonymous interchangeable capacity. Labor-power is an exceptional commodity, realized or in potential, because it is the place where the subject is split and offered in estranged form, that of abstract time. Over time, the artist's time is valued in the same matrix of any other labor-time rather than held outside in a logic of exceptional and irreducible qualification. Art making, otherwise far from commodity exchange insofar as it occupies a specialized domain of nonfungibility, comes to rely on this metabolic set into motion by the transaction and enters a heretofore occluded relation with capital. The result ratifies what art historian Marina Vishmidt sees as specific to "the Neoliberal art market, [where] art and labor, creativity and training, become harder and harder to tell apart. The growing proximity between art and labor starts to emerge as a zone of indistinction."[9] While art making is far from synonymous with labor insofar as it is not compulsory in the way that most labor is, "we are all readymade artists" insofar as artists themselves, not unlike their paid assistants or models-as-tools, are forged by social relations reticulated through otherwise unconscious market mechanisms in which labor-time (disguised as affective presence) is the primary object.

Modernism's ambivalent relationship to production and compulsory social reproduction might also be charted as a symbiotic entwinement with both. One obvious place to locate this dependency would be the figure of the model, so often gendered and balanced between paid worker and unpaid mythical muse—that is, between the scenes of production and reproduction but belonging properly to neither, and carrying a last trace of transcendental autonomy from circuits of value. The trope of the prostitute figures here as that which desublimates the muse and is instead conjugable with any other worker, remunerated for the metabolic labor generated by the skin of her back. Far from the liberated inspiration wrought by the muses, the prostitute is nonetheless nonproductive. In this regard the prostitute occupies an ambivalent place, a kind of accursed share of surplus and excess personified, a means of exchange without ends. The prostitute marks an interval, a leveling of metaphysics caught between the delivery of plenitude expected of eros and pressed into material circuits of transactionally exchanged time. It, this figure, could be an allegory for art itself, suspended between the fugitive cult of creativity and reality principle of material circulation. Modernism has been famously thought to be founded on this figure, insofar as Olympia is "the founding monument of modern art."[10]

The artworks and practices that this book explores cross modernity and media. They qualify as "global" in the same sense that capital is global, crossing geopolitical space to extract resources, just as cultural practices cross spaces and media to act as nodal points in signaling the reorganization of labor. The sale of labor-time, the crux of abstraction in the social field, forms a cultural unconscious, under the visible and denotative discursive spaces of politics and ideology. Chosen for their attenuated way of indexing the material circumstances of value extracted of others to be sold as abstract labor, these works innovated the medium, genre, or form into which they intervene. I take the artworks I examine in this book to be "vision machines" for understanding and working through Marx's curious term *universal prostitution*, imported into the sphere of art when it was taken up by Picabia as a title for his own groundbreaking work. I explore Picabia's appropriation of Marx's language as the artist's own plastic *description* of a universal operation of the sale of labor-power mediated in any number of ways by the market and the wage, with an acknowledgment of this permeation in turn infiltrating new forms of art and media. I take Picabia to be offering a description of the split subject of capital, strewn over circuits of reproduction.

However, this book will take as its starting point an older work, Seurat's new "abstract" technique, which he developed at a moment of intimate contact with new social forms and types, expressed primarily through his relation to the model who posed for his paintings as an early expression of the artist's preoccupation with the problem of social abstraction understood as the market-mediated sale of labor-time, or, in plain terms, *real abstraction*. Seurat forgoes both muse and prostitute to mobilize the worker as a vehicle through which to explore abstract painterly process. This is to say that in his work, aesthetic abstraction is an index of social abstraction at the level of process and making. The sale of time is the mis-en-scène in *The Models*.

Disarticulated and differentiated from thought abstractions through Alfred Sohn-Rethel's work (discussed in the previous introduction), real and concrete abstraction is a naturalized social field structured by exchange. It describes the unconscious yet total saturation of a market—and above all a labor market—that insensibly determines other social relations. At the opening of the twenty-first century, contemporary artists Claire Fontaine defined abstraction as a social condition performed through "exchangism." Claire Fontaine also leans on Sohn-Rethel's explanation of normative social relations compelled by a labor market that operates unconsciously, forging a dominant social unity that is overlooked in the particularities of everyday social life yet more silently causal scale than any identity or political group to the everyday lives of all subjects and objects that cross it. The market connects everything under the more self-evident spaces of politics and ideology, which present a fragmented and separated social order by contrast. Once at market, social and political identities are suspended under the compulsions of the transaction, and "the consciousness and the action of people part company in exchange and go different ways."[11] Yet while transactional actions and consciousness part ways in the moment of exchange, all of society is organized around exchange, under and outside the field of vision, where it creates an unfigurable totality. Claire Fontaine calls this an "imperceptible abstraction."[12] For them, "one could even go so far as to formulate the hypothesis that, just as the value-form contaminates the whole realm of objects, including those that aren't commodities, in the same way this value-form, that injects exchange value into behaviors, colonizes or infects *all* human behaviors (including the most spontaneous, emotional and disinterested ones)."[13] Autonomy itself takes on different meanings in relation to the "second nature" established by social relations rendered abstract through multiple cycles of what Claire Fontaine calls "exchangism," as these artworks explore. Here, "exchangism," or the market transaction in which goods and labor-time are valorized, quietly but structurally informs social relations at the very moment when they *seem* independent of the market, just as the artwork is entwined in the market when it appears most "autonomous." Claire Fontaine continues: "the paradox is that commercial exchange is in reality a social tie created by an activity that negates it. Because the use of money allows and authorizes every owner of commodities to abstractly (but concretely) pursue his own personal interests, without obstructions, without even thinking about his place in society."[14] They attribute to Sohn-Rethel their conceptual access into this "absurdity" wherein collective self-interest is negated by *unconscious* individual self-interest that constrains the remaining creative capacity of the subject.

Moving from Seurat to Claire Fontaine, we might ask: What happens to authorial intentions in the regime of exchangism? The space and time of a transaction both realize and negate the space and time of production as well as the contextual situation in which those involved in any given production process otherwise live. It equally nullifies intention because it is motivated by an *autonomous* logic disinterested in the everyday lives of social actants: that of price, profit, and circulation.[15] This other place driven by an autonomous, which is to say *automated*, metabolic generated by exchangism, suspends not only creative agency but the social relations existing outside the space of transaction itself, including family, community relations, identity, and affect, is indifferent even to production and consumption aside from how they affect the relation between value and price.

The term *universal* reverberates in Picabia's appropriation of "universal prostitution" as a cruel parody of art's promise to deliver an aesthetic experience that could claim to transcendental idealist universality per its Enlightenment theorization. Set into relation with "prostitution," it precipitates the fact that only capital, not aesthetics, totalizes (or universalizes) through its forms of abstraction. That from which art had held itself to be free operates "behind the backs of men" and universalizes through the value-form.

The claim has been made that the *thematic* of sex work allegorizes this condition once and for all and that this theme is the foundational framework of modern art, as T. J. Clark has argued.[16] Indeed, the thematic of prostitution has continued to be a popular trope in art making well into the present.[17] For instance, in 2002, New York–based artist Andrea Fraser presented a piece at the Friedrich Petzel Gallery, also in New York. Fraser, a feminist artist known for her commitment to the second generation of the critique of institutions movement in American art (1973–2000), exhibited an artwork titled

Untitled.[18] It presented a video-recorded sexual encounter between herself and a collector. Fraser had agreed to engage on physically intimate terms for payment; the brief affair was framed as purely transactional. A contract was signed by the artist, collectors, and galleries involved in the agreement. The transaction was to be to both parties' satisfaction and include a full night of one another's time. Its duration was recorded. The collector received one copy, the artist another, and three were placed on private sale by the gallery.

The situation unfolded by script in a civil key, indeed, with the affectively neutral tenor characteristic of contractual agreements. It placed limitations circumscribing the encounter, also intended to mitigate violence, danger, and risk. It also, Fraser hoped, would be understood within the genealogy of conceptual art and its critique of the fetish object. The contractual agreement, arranged by Friedrich Petzel Gallery, was proposed by Fraser as an assertion *against* the commodification of art. And yet the contract specifying the terms of the transaction is precisely what literally signed and thereby sealed the act's status as a commodity, that is, as dead labor congealed in a thing, extracted from the very skin of the worker's back to be congealed on a recording device to be made available in multiple iterations on a market. The work became a function of this contract, distinguished from a mere thing due to an agreement between seller, buyer, and distributor. This agreement afforded the piece legal status, ironically differentiating it from the illegal sale of sex.

As part of its exploration of real abstraction formalized in art, this book asks how and why (art) history summons the figure of the sex worker, from Manet's *Olympia* through decades of the "petit rats" of Impressionist and post-Impressionist painting, across the avant-garde's diagrammatic nudes, over midcentury capitalist realism and into new genres, above all performance. Why does the situation of human flesh offered—represented, indexed, mapped, and performed in the real—for money in a circumscribed transaction recur across the nineteenth and twentieth centuries, from modernism onward? Why is it the very signal of modernity and each successive revision, renovation, and update to modernism? Or to flip the question around, *why must timeliness as such take the form of transactional sex?* How does this transaction, the exchange of time necessary to render the service of sexual gratification for a contractually agreed sum, assume so many forms, from painting to the diagram to performance, over a century and a half? If at the outset of modernism, the sex worker became a way to thematize a social reality principle redoubled at the level of a self-reflexive acknowledgment of the material reality subtending representation (flatness), why has this knot—sex, money, social reality—inhered across media and aesthetic practice for over a century and a half, long after painting's hegemonic relevance? Why does the sex worker stand in not only for the foundational monument of modernism but also become the only vehicle by which to articulate the movement of history and, finally, to think about the medium, any medium, itself in its concrete, material facticity?

But what if we were to recognize the anonymous transactional space formative of social abstraction as the condition for the possibility of the work even *at its most distant* from this thematic? In other words, to what extent has the "universal prostitution" that Picabia chose as the title for one of his works, a work that does *not* represent prostitution or indeed any anthropomorphic content as such, nonetheless come to limn the very condition for the possibility of art making in its time? To what extent does Fraser's spectacular and perhaps even ultimately trite literalization take part in myopia about a universal condition—universal only because unconscious yet empirical, happening in a global space, namely, that of the market, that moves in concrete terms only behind the backs of men? Steyerl's insight in "Her Name Was Esperanza" is that this sale of love, that which is absolutely and totally irreducible, is common where it is least posited as "prostitution" in any transparent or figurative representational sense.

What does the disjuncture between Picabia's title and the breakdown of figurative representation in the work itself tell us about social appearances within abstract social relations? In 1924, Marcel Duchamp, progenitor of the paradigmatic avant-garde artwork the ready-made, gifted to the Yale University Art Gallery an artwork made by his friend and comrade Francis Picabia.[19] Entitled *Prostitution Universelle*, or *Universal Prostitution*, the drawing spelled out its replacement of composition and mimesis by a diagram, or something that looked like a diagram but also suggested machine parts. Picabia completed this drawing in the same year as *Fille née sans mère* (*Girl Born without a Mother*), which presents a machine part in lurid green against a gold-leaf background. Both works taken together offer a prescient analysis of twentieth-century labor avant la lettre. Summoning money, or gold, the work is oriented toward a breach in traditional modes of not only production but also social reproduction, or the production of the workers who through the sale of their labor-power produce value. The machine part nods to anonymous socially necessary labor-time, a cliché of modernity and the birth of the factory, but it also seems to imply that this value-productive, socially necessary *labor makes its maker* as much as it generates gold. The "subject" worker who labors has herself become not only machinic but also quite literally part of the machinery insofar as she is inscribed, via her labor-time, in the infrastructure. The worker is forged on the assembly line just as workers' labor constitutes the assembly line on which that work takes place, as well as the objects generated of that work. In other words, the workers produce not only the objects they are tasked to manufacture but also the very site of manufacture itself, which comes to extend into the spaces of social reproduction, constitutive of the subject. Picabia addresses this by noting the displacement of biological reproduction, an ontological origin in a woman, or mother, by a value-productive apparatus. In this sense, he speaks in advance to Greenberg's eccentric displacement from value production to the metaphorical "umbilical cord of gold."[20] What Marx referred to as the "hidden abode of production" doubles here as a site of social reproduction, the making of labor-power itself.

Its pendant piece, which Duchamp gifted to the Yale Art Galleries, draws its title from Marx's *Economic and Philosophic Manuscripts of 1844*. In this text drafted thirty-three years before the publication of *Das Kapital*, Marx used the term *universal prostitution* to describe the new condition of the laborer, better understood as the bearer and seller of labor-power in a new regime of production. "Prostitution is only a *specific* expression of the *general* prostitution of the *laborer*," he writes, "and since it is a relationship in which it falls not to the prostitute alone, but also the one who prostitutes—and the latter's abomination is still greater—the capitalist, etc., also comes under this head."[21] Here, Marx seems to be trying to contain the metaphor by saying that actual prostitution is an expression of the broader category: the sale of labor-power.

In *Capital*, Marx arrived at other terms through which to articulate the specific features of the new subject, the bearer of labor-power as a commodity alienated from the laborers themselves—which is to say, estranged from their own inclinations and tendencies, while dependent for self-reproductive sustenance on the basis of that very estrangement: "The second essential condition which allows the owner of money to find labour-power in the market as a commodity is this, that the possessor of labor power, instead of being able to sell commodities in which his labor is commodified, must rather be compelled to offer for sale as a commodity that very labor power that exists only in his living body."[22] Marx dispenses by then with the word *prostitute* but offers a definition of that which specifies both "prostitute" and proletariat. Both have nothing on offer—no object in which their work is objectified to trade—through which to gain access to a financially mediated form of subsistence (money, the wage) other than the immediate metabolic offered by their embodiment and the commitment of that embodiment to a temporal frame in which that embodiment might be exchanged for that most abstract representation of labor-time: money. Both occupy a split condition between locating this capacity in their own brain and body while simultaneously "alienating" that capacity or "handing it over to the buyer for him to consume, for a definite period of time, temporarily." In this way "he manages to both alienate his labour-power and to avoid renouncing his rights of ownership over it."[23] Here, while the workers, unlike enslaved persons, are in possession of themselves as their own property, the expenditure of labor-time is objectified as that which must be compensated to a minimal extent by pay in order for the workers to continue to exist.

For Marx this new form of labor—generalized, universalized value extracted by the measure of time—is epochal. It is the pivot of the capitalist mode of production and of modernity as such. Both prostitute and worker are sufficiently "free" from social bonds and obligations to offer their body to market mediation in order to gain access to subsistence. And this worker, "free" from slavery and any other means of subsistence, must sell and valorize this labor-power on a market in order for it to be realized as such and for the worker to replicate himself as someone who "has brought his own hide to market and now has nothing else to expect but—a tanning."[24] If Marx moved past this allegorical expression for *labor in general*, it nonetheless stuck as and, indeed, continues to resonate into the twenty-first century in advanced forms of aesthetic mediation, as evidenced by Fraser, Sierra, Steyerl, and others.

I will return to this enigmatic, opaque passage throughout this book. Picabia's work affords a moment to explore Marx's language, in relation to the eponymous work but also across his oeuvre. "Portraits" of a young girl from 1915 (figures I2.2 and I2.3) might be seen as a study for both *Girl Born without a Mother* and *Universal Prostitution*.

Chapter 2 will elaborate on Picabia's specific choice of borrowed words for the title of this diagrammatic drawing. For now, I would like to pause on Duchamp's having noted it. Duchamp inaugurated a new genre of "object" that is singularly responsive to the capitalist matrix of production and its replacement of the craftsman with anonymous labor and of artisanal skill with specialization in a larger *network* of production (figure I2.4). He was first to rethink the work of art through the ascendance of abstract labor-time over quality and technical expertise characteristic of the basic commodity. But Duchamp seemed to recognize in his friend's work a more lucid analysis

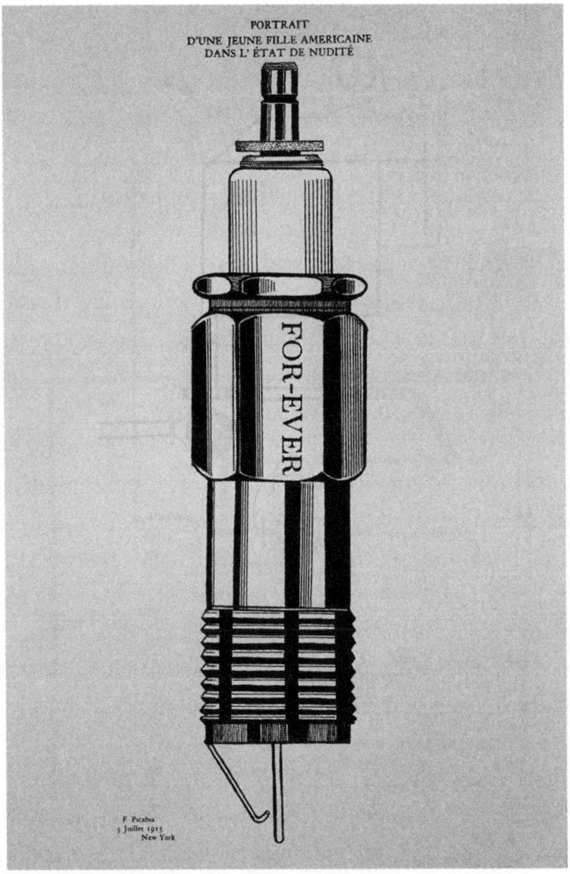

Fig. I2.2 Francis Picabia, *Portrait d'une Jeune Fille Americaine dans L'Etat de Nudite* (*Portrait of a Young American Girl in the State of Nudity*), 1915. © RMN-Grand Palais / Art Resource, NY.

yet: it was not merely the nature of the object that had undergone a radical transformation; it was the artist-subject. The new forms initiated by Picabia's work in homage to Marx identify the way that the subject-worker—or the worker as a subject otherwise living among the complexities of everyday social relations in all their plurality—is formed by the objective conditions that forge social relations in ways that are not apparent to those subjects.

The workers work to the extent that they organize the totality of their life in relation to the value extracted from the hours of their life in order to assimilate into a social system measured by marketized time—a system in which racialization, ideology, and history all play a part. In the logic of Picabia's work, the nature of labor as determinative of life becomes a total subsumption of life in which the human is turned into a machine, a technology

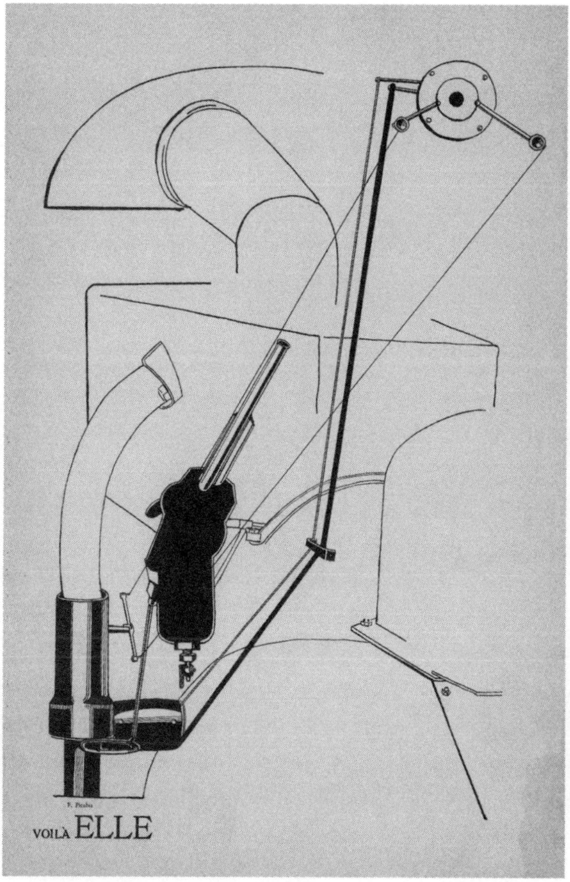

Fig. I2.3 Francis Picabia, *Voilà Elle*, 1915. Miriam and Ira D. Wallach Division of Art, Prints and Photographs: Photography Collection, The New York Public Library.

for the extraction of value. This is meant in a concrete sense insofar as labor-time becomes fixed over time as fixed capital, as equipment. Picabia foresaw a techno-capitalist future dependent on a kind of circular logic in which the workers contribute to a global machinery of value against their own self-interest, a compulsion driven by a social unconscious.

Having posited the model of the subject—once subject insofar as subject to and of a sovereign power, now replaced by the money relation—Marx reminds the reader that this new subject finds its place in an invisible totality.

> The totality of the process appears as an objective interrelation which arises spontaneously from nature; arising, it is true, from the mutual influence of conscious individuals on one another, but neither located in their consciousness nor subsumed under them as a whole. Their own

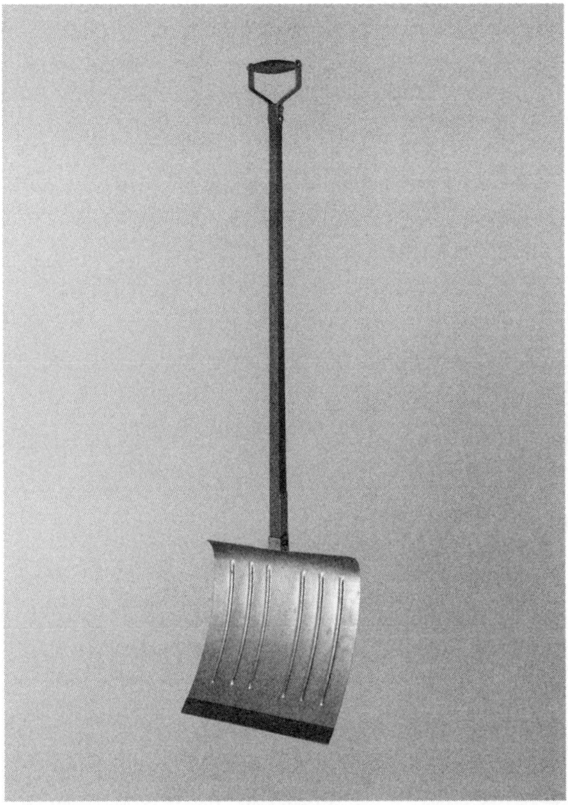

Fig. I2.4 Marcel Duchamp, *In Advance of a Broken Arm*, 1915. © The Museum of Modern Art / Licensed by SCALA / Art Resource, NY.

> collisions with one another produce an alien social power standing above them, produce their mutual interaction as a process and a power independent of them. Circulation, because a totality of the social process, is also the first form in which the social relation appears as something independent of the individual, but not only as, say, a coin or an exchange value, but extending to the whole of the social movement itself.[25]

Individual experience is blind to the totality set in place by the market in which social synthesis is constituted through transaction and where labor-power is sold "behind the backs" of conscious intentions. Abstraction, then, is a social relation. The aesthetic conjuncture marked by Dada and other avant-gardes (1917) echoes the degree to which the abstraction brought to bear by real subsumption in everyday life, where worker-subjects were forged in relation to the sale of their labor-power, comes to mediate aesthetic mediation; the artwork surfaced as signal and index—as opposed to reflection or representation—of abstraction at the level of the real, the "real abstraction" wreaked by capital that Marx elaborates in *Grundrisse* and against which he brackets off "aesthetic abstraction."[26]

But again, the better question might be to ask why aesthetic experience, bracketed off from the heteronomy of everyday life, should organize this issue through the figure of the sex workers who have nothing but their proverbial skin in the game, nothing but their labor-power. This figure stands for a set of social relations that can be understood and *objectified* as a diagram of a metabolic mediated by an abstract transaction and configured as value. The sex worker comes to allegorize anonymous socially necessary labor-time and market transaction and functions as a social technology elaborated to maximize the value-form that by midcentury would be understood as technology as such. What the artwork I analyze here illuminates is the way this "subject"—whose labor-time is embedded and constitutive of both commodities and the equipment to produce commodities—becomes part of the technology or medium through which to "see."

The ready-made might also be taken as a *theory of technology* and of the way anonymous labor-time's calcification into objects and equipment in turn requires a new orientation toward objects. Dada's response to modernity in the form of the ready-made has been called the theoretical object of the twentieth century par excellence, precisely for the way it articulates and indeed *theorizes* impossible-to-"represent" (because they are totalizing, diffusely) fundamental changes in the metabolic subtending and constituting everyday life.[27] But in the last instance, the fact that art continues to carry an irreducible excess of uncanny prescience belies explanation. The prefigurative and sensitive timeliness of the works traced in this book suggests that the artwork is often ahead of its own time to the extent that it is perceived to have a kind of premonitory vision. More realistically, the artwork signals that which has come to pass but defies denotation or even description until it has already been transformed, such that it appears to "fall out of time," or at least as autonomous and prefiguratively "reflective." As such, it recovers time but only in hindsight. This dialectic is heightened under capitalist manufacture and the total domination of the workday, beyond the technical hours of work.[28]

Abstraction—defined now as the total, if invisible, organization of society through the formation of the subject via the sale of labor-power realized as a transactional exchange—is expressed in technology. This dynamic motivates concrete lives such that its power is everywhere and unlocatable; its effects can only be traced. Art's askance location, neither transcendental nor instrumental, is potentially universal and yet bears a capacity to both grasp the movement of history and de-reify its formation. In this sense, this book is a theory of modern art and technology insofar as the latter emerges alongside a changing model of the subject under real abstraction—actually existing (if unconscious) operations in the social field. This social abstraction founded in the organization and specific composition of the subject produced *by* capitalist social relations is the condition of possibility for the putative turn to technology. Social abstraction is itself the prefiguration of technology—objectified and externalized relations. Technology, in turn, is merely congealed labor aggregated over the *longue durée*.[29]

Chapter 1, "Georges Seurat's Muses, Abstracted: Abstract Anonymous Labor and the Beginnings of Aesthetic Abstraction," traces Seurat's attempt to articulate a newly wrought social regime reticulated through metricized time expressed by the relationship between the clock, labor, and the wage. The accelerating sale of labor-power and its way of reconstituting everyday life on an almost molecular level is indexed in the formal and procedural experiments that the artist explored in painterly technique. I focus primarily on Seurat's last large panel, *The Models* (1888), for the way in which it situates the nude as a common worker—neither goddess nor prostitute—undressing for pay. The question of the mythical body—Venus or the Other in an orientalist vein—and the material reality of the sex worker, as Manet had posited it, is both canceled and radicalized in the figure of the wageworker. Seurat adopts the theme of the model as common worker, paid by the artist for her time, rather than a mythical figure as an iconographic framework to explore a social unconscious newly forged in the sale of anonymous labor-time. Seurat's uncanny sensitivity to the problem of social cohesion through separation, procedurally reperformed at the level of painting itself, conveys an understanding of labor-time as a matrix of abstraction. However, the way in which the final picture comes together through the synthesis of separated dots of color, the artist's well-known pointillist technique, indexes the contradictory way in which the very same social operations, namely, an expanding market of labor-power that estranges individuals and communities, that separates and divides, also paradoxically constitutes the only binding social synthesis in a reified world. The emergence of painterly abstraction in Seurat's oeuvre becomes a way to signal an otherwise impossible-to-convey social, which is to say real, abstraction. In its inquiry into the forms of separation and synthesis unconsciously demanded of workers who toil daily only to self-replicate, Seurat's abstraction both informs and complicates the era's more explicit figures of prostitutes in other painters' work (from Claude Monet to Edgar Degas), teasing out what "universal prostitution" might mean. Pivotally, if Seurat's attention to *structural transition* turned away from some of the more familiar forms of the day—namely, the prostitute—he nonetheless retained the genre of the nude. And this raises once more the question of gender as a way to try to figure the new modern worker. As Manet had done before him in *Olympia*, the common genre is mobilized to demonstrate the way modern time, wrought by labor, changes the *how*—not the *what*—of that which can be perceived and recognized in the field of the real.

Chapter 2, "Francis Picabia's Real Abstraction and the Beginnings of Futurist Cyborgs: The Prefigurative Avant-Gardes," turns to the work of Dada artist Francis Picabia, who in turn returns to the problem of the figure of the prostitute, this time through Marx's own language. Picabia's "mechanomorphs" elaborate the questions of reification and the subject in relation to the accelerated circuitry of value that seems to become independent of human agent. Alongside the mechanomorphs is Picabia's singular use of the diagram interrogating the gap between labor-power and its bearer. The question of abstraction, of the division between intellectual and manual labor, and its reification becomes a function of the machine, as Jason Smith has made clear in a series published by *Third Rail* on the burning question of automation in the era of artificial intelligence titled "Nowhere to Go: Automation Then and Now":

> It may be that the history of capitalism is the history of automation. Warnings about the perils of automation are as old as the capitalist mode of production. The first revolts of the workers' movement produced the myths of General Ludd and Captain Swing, and the insurrectionary forays of the canuts of Lyon. In their wake were left wrecked shearing frames and looms; proletarian arsonists targeted barns, buildings, and goods. Yet the development of the productive forces, and the implementation of large-scale machinery in capitalist factories, never quite made workers purely and simply redundant. To the contrary, over the course of more than a century, the demand for labor had grown exponentially, even as millions of peasants poured into cities, and entered into the wages system and the urban cash nexus.

Picabia's diagrams initiate a new formal device by which to think the "human" as a function of reification, a becoming-machine to lubricate value's machinery.

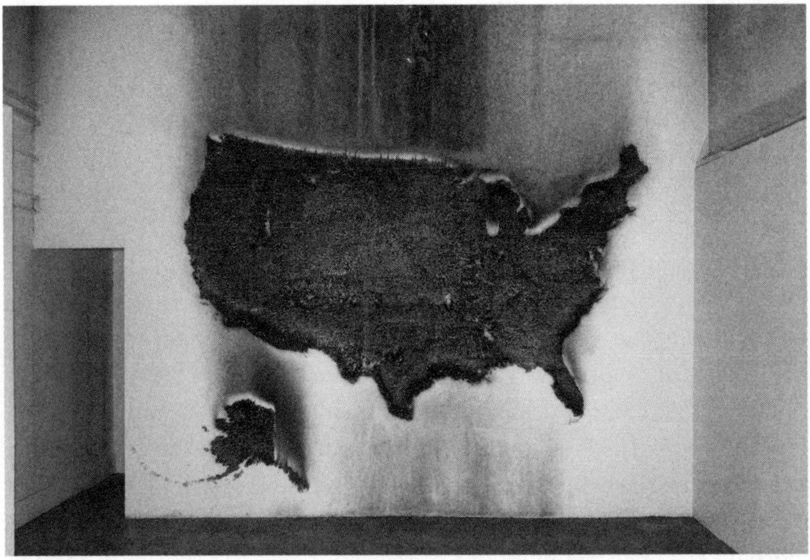

Fig. I2.5 Claire Fontaine, *America (burnt/unburnt)*, 2011. Burnt/unburnt matchsticks, dimensions variable. Queen's Nails, The Mission, San Francisco, 01.12. Courtesy of Claire Fontaine.

Chapter 3, "The Future of the Futurists: The Young-Girl En/gendering Real Abstraction," focuses on Tiqqun's *Preliminary Materials for a Theory of the Young-Girl*, a prose poem that elaborates the figure of the worker-subject within capitalism as begun by Picabia and Duchamp. I make a case for this hybrid subgenre in order to argue for why this particular formal and historicist device is necessary to convey meaning to a new generation of readers who are fully subjugated to capital yet interested in a counterpraxis and counterlogistics in order to thrive. This is where the avant-gardist manifesto or futurist prose poem gains greatest currency.

The fourth chapter, "The [Young-Girl] Worker as Equipment: Yves Klein's Living Paintbrushes," continues the analysis of worker-subject-as-thing through a case study of the midcentury French painter Yves Klein's use of the model. In yet another metamorphosis at the level of form, Klein declared the nude women working as paid models in his studio to be "living paintbrushes." In his 1960 text "Truth Becomes Reality," Klein explained how he turned subjects (already objectified by gender) into objects saturated in paint (à la Alexander Rodchenko) to apply pigment to a receptive surface while he himself maintained physical and emotional distance from the canvas in order to avoid expressive interiority and "psychology" of any kind. But a half century later, in an interview with the BBC in October 2016, one of the artist's former models from the 1960s, Elena Palumbo-Mosca, insisted that despite Klein's language, the women hired to work in the studio and who were applicators of paint did in fact engage in difficult intellectual labor, becoming interlocutors and assistants in multiple ways. As Palumbo-Mosca stated, "I was not a paintbrush because, in spite of it all, I did use my brain."[30] Chapter 4 continues the analysis of the division of intellectual and manual labor, a division heightened and objectified in a situation where one human asks another to become a tool for the manufacture of the work that was once understood to be a representation of her, that is, *the* nude. This almost alchemical metamorphosis of muse into worker and allegory-made-instrument emblematizes the thrust of this book's argument. Taking up this division as doubly determined insofar as it is historically and socially organized along a binary of gender—namely, as a condition that women are asked to bear with a (doubly devalued) double burden—I then take up the writing of avant-garde fellow traveler Pierre Klossowski to think though the contradictions unleashed in Klein's project. Klossowski's use of the term *living currency* to describe the particular value of women as bearers of value, a general equivalent anterior to and formative of money itself, is updated through a reading of Luce Irigaray's "Women on the Market," in which the author explores the originary source of value as such: women.[31]

Chapter 5, "Surplus Bodies: Santiago Sierra's Exploitive Remuneration," explores the emergence of "delegated" performance. In June 2001, Spanish artist Santiago Sierra gathered 133 men to take part in his project for the Spanish Pavilion at the 49th Venice Biennale. Sierra's "action," titled *133 Persons Paid to Have Their Hair Dyed Blonde* (figure I2.6), took place at the opening of one of the international art industry's most auspicious events. The criteria for selecting the men were as follows: they were to originate from Africa, Asia, or the Middle East and have dark hair. The participants were immigrants and refugees, legal or otherwise. Sierra directed the men to an area in the Arsenale where he bleached their hair, producing a visibly artificial appearance.

The bleached hair on dark bodies effectively marked each person as though with a yellow highlighter. The self-assigned role of the artist was to collect, direct, and manage these persons within the spatial parameters of the Arsenale only, in the institutionalized framework of the art exhibition, and before an audience. Thereafter, however, the yellow-headed persons dispersed, returning to their everyday activities: predominantly illegal street vending on

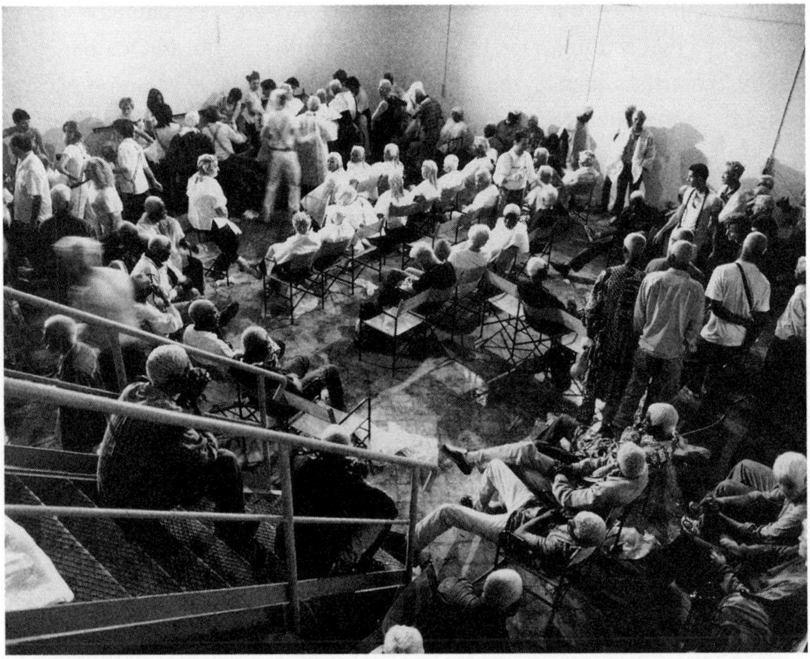

Fig. I2.6 Santiago Sierra, *133 Persons Paid to Have Their Hair Dyed Blonde*, 2001. © Santiago Sierra / VEGAP, Madrid / CARCC, Ottawa, 2024.

and around Piazza San Marco, a form of survival and daily self-replication. Sierra expands the genre of performance art, a genre already saturated in the contradictions of exploitive remuneration and the shifting nature of labor, to limn the racializing dynamic nested within the labor-capital relationship. As such, he probes the racialized extraction of labor power from surplus populations. Indeed, this artist introduced to contemporary art discourse the fact of surplus populations, those demographics formally unemployable for reasons having to do with state and identity yet held in reserve for their labor-power. Sierra located and identified a contradiction implemented by the state form to legally distribute the very value of human life and, within the brutal parameters of capitalist value, its very right to self-valorization. The key point here, at once critically expanding on lacunae in Marx's analysis and contributing to a larger structural understanding of the totality of capitalist social relations, is that any given labor pool is divided into those relations that are legally mediated by a wage and those that are not. This form of mediation is then rationalized by deference to categories of identity that retroactively legitimize the socially divisive brutality with which labor-power is extracted. The way that racialization and abstraction are co-constitutive is raised with urgency in this fifth chapter as well as in the conclusion.[32]

The book concludes with an analysis of Hannah Black's project *The Meaning of Life* (2022), which revisits modernist concerns around the mobility of the sign, opacity and transparency (of the material support, of meaning, of reference, of information) that had preoccupied aesthetic abstraction beginning with Cubist collage, now situated in social field structured by racialized concrete abstraction. The dialectic between living and dead labor, and between the social operations implicit in the gift and in theft in relation to the commodity, is demonstrated to be a function of racialization, proven by the uneven weight of the law in its adjudication of which bodies are allowed to live or made to die in a biopolitical regime founded on real abstraction. Needless to say, Black's work addresses the role of police in enforcing social relations set in place by the primacy of property and the unconscious syntheses ratified on the (labor) market. She explores how race itself is imbricated with real abstraction. Black's work offers a glimpse of what the "meaning of life," of eros and joy, might be, freed from the social abstractions enforced by the value-form.

1

Georges Seurat's Muses, Abstracted

Abstract Anonymous Labor and the Beginnings of Aesthetic Abstraction

> The abstraction, therefore, lies not in the thought of the sociologist, but in society itself.
> —Theodor Adorno, *Introduction to Sociology*

Already by the 1880s, Georges Seurat had responded to the seeming spontaneity of the Impressionist brushstroke by demonstrating painting to be a function of a highly quantified and calibrated process for which the artist charged by the hour, in mediated identification with the unskilled model exposing her body to fatigue for hourly pay.[1] *The Models* (1888), which took more than eighteen months to complete, was begun just as Seurat completed his previous major work, *A Sunday on La Grande Jatte*. The earlier picture had been read critically in its own time as a meditation on indifference, anomie, and the new social character of public life as a function of class and consumerist hierarchy in Paris during the 1880s. Here, in *The Models*, the earlier *painting* is repainted, repeated, *en abyme*, nested within this second social analysis. If the first picture described social anomie resulting from modernity, the second addressed the material source of this anomie. This duplication, in a second picture set in the artist's studio, might offer an account of the creeping sense of morbid indifference that seemed to saturate the social scene in the earlier picture. It might be taken as an explanation, in the form of a painting, of the behind-the-scenes conditions within which the earlier work was made, or what those conditions might themselves be "about" insofar as this cannot, the second painting suggests, be narrativized. The way the picture is doubled in the later work suggests a programmatic *demonstration* of painting's conditions, even of abstraction's beginnings, over any narrative. It seems to defy narrative and to be instead about the nature of the production itself. A picture about a depicted picture, the painting makes clear that it is a way of thinking about the conditions within which painting is possible. And because it signals a studio space where some form of labor and an attendant kind of metabolic exchange are necessary to painting, it suggests an exploration of the social conditions of exchange within which an artwork is made.

Seurat multiplies the presentation of scenes, nesting one within the site of its production in a way that demonstrates the degree to which technical operations at the level of painting itself—the pointillist technique generative of the first spectacularly successful painting—are related to the laborious, meticulous, at once skilled and skill-dismantling technique elsewhere, outside the frame.[2] This "outside" the picture, literally outside the earlier painting if inside the second, is the scene of work itself, insofar as the represented elements in the picture that convey the relationship between artist, model, and painterly surface articulate a late nineteenth-century capitalist social totality. Much has been made of Seurat's crossing the edge of the painting with pointillist dots and moving onto the frame itself. At the level of process, this signals Seurat's concern that the frame must not be read as a finite edge but rather as an index of the world outside the picture.

At the level of pointillist procedure and painterly technique, the artist mimetically inscribes the socially necessary labor-time—both the artist's labor-time and that of the model—to generate a totality.[3] In other words, by building the painting through separate points of color that synthesize in the eye of the beholder, Seurat is already allegorically performing the degree to which any totality within capital is a function of fragmentation and separation. This optical synthesis performed here and now before us in the form of a painterly essay is shown to be a function of fragmentation, separation, repetition, and (potential) anonymity—figured in the model(s). It affords a glimpse into the new worker-subject—the new worker that Marx initially identified as a universal prostitute, set to whatever scenario would fetch a wage. But what makes this figure—otherwise as singular as each "dot"—"universal" other than its abstraction as so much labor-time, regardless of the substance of its experiential life? In the figure of anonymity that any worker is, buyer and seller of labor-time are both unconsciously tethered to the transactional space of the market, which is indifferent to the specificity of identity or experience and which doubles as a site for the realization of capitalist circuits of production. Yet despite the social abstraction cast by the exchange of labor-time, this transactional space is also the crucible in which the modern subject is forged. This chapter, nested within the larger argument of the book, asks why Seurat's exploration of the emergent worker-subject is performed in painting and, once again, over the figure of the nude and the troubled representation of the naked female body. I'll then ask why the worker-subject, even in Seurat's empathic paintings, is imagined again, as in Marx's early writing, as a woman selling access to her body for a measure of time—visual access, in this instance. Why is this the primary way to imagine the worker-subject's sale of labor-time?

This chapter explores how painting probes the strangeness of the transactional sale of labor-time and its immediate effect—the inauguration of a new kind of worker-subject. Taking a detour into social art history and into Seurat's biography to explore the latter's circle of comrades among whom anarchists figured significantly, I trace the way that Seurat's social concerns were inscribed in his paintings at the compositional and procedural levels. This form of inscription, far from any transparent reflection, indicates much of the entwined relationship between real, or social, abstraction and aesthetic abstraction in early modernism.

Seurat referred to his paintings as *toiles de luttes*, "canvases of battle." This nomenclature already begins to indicate his prescience in recognizing that a new social form, a new ontology, had not only emerged but was being set into antagonistic relation to the very social order it engendered through its own labor. The new worker motivated a radical new form of painting from within the carapace of an old medium. This new form, were it to have any claim to cogency, would need to acknowledge social abstraction as the new matrix of everyday life. It would also have to recognize that antagonism—in canvases of battle—no longer operated as simple enmity or antipathy toward the social field but would, on the contrary, be a last resort to forging any kind of community against social abstraction. As Seurat's exceptional painting indicates, gender and technology stand at a crucial conjuncture in that battle, poised anew at the opening of proletarianized modernity insofar as they introduce difference, contradiction, and antagonism from within class structure. This comes to ramify across the century. Like a new "species of being" (*Gattungswesen*), as Marx put it, with a new ontological bearing, the proletarian emerged onto the arena of history in the late eighteenth century, a novel subject formed by and through the intergenerational experience of subjection to the wage, a new form of measurement of labor and self-expenditure reticulated to the clock.[4] But this leaves unanswered the question of the gendered worker-subject's origins, both in Marx's astonishing language—"universal prostitution"—and in Seurat's enigmatic *Models*.

Having been trained at the École des Beaux-Arts, Seurat explored the parameters of radical social change by first pushing the boundaries of the medium to meet transformation at its most molecular yet ramifying locus: the sale of labor. This ramified at the level of painterly form; representing urban scenes in traditional ways could not begin to indicate fundamental change in the totality of everyday life. Compelled to renew the medium at the even more molecular level of mark making, Seurat initiated aesthetic abstraction as a tortuous process of coming to grips with a very real abstraction newly, yet unconsciously, structuring the social field. Aesthetic abstraction at its inception responds to real abstraction, which cannot be represented in any transparent way. While it goes without saying that the artwork retains its opacity and its margin of difference from labor and from the commodity, this ultimate irreducibility does not seal off the artwork from coming to terms with new forms of work and new kinds of workers—above all at the levels of process and practice.

Through this "struggle," Seurat gave form to one of the earliest instances of aesthetic abstraction. Generated through heated dialogue with comrades in the sciences of vision and physiognomic optics as well as those involved with the ultraleft regarding the means whereby art and politics might be part of any social mediation, Seurat's work elaborated a modality of aesthetic abstraction set into dialogue with concrete social abstractions that structured modernism (and post-modernism) from behind the scenes. Based on the theories of Michel Chevreul and Charles Blanc—that is, on physiology and optics—Seurat demonstrated a way of allowing the picture to be reconstituted in the act of viewing as a totality of optical relations. Reconstituted in reception, the pointillist system may suggest division as the modus operandi of industrial manufacture, but it also accomplishes a form of perceptual synthesis that summons other forms of synthesis—namely, synthesis as a function of consumption and circulation. This painterly analytical breakdown and reconstitution also signaled something of Seurat's larger political aspiration that a radical empiricism at the level of vision would translate into potentially revolutionary forms of sociality. While writers across the decades—from Meyer Shapiro, Norma Broude, Linda Nochlin, and John Rewald to Jonathan Crary, Carol Armstrong, Michelle Foa, and others—focus on Seurat's technique as an expression of social anomie, I turn to how, on the contrary, his technique thinks the changing nature of synthesis within abstraction.

With *The Models*, Seurat replaces the last traces of realism, a pictorial episteme originating in mimetic illusionism long ossified into a rigid discourse that most nineteenth-century painters from Gustave Courbet to Claude Monet were dismantling, but Seurat dismantles and replaces traditional (social) realism with a mode of painting that self-reflexively emphasizes the practice and process of its own laborious repetitive making over the neoclassical figurative depiction of objectified labor. This process, *seeming* to abstract the concrete world about which it speaks, actually *performs* the reverse: it affords a way to see and think the actual abstraction of everyday life and how that abstraction is a function of an unconscious social synthesis endemic to the structure of capitalist social formations, which, in case the phenomenology of the process is too opaque, remains grounded in a referent: labor-time. *The Models* does this as much through what it presents as *how* it is presented, turning from narrative realism to composition itself. Seurat's studious interest in the science of color offered one technical route to rethink composition and process in the era of capitalist social recomposition, which in turn afforded the artist a way to think about social composition and painterly composition as indexically entwined.

Seurat worked through the problem of abstraction, in both the aesthetic and social sense, within a circle of close colleagues and comrades from leftist and scientific communities. This close-knit circle included the woman who modeled and worked for him, whom he met through anarchist circles shared with poet and writer Félix Fénéon. Jonathan Crary has carefully reconstructed the extent to which discourses around physiological optics had entered broad discussions among wider social circles and remarks that these concepts "were part of a large and collective body of psychological and neurological concepts that by the end of the 1880s had become widely familiar and influential."[5]

In 1884, Seurat attended Charles Henry's first lectures at the Sorbonne, where the latter "filled a little blackboard with equations and figures in which he used dress-mannequins draped with varicolored clothes in order to illustrate points in the theory of colors."[6] Henry was an autodidact who lectured at the Sorbonne and who was interested above all in the rationalization of labor but who framed a secondary research path into labor through theories of perception. Henry not only helped Seurat discover mechanisms to reveal the "rationalization of labor" being undertaken by capitalism; he envisioned a system of correspondences between color, line, and emotion that would ultimately "expand the agreeable within us and outside of us, and from this point of view its social function is immense in this time of oppression and blind conflicts."[7] In attendance at these lectures along with Seurat were Paul Signac and Camille Pissarro. According to Georges Lecmote, "Seurat patiently drank them in and later explained them to Pissarro."[8]

Although Seurat attended his talks, he did not personally meet Henry until 1885. By that time, Seurat had begun exploring in paint the degree to which composition might relate to the social formation of capitalist labor that both men were exploring. While the utopian aspiration to correlate form and social intervention did not come to fruition, and while Henry himself, according to Crary, was more on the side of instrumentalizing rationalist theories to arrive at efficient value-productive models of labor, a Taylorist *avant-la-lettre*, Seurat's work affords a view into abstraction as articulated by an artist who handled the question like a scientist. Abstraction as a problem crossing the scientific, social, and aesthetic registers is imbricated in a larger social unity, however unconscious, wherein the economic, political, and aesthetic de- and recompose in a totality. This painterly artistic research poses an explanation for how individual subjects are situated in relation to a totality to which they have no conscious access—that is, the social unconscious structured by transactional social formations on an increasingly determinative market.[9] Some, in recognition of this inaccessible unity, have gone so far as to state that "the emergence of modern art dealing is a particular subdomain of capitalism, but one which sloughed off its artisanal skin by integrating financial strategies with a cultural repertoire."[10] The relationship between the aesthetic proposition and an economic unconscious structured by the sale of time itself runs like an undercurrent across modernism and into our contemporary era.

The pages to follow explore this early scene of social and aesthetic abstraction as a flashback, looking briefly first at an example of its twenty-first-century reiteration in a different technical support. Hindsight offers a kind of clarity that the blind field of lived time within the second nature of the real abstraction of everyday life cannot.

The Clock (2010) (figure 1.1), a paradigmatic contemporary artwork by Christian Marclay, advances a more recent exploration of abstraction as an articulation of invisible concrete abstraction. The piece stitches numerous film clips of clocks into a twelve- to twenty-four-hour—depending on the iteration and installation of the work—video projection. Marclay's deliberate recombination of a wide variety of source material, of almost infinite quantity and ultimately "the same" through the range of difference, generates a seamless flow of visual information in which the object pictured (the clock) moves in synchrony with the timing of the support itself. A time-based medium, that support is a lens-based mode of capturing, recording, and projecting that which already lends itself to time at the level of mediation and form. In other words, there is an at once reflexive and indexical relationship between form and content, support and object. The clock is a figurable way of representing time to the camera, itself a fundamental step in the elabora-

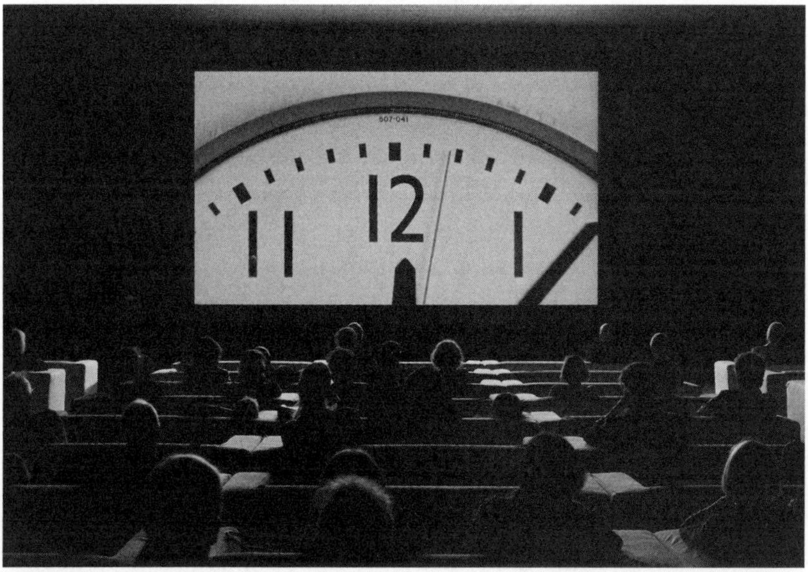

Fig. 1.1. Christian Marclay, *The Clock*, 2010. Tate, purchased jointly by Tate, London, with funds provided by the American Fund for the Tate Gallery; Centre Pompidou, Musée national d'art moderne, Paris; and The Israel Museum, Jerusalem, 2012. © Christian Marclay. Photo © Tate.

tion of time-based visual media such as film. Rosalind Krauss has referred to Marclay's painstaking suture between image and time as the pure synchronicity of disparate forms: that of representing time and the other of seeming to produce time, or "synch-time." At the same time, the division and separation of any number of images from their "original" context into an almost liquid-like delivery substitutes fragmentation with a new kind of combination that hypnotically begins to feel natural over time. Synch-time, the suture of the image of the clock to time via the camera, affords a way by which to present an otherwise disciplined and fragmented mechanical process resulting from separation and division as fluid presentation of synthesis.[11]

While *The Clock* initially generates disorientation with its excess fixation on rationalization, it comes to be almost mesmerizingly soothing over time. It could lull the viewer to sleep as much from fascination as boredom. While clock time is a formal organizing principle of everyday life, the piece occupies and bends normal clock time. The piece is almost "invisibly" split from within: the seamlessness and fluidity of the edits montaged together in flowing time-based movement contradict the *picture*, the visual register, presented in each moment. Fluidity stands in resistance to the banality of the mechanical order denoted by the image of the clock. This stealthy cognitive-perceptual split might be said to elaborate itself over the course of the piece insofar as the seamless flow suggests one affective relation, while the turgid repetition of the same icon, a clock, again and again becomes, after a while, stultifyingly dull. This internal, initially imperceptible, division and reversal might be said on the face of things to "reflect" life within capitalist abstraction. Unfortunately, the situation Marclay articulates is at once much simpler than any transparent "reflection" and much more complex. *The Clock* moves through twenty-four hours of one-minute clips drawn from existing film stock of clocks. This particular segment of time is not arbitrary or neutral; it is "reflective" insofar as it internalizes the legally entrenched commercial conditions in which it locates its legibility. Were each clip to be any longer, Marclay as the "author" would be in tremendous financial debt to the copyright holder of each and every source from which each clip is drawn. In this instance, time is money; money is time. The piece, for all its numerous allegorical capacities, has herewith materialized its awareness and flight from that socially normative legal constraint itself supporting the flow of capital as such above and over any particular individual or lived situation.

In her essay "Clock Time," on Marclay's exploration of the way that a "new" medium is structurally informed by and responsive to the totalizing logic of clock time, both index and allegory of capital's near autonomy from experiential time, Krauss notes that "the illusion of movement overrides the film frame's appearance, creating the visual slippage we call 'the movies,'" in such a way that viewer and screen move into a symbiotic relationship. Other to narratival suture, Marclay's hypnotizing synch-sound is different from narrative identification. However, as image and time move together in a rhythm that compels as much as it estranges, it is as though viewer and image were newly at every second constituted by the other. This indexes a temporality of production, a productive ontology summoned moment by moment. This is an economy of interpellation within which the subject recognizes themself as the one addressed by the image, not to enter into a story with personifications and characters so much as simply the generator of infinite plenitude assembled of fragmentation. We come to identify with its source, the visual data streaming on the screen.[12]

This highly artificial redundancy comes not only to influence; it *comes to define the viewer*. In a strange and unexpected reversal of all we have come to hear about medium specificity—about a still medium such as painting or photography in contradistinction to time-based mediums like music, literature, and film, each of which constrains and therefore motivates specific ranges of possibility—Marclay's inundation of apparent movement suggests another kind of constraint, an abstract constraint, nowhere near as self-evident as merely spatial (as in painting and photography) or temporal (as in music, narrative, time-based media).

Krauss emphasizes the way that Marclay acknowledges "the technical support," in contrast to any artisanal hands-on support, as a means of carving a specific experience of that which it purports to be "about": clock time. This might be differentiated from numerous other kinds of time: cyclical time, narrative time, et cetera. Again, this experience is split between the seamlessness of suture and the staccato movement of each moment registered by each clock. *The Clock* enacts this reflexive yet split path through the historicity of perception itself in modernity through recursive reference to that adjudicator of value: time. Drawn from late nineteenth-century to contemporary source materials, the footage references the era of capitalist time: value squeezed out of a suture between labor and time. If science and physics stipulate that density is mass over volume, profit derives from accelerating the relation between the expenditure of labor-power and time. This relation is represented by the value-form, although Marclay's *Clock* circumnavigates this "hidden cause."

Marclay's piece picks up the structural logic of production itself, even as we watch the artwork unfold in real time, bearing witness to its own production and producibility. Marclay picks up the medium through which value is produced and measured in an estranged mimicry of the process of production in general, given that there is no other "content," no narrative and therefore no conflict and closure, finally: nothing but production in infinite process, its repetition perceived as rhythmic or fluid, its technicity perceived as almost organic, random order offered as *necessary*—in short, heightened productive temporalities become a kind of second nature.

This mimetic economy *sutures* the viewer to the work.[13] But unlike the use of suture to connect the viewer to the artwork or culture product (such as cinema, television, or any other lens-based form), Marclay not only connects (montage) but disidentifies through the deadening repetition's odd relation to a fluidly presented yet infinitely internally differentiated range of objects: an infinity of clocks. The clocks, in their immense range, are at once different and yet utterly the same, in measurement to the same law. This reveals and estranges time itself as a social synthesis, medium, or support organizing all of perception. After a while, much less the twelve- to twenty-four-hour duration of the piece that is an entire day broken into synch-sound, reflection on the technical support might facilitate recognition that the mundane understanding of time is highly artificial. What is, on the face of it, not unpleasant becomes a jarring presentation of the anything-but-natural presentation of time. Marclay suggests that the perception of time is itself a function of the modern forms that issue it: clocks, mechanical devices, give rise to time, and time itself—whatever that may be—is simply not self-evident, at least not in any unmediated way.

If time is thus naturalized, Marclay reminds us that this seeming "nature" is a second nature derived from a highly differentiated, abstract structure that subtends the field of the real prior to its apperception. This seismic yet molecular shift in the advent of abstraction at the level of the social field, signaled later by the ready-made, originated in the nineteenth century, notably in the way that many of its most searching artists tried to articulate this ontological change in the "nature" of things—once they have become second nature. While Marclay questions the mechanical and digital support as a function of capitalist time, Seurat had already tried to address the ontological changes at the heart of the metabolic of everyday life through a soon-to-be-obsolete artisanal medium: painting and the brushstroke.

Seurat's *The Models* (figure 1.2) mobilizes the pointillist technique that appears in the painting within the painting, this time building up the image of women in various poses and stages of undress. They take their places in what is clearly the artist's working space, as denoted by the numerous pictures hanging on the wall, including *A Sunday on La Grande Jatte* (figure 1.3). Rhyming it, there are any number of quadrilinear forms on the wall to the right. In the long tradition of painting of artists' studios, beginning with Diego Velázquez's *Las Meninas* and its many pictures within the depicted room, the painter could not make any clearer the nature of the depicted space as a place of work. But unlike the former's meditation on secular power and the location of sovereignty, Seurat's studio scene points to the artist's work insofar as it sets artwork into a network of questions about the material conditions of the work's possibilities, however banal, however far from the breathtaking drama of courtly political life. It entails first and most manifestly the labor-intensive work of repainting an earlier work, to the point of tedium.

Although the painter's own repetitive work and the labor of replicating prior realized work enter into resonance with newly generalized anonymous, proletarianized labor, the process constitutive of the work, include this second time as we step further back to see the scene in which the prior scene

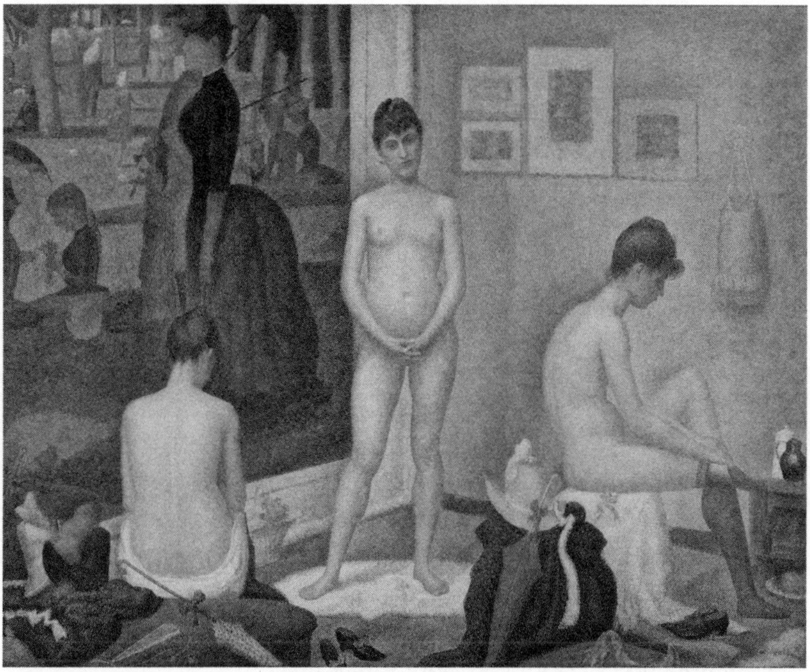

Fig. 1.2. Georges Seurat, *The Models*, 1888. © The Barnes Foundation, Philadelphia, PA.

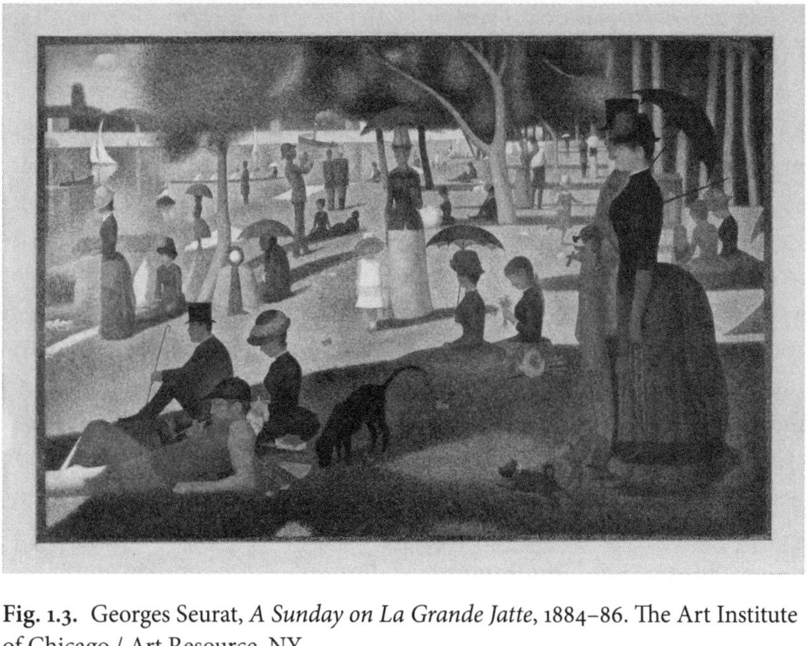

Fig. 1.3. Georges Seurat, *A Sunday on La Grande Jatte*, 1884–86. The Art Institute of Chicago / Art Resource, NY.

was made, the labor of an *other* whose labor-time is inscribed in the product. At the level of its presentation and re-presentation of the earlier work, Seurat offers a "representation" (although this will be shown to be far from clear) of the eponymous models. They are the figures whose work as models makes the composition of the picture possible, not unlike the actual living woman or women (more on this later) engaged in banal tasks, such as sitting for the picture in various states of dress and undress, who will be potentially immortalized in an artwork, overwriting the banality of their hourly work but doing little to mitigate material necessity. The question of the models' embodiment, their somatic endurance and material self-replication, is indicated in the studies for *The Models*, in which the artist included the image of a small stove, thereby acknowledging the need for thermal warmth on the part of naked bodies in the real space and time that makes the final picture possible. In the final picture, the state of warmth and comfort are noted insofar as the bodies of this woman or women are surrounded by various accoutrements telling us that very practical gear of everyday life. Practical daily gear like stockings and umbrellas were all shed for the task performance at hand. Seurat notes these objects as signs of social bodies leaving "life" to enter the scene of work necessary for his painting to be made.

As noted but maybe deserving a moment's pause, studies for the final work indicate that Seurat considered ways to address material circumstances, such as shelter and warmth, symbolically. In *Study for "Poseuses"* (figure 1.4), a stove absent from the final version of the painting anchors the scene. This study explicitly *denotes* the material and financial issue of the thermal warmth and caloric consumption necessary to daily self-replication in the metropolis in the late 1880s. Seurat did numerous studies of this little stove, seemingly incidental, thereby quietly marking its significance. The inclusion of a stove in the otherwise spare room in the study would be one way to address the material facticity of warmth and energy. But the way that the studies isolate the stove and a girl, one of the titular models, suggests an allegory, if not a correlative identity, between young girl and heating apparatus. The women spend their energy to make the work of the artist possible, as the heat in the room generated by spent energy makes their presence in the room and in the work possible. There's a nested logic of production and its equally generative logic of reproduction, whereby stove and girl come to double as a resource to be extracted. The painting could be said to be "about" the expenditure of energy, of resources and the shared work-time of artist and model(s). One might guess that Seurat omitted the stove because he hoped to move from narrative form, or a story about the expenditure of embodied labor-time, into

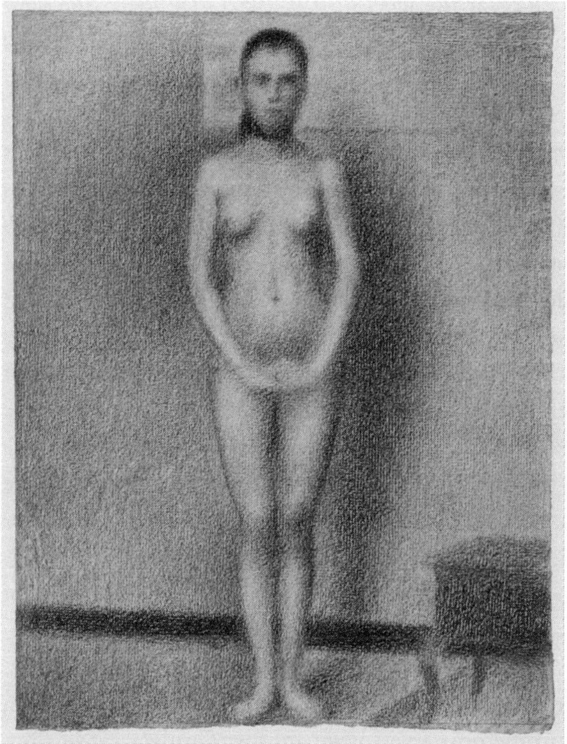

Fig. 1.4. Georges Seurat, *Study for "Poseuses,"* 1888. The Metropolitan Museum of Art, NYC.

a demonstration of synthesis, thereby mapping the iconography comprising a story onto the painterly mark, the grapheme itself, to perform the deskilled and reskilled process of pointillist division and resynthesis, the labor constitutive of this painting and the former painting, *La Grande Jatte*, that this current situation presented in *The Models* made possible.

But again, the nagging sense of enigma hovers over *The Models*, emphasized by the internal tension between "originality," seriality, and mimesis set into motion by the relation between the present painting and the redoubled past painting within it for which it serves as predecessor in some present imaginary space. There's something unnatural about the scene of work. Set into equivalence with the painting depicted inside the painting, the scene in the studio that is meant to offer us the "behind the scenes" reality of the artist's and studio workers' practice and the material process that is constitutive of an artwork instead slips *en abyme* into a dubious, equally intangible, speculative, and finally logically impossible temporality. The picture for which this picture serves as hidden abode and place of origin has already happened.

There are other questions at the level of basic narrative logic, the very logic that Seurat's paintings both dismantle and defy. For instance, how many women are in the picture? Does each represent a separate figure in *La Grande Jatte*? Does it matter if there is correlation to be assigned to identities? The figure at the left with her back turned faces the woman in Seurat's earlier picture, who in turn faces toward the eponymous bank in profile. This spatial relationship between the seated woman, her back turned toward us to face the earlier painting, might insinuate her role in the realization of that first picture. Meanwhile, the women on the right whose faces are shown appear to be twins, or doppelgängers, and unrelated to the earlier painting. In all, it seems moot whether we are looking at one or three women, and this itself is part of the picture's analysis of contemporary social relations. Much of the literature concurs that all three women are iterations of the same model, or one woman in three poses. Eric Alliez sees the painting as the presentation of three aspects of one laboring body.[14] However, there is no final consensus.

Ironically, despite the fact that her back is to us as she faces the scene of indifference, this woman whose verso we face might look somewhat familiar, more so, strangely, than those who are more visibly facing the viewer, especially to the viewer accustomed to looking at pictures and for whom a quality of resemblance in the pose may evoke another familiar image—but which? The turned-away figure, as noted by Roger Fry and others, rather loudly references a picture hanging in the Louvre, titled *Bather in a Harem Interior*, painted by none other than Seurat's teacher, Jean-Auguste-Dominique Ingres, in 1808.[15] She, this woman whose back is all we see, thus takes her place in a history of painterly citation, of representations denoting other representations. Needless to say, given that the old master Ingres never left France, the Turkish interior of the eponymous bather is pure fiction. But the scene of painterly work here and now in this picture, by Seurat, is quite concrete. And yet citation, a picture referencing a historical picture, reintroduces doubt about the very nature of realism. If Seurat is painting a much earlier painting, how is he addressing social change? If we want to tell ourselves that Seurat was looking at the daily worker models in the room, how does this canonized painting of sumptuous sensuality par excellence factor in? This once again raises the primary question of this book: How do we determine what is abstract and what is concrete under essentially abstract social relations? And how does the work of art, itself an index of its time, offer a compass through this abstracted, blind field?

Seurat's self-reflexivity at the level of process continued to be bound up with citation, as Fry and others have noted, and in a long tradition of French history painting. The decision to make explicit reference to Ingres's *Bather* in the figure of the model on the left with her back turned strikes me as a way of distinguishing her from the other two who are facing the viewer and can be identified as obvious replications of the same woman, or a representation of twins. Natural or cultural, these two raise the question of doubling and of reiteration. They do not afford any greater transparency into the picture's meaning, at least not on a narratival level.

While these two are accessible to our vision, there is nonetheless nothing familiar about them. They are either looking out at us or available in profile. Uncannily, the peculiar way in which they resemble one another while situated in different angles to vision, reopens the nagging possibility that this might be one woman in two different poses. This quality of unstable resemblance and uncomfortable mimesis takes its place among several terms in the painting that are equally disorienting, equally rendering impossible any notion of a solid or "original" term in relation to its "copy," beginning with the painting within the painting. The women are likewise set into uncertain seriality and sequence. This multiplied ambivalence pushes past basic painterly self-reflexivity to generate a sense of discomfort and doubt. Who or what is copying who or what? Does this quality of the double issue from a manufactured space or a natural origin? Where is the stable object of depiction? What, precisely, is being depicted? The consensus is that Seurat is depicting the model or worker's time at work, as a model. That reading is certainly supported by the fact that the picture is quite precocious and early to represent a woman in a state of undress who is neither a fictional nor mythological figure, nor necessarily a prostitute. Seurat's models are neither mythological nor cultural other. That they are Frenchwomen is loudly announced by the red and blue among the garments carefully set aside for the hours of task performance. But what might be said about this worker who is clearly neither a goddess nor a secular exotic à la orientalism, other than that she is a generic, anonymous body with self-reproductive needs, such as thermal warmth in analogy with resources such as remuneration and nourishment? The painting is ultimately indifferent to identity outside the anonymity and interchangeability—in short, social abstraction—as a function of modern work. Singular or plural. What might possibly qualify her as anything other than a contingent node in the expenditure of energy in the service of production destined for market valorization, a transaction of the kind the earlier picture must have either undergone or was about to undergo, to merit *this* picture, here and now, of its production.

By rendering impossible any way of deciding on the woman as singular or plural, the picture emphasizes its indifference to her identity, context, experience, or interiority. The modern proletarian is above all as qualified by her anonymity as by her capacity to be dispossessed of her former means of subsistence and reskilled to assimilate to urban life.

Yet another aspect of abstraction seeps into the picture. As this woman (or three women) slides from uniqueness to interchangeability, her (and our) indifference to her as anything other than a means to an end begs the question of that end. The models are contained in a space that finally emerges as constructed and artificial. Seurat acknowledges painterly realism in his nod to classic spatial construction, but the vertical, horizontal, and orthogonal planes of the depicted space do not add up to perspectival space. Whether a copy or not, whether an "original" space in which the kind of work that comes to be hung on the wall of the studio after its putative display before a public or another such object itself intended for exhibition and ultimately exchange, the painting is telling us in no uncertain terms that the ostensibly "real" space of the room is itself already abstract, no less or more abstract than the picture hanging inside the picture. The "real" and the depicted scene are equally manufactured, equally unnatural. And the women are equally equivalent in their seriality and interchangeability.

The grapheme set into *working* relation, with each mark separated and recombined in perceptual synthesis, begins to conceptually and perceptually rhyme with something about the forms of separation and division performed in the presentation of social formation in the picture. The women slide into a kind of indeterminacy between identity and anonymity, uniqueness and interchangeability, finally reaching a point of interpretive stillness for the viewer, only to decompose again into the same set of questions.

Seurat folds the depicted scene of remunerative labor—after all, this painting may be the first to place front and center the subject-worker whose time is spent in service to the author—into the procedures by which the painting is made. This is a reminder that Seurat inaugurates a new form of *painterly* labor to explore new forms of actual value-productive labor, or rather that the mimicry of labor becomes a way to talk about the painting's method of fabrication—another kind of self-reflexivity at the level of process. The rhyme between method and image once again confirms the degree to which Seurat's search for new forms of aesthetic mediation was motivated by new social formations.[16]

What we think we see, made possible through the optical synthesis of Seurat's technique, adds up to so many depicted objects in this practical and concrete painting about painting and begins to decompose.[17] The very labor-time presented to our vision at the level of depiction and form begins to feel fragile due to the very same assurances that deliver the material to view: the pointillist technique that guarantees a final picture also seems to render that which it presents as strangely contingent. Like Marclay's smooth, seamless synchronization of clocks to montage, the elegant color synthesis wrought by the pointillist grapheme begins to show us a content as mannered and artificial as the technique itself.

If the moment in which the picture is viewed completes the optical synthesis that Seurat worked toward, then the uncertain depiction of women tells us something about the painter's relation to forms of labor, and new social forms more broadly, that also becomes part of the visual synthesis with which to suggest social fragmentation and recomposition: the model. Her work is, after all, a source and site of his labor. The painting could not be completed without it. Once again, the inclusion of the earlier successful painting, *A Sunday on La Grande Jatte* (figure 1.3), nested inside *The Models*, makes the doubled relationship between the model and the woman in the painting within the painting ample: production of that painting necessitated a similar form of labor, a form other than the painter's pointillist work. And that form of labor on which painterly process rests finds its origin in market transaction. The model is paid to undress and to stand reserve. This point of sale is fundamentally necessary to the work, as the artist seems to be demonstrating in this second picture about the manufacture of the first. It was as though Seurat were confronting us with anonymous labor-time, put on sale, as the primary ingredient in the optical (and social) synthesis toward which the work strives. The model's presence is a *source* of visual synthesis telling us something about the matrix of modern social synthesis, structuring social experience and social relations regardless of any individual or collective intention. The uncertainty around the models' number and identity, the inevitable recrudescence of anonymity at the center of the painting, moves the open secret of real abstraction to the forefront. The scene of production leans already on a place exterior to it: the labor market that compels the worker to the place where a metabolic transformation takes place, transferring that labor-power purchased in potentia into the actual value added to the commodity.

As Alfred Sohn-Rethel notes in *Intellectual and Manual Labour*, consciousness is preoccupied with that which stands before its immediate perceptions.

These are the content and substance of lived social relations, however fragmented or carefully composed. However, standing outside and often above this consciousness is another kind of unconscious, namely, that motivated by material concerns operative under political, social, and other conscious motivations for purpose and action within everyday life. These "economic" intentions are economic on a register so at once ubiquitous and banal as to be experienced as all but invisible in the lived space of the social. At the same time, the point of sale around which the worker lives life is fundamental to the replication of every other moment. At the level of immediate consciousness, the content of concrete social relations seems to overwrite the anonymous, abstract, and ultimately autonomous (of human interest) nature of necessary compulsions under capital, which form a social unconscious that sutures together otherwise unrelated identities. These become intertwined, unconsciously:

> While the consciousness of those involved in exchange plays a role as their private consciousness, as isolated subjectivity, their actions remain objectively social, though unconsciously abstract and non-empirical. What conceals the abstractness of their activity from those involved in exchange is precisely their consciousness. The sensuous perception of the empirical qualities of things through the eyes, the ears, the sense of touch, etc. Against this, the value-relation of the products of labor within which it appears, have absolutely no connection with the physical nature of the commodity and the material [*dinglich*] relations arising out of this. The abstractness of exchange thus applies to the activity and precisely not to the thoughts and consciousness of those involved.[18]

However, objective conditions are driven by socially necessary transactions independent of experience and will, above all the necessity of the sale of labor-power itself. "Abstraction" emerges as much in the separation and resynthesis of whole demographics required by each new wave of proletarianization, as it does in the particular individual's divide between action and thought occasioned by any given transaction. Just as the use-values or qualities of the commodity are temporarily suspended when the manufactured object is sent to market, so too any specific qualities of the worker outside of their utility to the point of sale. And yet all of life comes to revolve around this momentary point of sale that cancels out all of life: "Only in this way does it become evident that the real abstraction of exchange asserts itself in two entirely different ways: on the one hand, in the economic abstraction of value, and on the other hand in the conceptual and cognitive abstraction of thought."[19] However, abstraction is the effect of the action of men and not of their thought. It takes place "behind their backs," at the blind spot, so to speak, of human consciousness, where their thinking and efforts are absorbed by their acts of exchange.[20]

In other words, this *real* of real abstraction is tricky to locate because it is to be found in the self-effacing "sacrificial economy" of labor itself. Abstract labor—and subsequently, all capitalist abstraction—emerges from processes that refashion human expenditure as a measurement of quantity that is transparent to exchange. So, while Sohn-Rethel's emphasis on the surreptitious nature of a market unconsciousness finds its explanation for abstraction in the indifferent transactional logic of the market, it is specifically the sale of labor-power as a function of time that comes to be overwritten in the moment of exchange that seals abstract social relations. This results in a split condition not unlike that between the unconscious and conscious mind, or between concrete experience and value's abstract compulsions to replicate itself. Why does the source of "real" abstraction a priori slip away from consciousness, itself equally abstract as a distinguishing feature of the species' capacity for thought independent of material necessity? This disavowal, in turn, becomes a primary matrix of social relations insofar as seemingly natural social relations revolve around a primary abstraction for its material reproduction. Capital grows independently of social interest in asymmetry to the way in which the social relies on capital to exist. Seurat's work indicates this recomposition of social order collectively and individually. While the earlier painting, *La Grande Jatte*, attended to collective social abstraction, the latter one, *The Models*, looks at the split within the worker subject between their social being and their utility as the bearer of labor-power measured by time. And while he does this at the level of iconography and compositional structure, the application of paint rationalized by separation and recombination indicates the at once molecular yet saturated extent to which the capitalist mode of production had swiftly metamorphosed into a seemingly second nature, reconstituting each object and the relations dis/connecting them.

To summarize, this unconscious space summoned by the presence of interchangeable women who have been offered payment to pose is not the unconscious theorized by psychoanalysis; it is rather that which motivates social relations under capital despite any individual free will or intention. We may be looking at the scene of production, but Seurat's work signals the effects of the market casting its long shadow over production and reception insofar as the models' time must be purchased and, in theory, the picture itself is made for a market.

The studio space might be understood as a relatively intimate space. After all, it is populated by naked and vulnerable humans. And yet the inability to distinguish the woman/women's identity in relation to the interchangeability of repetition suggests the effects of depersonalization. The space and time of a transaction involving the sale of the women's time may differ from both the space and time of production as well as the contextual situation in which those involved otherwise exist, that is, in their daily lives. Again, the transaction making this scene of production possible is anonymous, impersonal, and impervious to experience, much less consciousness. It forges an unconscious matrix indifferent to reflective determination, a.k.a. free will. We are reminded that any given transaction, including that of hiring a woman for the limited aspiration of making a picture, cancels community and replaces it with a capitalist unconscious: a market.

The transaction achieved in the sale of labor-power marks the first divide between labor itself, which is to say its capacity to generate surplus and profit for the capitalist in the transformation entailed by the expenditure of labor's energy, and any truly free self-determination on the part its bearer. This primary division mediates and echoes any number of epistemological and social categories going forward, cleaving human activity into reflective labor and manual production (agrarian, industrial, etc.), each of which require a different vector of mediated cognition with relation to the product. This division forms the first separation among human activities which causes divisions among faculties, disciplines, crafts, and modes of production, as of identity, beginning with gender. Again, Seurat's model's anonymity and interchangeability emphasize the market's disinterest in her particular relation to the nature, quality, or specificity of labor other than that her capacity for some forms of work over others is marked by and in turn marks her social belonging.

Key to Seurat's exploration of the open secret of real abstraction is the open secret of the women who sat for *The Models*. As enumerated earlier, the women in the painting are inscribed into its composition in different ways; one of the three is fully opaque to viewers, her back turned, in citation of Ingres's *Bather*. While the other two who face us indicate a form of figurative transparency that in turn dissolves in the ambiguity of their possible doubling. This already reminds us of the particular problem to which Seurat returned recursively, in this painting and in *La Grande Jatte*: social composition. Moving now from the artist's address of broad social recomposition in an age of anonymity and proletarianization to the individual life of the models, it might be time to turn to the artist's personal interests. One of the women who worked as a model for his picture bore an immediate, intimate, and concrete relationship to Seurat. She has been identified as his model and long-term companion, with whom he also had a child. This specific woman was kept secret from most of his artist associates, and certainly from his family.

In his essay "On the Origin of Abstraction: Seurat and the Screening of History," Alastair Wright carefully reconstructs the passionately fraught years of the early 1880s. In the process, he shows how Seurat's early development might be correlated, month by month, to radical leftist thinking as it swiftly matured moved across the history of the Commune.[21] Among figures associated with its formation, Louis Auguste Blanqui, who had fomented insurrectionary politics since the revolutions of the 1830s and 1840s, and Marx, noted as the figurehead of a class-conscious workers' movement in France, surfaced to the forefront of debates Seurat participated in. In the next generation of communards, Louise Michelle personified an early gendered class consciousness. As a symbolic figure in the ensuing discourse and its dialectical entwinement of history and of myth, Michelle stood in for the "*petroleuse*" of the Paris Commune.[22] Knobloch, drawn from those "types" of women associated with the politics of the *petroleuses*, was a secret made "open" only in one of Seurat's paintings: *Young Woman Powdering Her Nose* (1890). Seurat met Madeleine Knobloch among anarchist circles in Brussels in 1886 and again in Paris, where she also lived.[23] Most of the painter's comrades in those final years of 1886–88 came mostly from the milieu that had formed in the aftermath of the Paris Commune, many of them living as refugees in Brussels.[24]As she shared his ultraleftist views, they agreed that she should keep her secret from his authoritarian family. He even, counterintuitively given the trust shared between them about both aesthetics and politics, concealed Knobloch from Berthe Morisot, who, according to Fénéon, was Seurat's closest confidant among the Impressionist painters. Morisot had encouraged Seurat's exploration into both optics and social theory, evidenced by the fact that his colleagues decided that among them it would be she who would climb the six flights to Seurat's studio to persuade the painter to finally stop working on *The Models*. He was reported to have felt unsure about letting the public see the picture. Her role in overcoming this anxiety speaks to the documented nature of the comradely intimacy between them. But despite this closeness, she did not know about Knobloch or their child. He also hid Knobloch from Paul Signac, as well as from Camille Pissarro, who accompanied him to any number of gatherings and lectures.

According to historian Joan Ungersman Halprin, Fénéon was unique among Seurat's comrades and associates to know about Knobloch's presence in Seurat's personal life. One can speculate that Seurat's painting was the only way he had of mediating the strict social binary Griselda Pollock and other feminist art historians have written about—namely, the division of women into "*femmes honnete*," the newly minted bourgeoisie, and the women on history's other side, the proletariat more often than not involved in sex work.[25] It suggests that convincing his family and friends of his and Knobloch's anarchist critique of women as property may have been too complicated.

This secrecy is made adequately evident by the way the figure for which Knobloch modeled is turned away. Discussed earlier in this chapter, the depicted woman whose back is all that is visually accessible cites Ingres's *The Bather*, which was already hanging in the Louvre by then.

In this painterly matrix of interchangeability, social de- and recomposition, abstraction, and synthesis, situating this figure as a citation of Ingres's *Bather* significantly elevates her, distinguishing her from the others by virtue not only of her estranging pose but also of her resonance with this cherished earlier work completed by Seurat's own mentor and already a site of collective cultural and even transcendental value, now conjugated with a protective opacity. In sum, Seurat's companion is hidden from quotidian identification only to take her place in the diachronic register of historical meaning and collective significance. This opacity both shields her and exalts her in contrast to the question of interchangeability and doubling that becomes all the more tangibly insistent on the part of those figures who are immediately visually available to the viewer, and whose identity is withheld not by protective anonymity but rather by the anonymity of abstracted social relations forged in relation to a market unconscious.

Here, *that which is visible is most abstract*, while that which has turned its back to the viewer in a gesture of seeming opacity is concrete, situated in the painting through reference to the history of art itself, if not to the painter's immediate emotional, erotic and domestic life.

Seurat's *toiles de luttes* thus address the *unconscious* matrix of abstract social relations. This unconscious matrix, in turn, is the impersonal way labor-power is sold, indifferent to its bearer, expressed through the labor of painting itself as it bears a different relation to the depicted worker-subject. Seurat's pointillist technique internalizes the division of general labor into anonymous, deskilled, and repetitive tasks by mimetically exacerbating the nature of anonymous work through the application of separate dots organized to offer a synthesis as the final "product" in the viewer's eye. At the level of process, Seurat incorporates the productive regime of the late nineteenth century as a function of anonymity and the changing composition of skill and fragmented process. This exploration stakes its position at a molecular level, that of the grapheme.[26] But what the grapheme sets out to indexically explore is shown to be motivated by a secondary problem, one in which gender and labor are co-constituted. That Seurat pictures the abstract sale of abstract labor as performed primarily by women will be taken up next. This framework once again raises the question of why the worker and that which constitutes the worker's relation to the social field should be figured as a naked female body.

The dialectical inverse of the worker, the flaneur was the very figure of Modernism partly as a result of the poet Charles Baudelaire's exploration and celebration of it as standing in for a new era of human relations and experience.[27] For Baudelaire, this figure articulated the subjective side of modernity as a totality of new sensations and temporalities: speed, change, dynamism, ephemerality. As most of the cultural history of modernism would have it, this social type immortalized in poetry and prose by Baudelaire had emerged in a gap between classes that the new social landscape had organized. As a subject-position occupying the gap between middle-class productive "values" and a proletarian whose time was entirely captured by the clock in service to value, the flaneur's primary inscription as a social type was of personifying and expressing a liberated relation to time and the market. Having no interest in work but possessed of the time and means to explore a dynamic new social field, the flaneur was the inverse of the worker-prostitute—we will return to the gendered part of the conjuncture momentarily—wholly subjugated to transactional exchanges in order to exist. To some degree, the flaneur, like the bohemian, as neither capitalist nor worker, was an avatar of the politics of the refusal of work. The flaneur refused the regulatory discipline of the working day and its organization of time into instrumental blocks.

The flaneur was therefore already coded as masculine by 1860 in the poetry and prose of Baudelaire, who most spectacularly located and analyzed this emergent type, the flaneur, as mascot of a newly minted bohemian nonclass, in 1863 in "The Painter of Modern Life."[28] While the poet sketched any number of specifically modern forms of experience, from immersion in department stores, among prostitutes, with new kinds of commodities and packaging, fashion, and makeup to walking the grand new boulevards of a Hausmannized Paris, his rubric was not capacious enough to account for a possible woman flaneuse.[29] The absence marks a contradiction specific to the way that capital genders bodies through an apportioning of value and valued time. It is as though at no point did the working woman cross over into bohemia as an agent of experience, seizing forms of self-inscription into the currents of modern life. Are these questions vulgar reflections of Baudelaire's individual sexism or a symptom of aporia in the social field, an uneven modernity elaborated over the axis of gender? Baudelaire aside, can there be a flaneuse?

This question situates the singularity of Seurat's contribution to any subsequent understanding of the relationship between labor and gender in modernism. With the exception of Seurat's *toiles de luttes*, and most specifically *The Models*, modernist culture looked to the male flaneur to allegorize not the newly generated worker but rather the newly minted *consumer*, the person newly set onto the stage of the urban metropolis. The flaneur paradoxically forces the question of what constitutes "freedom" in a politically free and economically unfree social matrix where the worker paradoxically purchases political representation at the expense of economic unfreedom. Baudelaire's voice has both described and partially constituted an originary matrix of modernism, a matrix woven by axes of class and gender that in turn maintain and heighten the contradiction between class and gender.[30]

One early theorist of gender as a function of the division of labor, Friedrich Engels, in *The Origin of the Family, Private Property and the State*, investigates the origin of the institution of marriage from hunting-gathering to agrarian societies. He identifies the co-emergence of marriage as it is recognized to function symbolically and materially in the last millennia alongside the development of the value-form and the advent of property as it is currently understood. Tracing the genealogy of marriage as an enclosed unit of reproduction in early societies through civilization into contemporaneity, Engels introduces in a single stroke three terms: value, labor, possession. Value, labor, and possession are the three facets of the wife-form: "just as the wives whom it had formerly been so easy to obtain had now acquired *an exchange value* and were bought, so also with the forces of labor, particularly since the herds had definitely become family possessions."[31] Transitioning from hunter-gatherer cultures to animal-rearing societies, predicated on rules around mating and taboos, a new notion of lineage and thus property emerged. Finally, after successive such transitions, in which a plenitude of female bodies fell to occasional scarcity, women acquired exchange value in supplement to their use-value. For the first time, men had to compete for access to women's bodies. At this moment, women's bodies came to be understood as property convertible to currency both on behalf of their own bodies and as bearers of children. This ultimately resulted the institution of marriage. The "mother right" or passage of inheritance and property once operating along a matrilineal axis is organized for the first time around patrilineage.[32]

Engels, in deference to Lewis Henry Morgan's work *Ancient Society* (1877), suggests that this—the conjugation of women and property—is the historical moment from which money originates. In order to guarantee that the children of their wives were indeed their "own" biologically, men required absolute fidelity. This fidelity was of course not to be understood as reciprocal until the twentieth century, even if then. Marriage was the first thing to come of a new structure of property. And with marriage, reciprocally, a new form and typology of property emerged—the substance of which were women and children. The latter, in turn, were for the Greeks and Romans synonymous with slavery. This marks the passage from collective, communal marriage to marriage as an economistic form of the mediation of value itself. As Engels writes, marriage "was the first form of the family to be based, not on natural, but on economic conditions—on the victory of private property over primitive, natural communal property."[33]

Three of the most significant objects of inquiry in the elaboration of a Marxian discourse in which Engels shared enter the scene as a co-constitutive knot: value (exchange and use), property, and possession. To this one might add identity. The latter is a legal-juridically generated category born of subjugation to a sovereign understood along an axis of lineage. Engels marks the origin of class antagonism in the shift from "mother right" to patrilineage and with it the division of use-value and exchange-value, the notion of property and possession (of persons and things). Reification and abstraction are both dialectical syntheses of new social relations caused by the shift from "mother right" to patrilinear exchange. For the first time, humans and children became property, *things*.

Abstraction, then, as marked by the transition from "natural" to "economic," as Engels puts it—is organized around gender, sexuality, and reproduction insofar as these concerns formed in conjuncture with a market. And if we are to investigate the class-generative dynamics of gender at the dawn of modernity in Paris, capital of the nineteenth century, we might ask, equally urgently, what happens to the common, otherwise employed laborer now newly gendered along the axis of the wage and the mediation of the market? A century later, feminist writers again took up the problem of gender as a function of labor, value, and property to try to limn the categories of both labor and gender. Mariarosa Dalla Costa and Selma James highlight the antagonism the capitalist mode of production generates to set men and women against one another. This social antagonism resulted from a fundamental material contradiction and its attendant crisis: the male worker is "free" to sell his labor-power and to purchase goods and services with the remuneration he gets for the sale of his labor-power; the female worker is not free in the same way, either to produce value or to consume it. The market mediation of labor-power along the axis of gender does not adequately explain this gap. Dalla Costa and James note the difficult transition from patriarchy to *capitalist* patriarchy in the recomposition of the dynamic between workers and capitalists. This decomposition wrought by the capitalist mode of production and its transition to quantified anonymous labor that qualitatively (as well as quantitatively) changed the power dynamic between genders marked a transition Dalla Costa and James describe as the epochal shift from oppression to exploitation: "The unfree patriarch was transformed into the 'free' wage earner, and upon the contradictory experience of the sexes and the generations was built a more profound estrangement and therefore a more subversive relation."[34] Gender is a relation to the market, mediated by the market. Gender, then, cannot be figured in the trope of the flaneur, which is already antagonistic given the gendered division of labor.[35]

Set into circulation in the expanding urban arena, the object of the flaneur's pleasure may not have any purchase on her own pleasure, at least not on the same market, not in the same street. On that market as an object, how can she overcome a doubly split position, as both worker and recompense for the new experience of waged labor, an object of consumption for the new proletarian in the new regime of the city? How does this doubling and splitting mirror the already split (male) worker?

In supplement and distinction to the flaneur, the imaginary of early modernism is consumed with the figure of the sex worker, the trope motivating "the foundational monument of modernism," or Manet's *Olympia*. Why would this figure, the female sex worker, rather than that of the stone breaker, child worker, or subproletarian, serve as primary displacement, trope, and figure of a new mode of production and distribution? Within a Marxian analysis, sex workers are not workers as such; they are not value-productive workers. Rather, they are non-value-productive and nonreproductive. And yet Marx relied on them as a reference to formulate the imminent capitalist mode of social relation in the urban metropolis where proletarianization forced a necessary division of both gender and labor. The sex worker at the turn of the last century functioned in abstract terms, given his or her place in the social totality and fabricated for nothing other than surplus-value extraction and multiplication, a kind of social and economic accursed share and necessary social excess in the form of a practicing subject. A sex worker is not quite a slave to be traded for money without the mediation of the process and practice of her time. As such, the sex worker is a walking contradiction, both like the worker whose labor constitutes modernity itself and unlike this surplus-value-productive worker, for the sex worker lubricates and facilitates the surplus necessary to keeping the order in place. This is to say that the figure of the prostitute suggested by Marx is the worker whose entry into "prostitution" is compulsory, structural, necessitated by the social modes put in place by the dominant mode of production at the level of the social matrix, the sale of labor-time itself, far from any form of self-determination. As such, Seurat's models in the eponymous painting presage the personification of capital elaborated in the figure of the Young-Girl in chapters 2 and 3.

2

Francis Picabia's Real Abstraction and the Beginnings of Futurist Cyborgs

The Prefigurative Avant-Gardes

In 1948, the architect and historian Sigfried Giedion published a book titled *Mechanization Takes Command: A Contribution to Anonymous History*, in which he described the new built environments of everyday life as mimetically inscribed in the logic and even the "aesthetic" of the machine. This re-elaboration of the built environment was caused, for Giedion, by the fact that "mechanization has taken command" of the American economy after World War I, coming to inscribe itself into the fabric of everyday life through design and production. Everything from white-collar offices to domestic space to designed objects emulated the machine, which came to metaphorize modernity as such. While the machine is itself a result and product of lived labor-time that accelerates the production process and often disciplines and subordinates living labor, its ontology and origins in lived labor drop out of the appearances of everyday life. Objects of design emulate the apparent results of production rather than the processes in the hidden abode of production that rendered them. Inscribed into the very making of the object and therefore no longer visible in the immediate encounter with the object, labor is overwritten and productivity as such is attributed to the machine as though it had issued from magic. The immediate misprision is heightened in described encounters with the "machinic object." That labor is all the more invisible because it is diffused, anonymous, social, and distributed. The occlusion of living labor constitutive of the machinic object is all the more difficult to locate for being saturated in a new urban built environment and a new social ecology. But this seeming imperceptibility is reified by the fetish, and in this context, the machine fetishized in its conventionalization.

The logic of the fetish is clearly an explanation for the vogue in machine aesthetics, even as it comes to stand in for "modernism." In Giedion's dazzlingly thorough analysis, the subject equally compelled to mimic the machine does not factor into the account. Some artists seemed to notice this skipped step in the ontology of new objects taken to signify a brave new world. While others would come to see the way in which the operational logic of the factory floor came to inscribe itself invisibly in social relations, creating a "social factory" through all of society, an official, institutionally supported version of modernism adopted a fetishistic aesthetic of the machine understood as a manifestation of ideal platonic form.[1] Again, the occlusion of living anonymous labor-time constitutive of those objects, on a mass scale, was the condition for the possibility of an emergent aesthetic within institutionalized notions of design that fetishized the commodity (and the commodity productive of other commodities) while pulling those objects out of the social reality of their making, in which labor is the primary commodity distributed across circuits of value. And yet the avant-garde, regardless of the institutional attempt to subsume its experiments back into official culture, directs us back to the problem of labor-power in relation to production and form, in particular machinic form as it is inherently historically bound up with the acceleration of the extraction of labor in the first decades of the century.[2]

But more than thirty years earlier, a more critical vision of the machine that situated it as a function of dead labor in a capitalist metabolic emerged from the ranks of the avant-garde. From 1916 to 1917, Francis Picabia worked on a mixed-media drawing that he titled *Universal Prostitution* (figure 2.1). On the face of it, *Universal Prostitution* looks like a machine part standing vertically against an undifferentiated field, connected to another machine part through a series of tubes and pipes spewing disjointed words about the human body. Language issues from the machine and slides like goods on a factory belt, sliding horizontally in tension against the iconography of a machine part that echoes the vertical rise of the frame. What appears to be a cord or wire stretches from the main machine part to the other. While some of the parts are presented as though capable of occupying three-dimensional space, qualified by modeling and chiaroscuro, they do so in a vacuum, against a flat and undifferentiated void. Its flatness is once again ratified by the words that cross the surface. The terms *convier*, *ignorer*, and

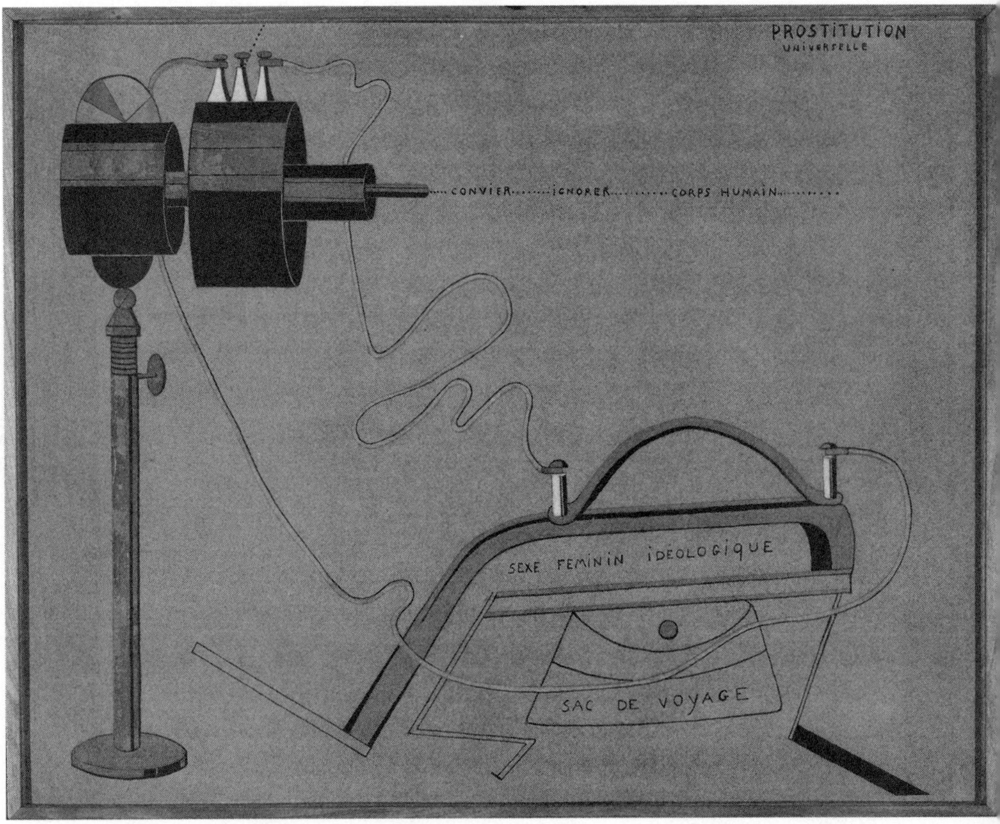

Fig. 2.1. Francis Picabia, *Universal Prostitution*, 1916–17. © Yale University Art Gallery. Gift of Collection Societe Anonyme.

corps humain are strung along a horizontal axis on the top third of the visual field and appear to issue from the main machine part, appearing under the language of the title, *Prostitution Universelle*. Translated literally, this text insinuates a kind of frustrated seduction, a striptease in which something is at once precipitated yet ignored, turned away. And from the secondary machine part on the lower third of the picture plane we read "Sexe Feminin ideologique." If these gears and technical equipment depict anything at all, could it be an apparatus akin to female reproductive organs? But any such vulgar reading is foreclosed from the start. We are just as well looking at an ideology (but ideology as such is a priori intangible), which stands against any material, experientially available limb or organ.

From the vantage of description or representation, the piece is nonsensical. And yet its exit from representation on the one hand and aesthetic abstraction on the other indicates the degree to which an altogether different kind of motivation drives the work. This is to say that it suggests a form of access to the real movement of history, which in turn spurs and activates a new kind of formalization and articulation that is neither symbolic nor merely stylistic. Gifting the drawing to the Yale University Art Gallery in 1924, Marcel Duchamp surely recognized the extraordinary ramifications of Picabia's insights, among which is a surprising mobilization of a new form of drawing: the diagram, drawn from industrial engineering and thus demonstrating an economy of indication more appropriate to an emergent worker-subject, one produced by an abstract and invisible, yet concrete, capitalist totality.[3]

A number of studies of Picabia's work within the context of machine aesthetics, most notable among them Amelia Jones's and Jennifer Jane Marshall's, posit a *mimetic identity* between aspects of the artist's turn to machinelike imagery and the exponential rise in the use of machinery necessitated by expanded industrial production and of warfare in the first decades of the century, above all in the context of World War I.[4] According to Jones, "While readymade objects or pictorial renditions of machines obviously comment in some way on industrial rationalism . . . they still function within the framework of aesthetics. Such works mark the confluence of industrial rationalism with aesthetic rationalism, both of which function to contain the threats posed to modern subjects by urban industrialism."[5] Here, Jones imagines a traditional subject who experiences the machine as an immediate ontological threat. Cultural responses in art, such as Picabia's and Duchamp's, are a way to come to terms and "contain" that ontological threat. The notion that the subject is already reconstituted by the practice of the sale of anonymous and often deskilled labor-time occludes both the degree to which this machinic and rational industrialism is produced by humans and re-produces them in turn in the metabolic of labor. The abode of production remains hidden in Jones's account, as does the issue of the sale of increasingly socially abstracted labor-power reorganizing the self as such. In this account of the representation of identities, Jones sees another work by Picabia, *Portrait of a Young American Girl in the State of Nudity* (1915), which offers a picture of a spark plug for a car under the language of the title as the artist's self-portrait. Jones sees Picabia spilling his perceived failures along with his alcohol abuse and womanizing into the picture plane as a projective space through which to work out the nuances to a wounded interiority of an organic subject. The work itself suggests the dismantling of any fixed ontologies, self or other, organic or machinic, linguistically anchored or representational—but what is the register of representation? Portraiture? Machine illustration? Although she avows the post-Cartesian subject of trauma, labor anonymized and set into relation with industrial machines themselves forged of labor-time do not factor into the problem of locating a subject to begin. Jones and Marshall focus on machinelike form as it enters the discursive space of aesthetics, the museum, as a modality of aesthetic idealism (Marshall) or as a way of expressing traumatized wounded subjectivity that results from the individual, understood in liberal terms as an agent of free will, in a traumatic encounter with the machine.

Other studies, among which George Baker's is most exhaustive, look at the structural logic of the artist's work, not least its tendency to evoke a circuitry quite other to either mimetic representation and its concomitant tendency to illustration. According to Baker's authoritative study on Picabia's oeuvre, this title derives from a passage in Marx's early *Economic and Philosophic Manuscripts of 1844*.[6] Baker attributes this choice of title to the artist's emotionally intimate relationship with Tristan Tzara, the poet most vocal in renouncing anarchist politics (if not anarcho-symbolist poetics) in favor of state- and party-affiliated communism in the 1930s.[7] Tzara's migration across political spectrums of the left sprung from his awareness that the tyranny of the market equaled or indeed outdid that of the state in mediating individual and collective self-determination.[8] Baker acknowledges Arnold Pierre's research, which had linked the phrase and others inscribed on the painting to a 1903 book by Remy de Gourmont. While Baker finds Pierre's connection credible, he nonetheless returns to Marx's mobilization of the phrase in *Economic and Philosophic Manuscripts of 1844*.[9] Baker notes above all the relevance of these precise words to the formal operations that Picabia sets into play, which for him trump both iconographic reference and philological illustration.[10] Both words (Marx) and artwork (Picabia) reach toward a functional dynamic constitutive of a new subject for which any other language or form of expression is inadequate.

The source for the title mobilizes this eponymous language no less eccentrically. Marx's *Economic and Philosophic Manuscripts of 1844* evoke the trope of "prostitution" to articulate the specificity of the sale of socially abstracted living labor within the structural logic of capital. This was the most suitable figure of language available to him to describe the sale of labor-power generative of value realized on the market, and the social position of the bearer of this labor-power—he who hauls his flesh to market with the hope of turning this labor capacity into a form representative of his labor-time (money) and by which he might in turn "earn" back the very *living* expelled in labor-time in order to service. It is my own gambit that Picabia read the following passage as much for its connotative content as for its rhetorical movement:

> Prostitution is only a *specific* expression of the *general* prostitution of the *labourer* . . . since it negates the *personality* of man in every sphere—is but the logical expression of private property, which is this negation. How little this annulment of private property is really an appropriation is in fact proved by the abstract negation of the entire world of culture and civilization, the regression to the *unnatural* simplicity of the *poor* and crude man who has few needs and who has not only failed to go beyond private property, but has not yet even reached it.[11]

Here, the prostitute stands provisionally for the proletariat. Suspending gender for the moment, "prostitution" is proletarianization, or rather, to be historically if not structurally accurate, proletarianization is cast by Marx as a form of prostitution. Its condition entails the reduction of the person to that which is for sale for its capacity to be set to labor-time in the production of value, and the way in which this reduction means that the person's embeddedness in their collective condition—its cultural qualities, attributes, and other characteristics—becomes irrelevant in a market that is indifferent to anything but the immediate instrumental use of labor-time. This reduction, Marx notes, is not natural but rather is a "crudeness" caused by the limited interests of the market requiring the reduction of the person to the point of sale.

Marx, not yet the "scientific Marx" of *Das Kapital*, does not pause to reflect on his startling metaphors.[12] How in the world could the masculine-coded sale of equally masculine-coded labor-power possibly be conjugated with a word that, until recently, has been attributed almost entirely to women? Marx does not naturalize the category of prostitution by gender any more than he naturalizes the sale of physical capacity for nonsexual physical labor as an attribute of men.

But why would that language have been specifically interesting to Picabia? Rather than attempting to mimic the morphology and aesthetic design of machines as Jones and Marshall have argued, Picabia renders conceivable the changed nature of the subject (individual and collective) in which worker and machine enter a relationship whereby value is drawn from the human worker and invested into the object, as measured through labor-time. This relationship remains abstract and impossible to figure along mimetic lines.

Picabia picks up where Seurat left off. If the previous chapter traced the inscription of the worker-subject as a function of increasing social abstraction into the compositional elements of painting on the brink of full aesthetic abstraction, then this chapter locates the calcification of this acknowledgment of social abstraction into new paradigms of aesthetic abstraction: the readymade and the diagram.

Gifting the drawing, Duchamp surely recognized the extraordinary ramifications of Picabia's insights, among them a surprising mobilization of a new form of drawing, the diagram drawn from science, technology, and industrial engineering, which introduced a new logic of meaning that he, Duchamp, also sought to work through with his own inauguration of the readymade. While Picabia may well have arrived at a new course of articulation through his engagement with a Marxian understanding of abstraction, mediated by his friend Tzara, he seemed eager to shift the application of this modality of graphic inscription from its articulation of things in industrial design, or data, toward an exploration of what it means to be individuated in the context of a radically changing world. But artists do not illustrate theory; they generate new idioms that only later come to be understood as paradigmatic of the avant-garde. Picabia, like Duchamp, found a way to convey an unlocatable—because fully saturated—omnipresent new ontology of everyday life under that which had been universalized yet remained invisible: the operations of exchange through which labor-power is sold as a commodity. This is to say that he hit on an index of a fully elaborated *social technology* yoked to circuits of the reproduction of labor-power. Picabia could be said to theorize the new technology productive not so much of commodities but of the form of life, of consciousness, that in turn makes those commodities.

What follows is a reading of three central works by Picabia—*Voilà Elle* (1915), *Fille née sans mère* (*Girl Born without a Mother*) (1917), and *Portrait d'une Jeune Fille Americaine dans L'Etat de Nudite* (*Portrait of a Young American Girl in the State of Nudity*) (1915)—alongside his and Duchamp's respective versions of *L.H.O.O.Q.* (both completed in 1919), to advance a reading of Picabia's turn to the mechanomorph or machine-part-as-portraiture and to the diagram, the two paradigmatic tactics for which Picabia is most credited in the history of the avant-garde. This chapter argues that Picabia's *Universal Prostitution* elaborates a condition explored throughout this handful of works, that is, a condition of ontological uncertainty and transformation at the very level of labor and anthros with the emergence of a new worker-subject. Consciously or otherwise, Picabia through these aesthetic propositions recognized the degree to which the subject-workers are forged by the sale of the commodity labor-power estranged from them. This is in and of itself fairly self-evident. What I hope to show, before returning to *Universal Prostitution* (1916–17), is not only that new forms of art were motivated, as was Seurat's work decades prior, by social abstraction or the displacement of traditional social relations by the exchangism and unconscious social synthesis of market relations but that this form of abstraction had already become a *technology*—not a new instance of engineering or production but a *social* technology in formation with productive machines. Mechanomorphism cannot be said to contribute to the research and development of more objects and more machines in any simple sense, but they did observe and augur the changed nature of the subject and the collective.[13] The challenge, it seemed for Marx and Picabia alike, was how to figure a profoundly new metabolic of production and relation to nature and with it, a subject produced by and responsive to this metabolic. Picabia's mechanomorph not only prefigures the much later phenomenon of the cyborg but also reveals its advent to be a function of the displacement of subjectivity by the value-form in a way that would come to aggregate in fixed capital, in technology, over the century. As such, Picabia's contribution to art complicates the usual narrative that technology is an object of interest only to right-tending elements of the avant-garde.

Girl Born without a Mother (1917) (figure 2.2) presents a machinelike figure delineated in garish green against an undifferentiated gold background. Gold, from the late medieval to early modern period of Western art, had been a way to reflect the wealth of the patron. Money, then, is the matrix of the "figure" against which it, the "girl" born, is "without a mother." Trading the iconography of the factory floor for the biological origins of the maternal body, the piece could not make the displacement of human contingency by a machinic order organized around market valorization any more transparent. That productive machines set into circuits have moved into the framework once held firm by the privileged human form is tethered in no uncertain terms to the otherwise visually mercurial plenum of gold against which this machinic subject appears. Anthropocentrism is eclipsed by the value of production itself, autonomous of human interest and indifferent to it. This reading is in and of itself crude enough, but Picabia builds on the ramifications of this piece.

While the machinic thing is itself a result and product of lived labor-time that accelerates the production process and often disciplines and subordinates

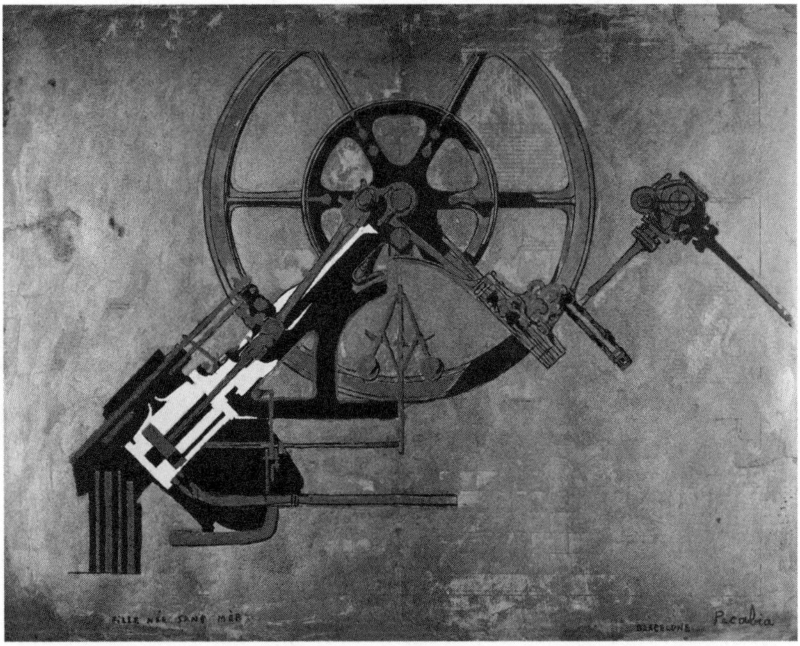

Fig. 2.2. Francis Picabia, *Fille née sans mère* (*Girl Born without a Mother*), ca. 1917. Gouache and metallic paint on printed paper. 50 × 65 cm (framed 90.8 × 75.9 × 3.8 cm). National Galleries of Scotland. Purchased 1990.

living labor, its ontology and origins in lived labor drop out of the appearances of everyday life. Objects of design emulate the apparent results of production rather than the processes in the hidden abode of production that rendered them. Congealed and no longer visible in the immediate encounter with the object, labor is overwritten and productivity as such is attributed to the machine as though it had issued from magic. Summoning this "magic" only to demystify it, the work acknowledges the social reproductive nature of labor itself, as it is invested in its value-productive object and in how it in turn re/produces a subjectivity amenable to it.

Two years earlier, *Portrait d'un Jeune Fille Americaine dans L'Etat de Nudite* (*Portrait of a Young American Girl in the State of Nudity*) (figure 2.3), made for the photographer Alfred Stieglitz's gallery 291, is a "portrait" insofar as the object figured on the visual field fills the frame in a genre convention specific to portraiture and insofar as Picabia guides us by the title. For clearly there is no girl in the picture; there's a tool. A generic industrial representation of a machine part fills the frame, rising vertically within the picture

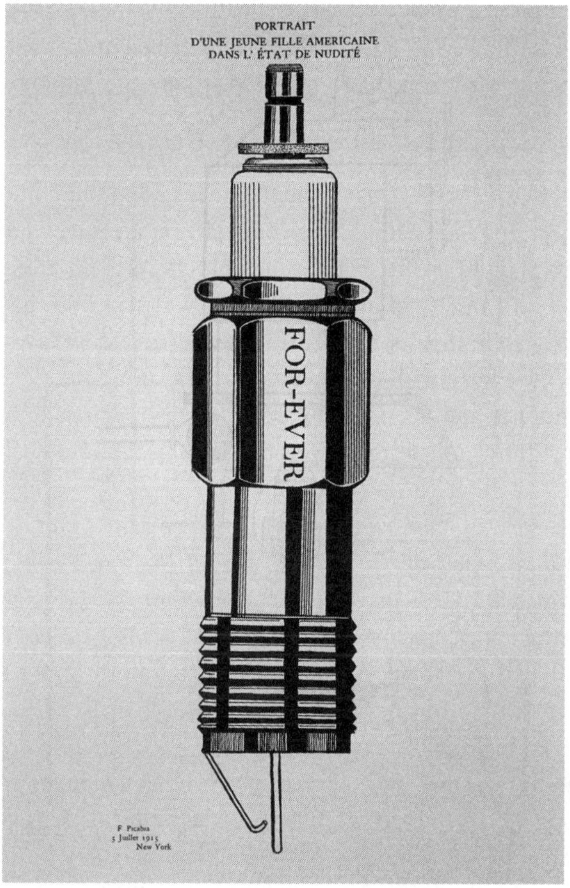

Fig. 2.3. Francis Picabia, *Portrait d'une Jeune Fille Americaine dans L'Etat de Nudite* (*Portrait of a Young American Girl in the State of Nudity*), 1915. © RMN-Grand Palais / Art Resource, NY.

plane, oriented to the wall as though an inanimate object could sit upright. But the thing shown is just that, a random thing. In fact, it is the illustration of a common spark plug, the tool that ignites the combustion machine, or motor, to make an automobile move. This object that sparks or "ignites" a vehicle of transfer might be read as an allegory of sexual desire and its objects of motivation. While there's no doubt a circuitry related to the pathways of desire that come to mind as a horizon of meaning, the picture plane refuses to lend itself as a space of projection or of narrative. Near the center of the picture, the word *For-ever* floats as though to ratify the *presence* of this strange thing and somehow elevate it to the level of a portrait as a form of apodeictic preservation for all eternity of a privileged being. But of course, having learned the lessons of language from Cubism, the word anchors only the flatness of the picture plane and the unreality of the thing. Somewhere in Picabia's contribution to the flicker of "presence" that is inscribed in the very forms of representation that ward it off, a new question around the ontology of the subject surfaces.

Picabia's other "mechanomorphs" address the reification of the individual in relation to the productive technologies over which he is said to stand but which come to stand over him. These include a "portrait" of Stieglitz, who managed to make of photography an art form through his efforts to promote the mechanical medium in a variety of discursive frameworks, in both his gallery 291 and magazine *391*. In this "portrait" captioned *Here, This Is Stieglitz, Here*, Picabia presented Stieglitz the man as a camera, an object. The ostensibly skilled practitioner and his medium are set in this portrait into a strange mutually constitutive indeterminacy as far as subject and object position are concerned.

A half decade before *Portrait d'un Jeune Fille Americaine dans L'Etat de Nudite* (*Portrait of a Young American Girl in the State of Nudity*), Picabia created a work titled *Voilà Elle*. This too was a mechanomorphic portrait done for 291 and its attendant periodical magazine, *391*. The reading order of the composition might begin anywhere. In the upper left, the word *Femme!* appears. From this issues a kind of calligram in which words make up an emergent picture that nonetheless fails to assume any recognizable contour. The words that constitute a vertical axis around which other language is arranged are onomatopoeic: *Hurluberu* might express a sound or sensation. The language branching off from this column of letters issues forth any amount of misogyny: "cerebral atrophy caused by materiality" and "she has no fear of pleasure." Under this cacophony of questionable language, the word ELLE floats, in capitals, and again *voilà* ELLE to its right; beneath a by turns two-dimensional diagrammatic, and three-dimensional mimetic, a depiction of a machine, the word is redoubled. "She" is distributed and multiplied in this cacophony of registers—symbolic, pictorial, diagrammatic—in which there is no subject.

Taken together, this group of works from 1915 to 1920 poses a critical question: who, or what, is a subject, much less an agent? This question of the location of agency in relation to capitalist structural determination organized around the sale of labor lubricating circuits of value production, circulation, and consumption has preoccupied a century of writing after Picabia's startling work. Jacques Rancière offers a theory of the subject (within capitalism) both as a vehicle to capital's structural self-replication and as *an interruption to a social structure necessary to capitalism*. Here, Rancière makes a requisite nod to Marx's phrase "hidden abode of production." However, that which is hidden is not the origin of value so much as its agent. Rancière posits the ultimate *impossibility* of locating agency, as it might be understood within modern democratic notions of the self, within capitalist totality.

In lieu of *locating* the subject in any one place, Rancière *maps* a *process* of subjectivization mediated in relation to production, to the commodity, and ultimately to the value that form makes, which in turn makes the question of the subject—as it had previously been thought—utterly superfluous. He introduces the following insight: this "absent cause" appears to be absent within the social field insofar as the identity of abstract labor and that of concrete labor are collapsed and confused: "This generalized and abstracted misidentification expresses the *structure* of a certain mode of production, of the capitalist mode of production."[14] This absent cause is not work but the way in which labor-power—objectified, anonymous, and metricized—enters the social field disguised as the individual laborer, which operates as a personification of the commodity labor-power valorized on a job market.

The worker is a split condition. Labor is presented socially in an anthropomorphic register that cannot help but conflate the concrete labor bearer with their labor-bearing capacity, and that capacity articulated in one form: money. Social relation in a social field expressed among agents misses two primary moments that abstract the individual from his social context: the abstract measure of labor-time as much as its point of sale on the market. Labor abstracted, once as socially necessary labor-time productive of value and then again as the commodity labor-power, suspends the personal and collective experience of the bearer of labor-power, replacing it with a "second nature" naturalized thus by two circuits.[15]

Rancière explains this glitch in the perception of labor, caught in an interval where the bearer of labor-power becomes confused with the labor-power itself, as a skipped step between subject and object. This collapse might offer the beginning of an insight as to why Marx first analogized the proletariat as "universal prostitution" in the *Economic and Philosophic Manuscripts of 1844*. While individuals have always been subject to power—indeed, as Étienne Balibar has noted, the word *subject* derives from subjection to a sovereign power—capital is the crucible of an internally split subject forged to suit a new mode of production that is ultimately not reciprocally interested in their flourishing: "The inversion of the inner structural determinations, which bear witness to the constitutive character of the relations of production, in their forms of manifestation, thus appears as a fundamental characteristic of the process. It is this law that determines the development of its forms."[16] In short, Rancière provides a theory of reification that nuances that of Lukács, who elaborated the term. Key to this discussion is the way in which concrete and abstract labor are unified in the moment of exchange. I will return to exchange later.

In sum, the generalized sale of labor-power—an abstracted commodity indifferent to its bearer whose individual experience is but one concrete instantiation of a much vaster pool of anonymized labor—displaces the individual as the seat of sovereignty. The individual, in a way uncannily familiar to those acquainted with Picabia's work, becomes a function of a set of processes and movements necessary to valorization. The "self" comes to be theorized not as a repository of interiority, experience, cognition, memory, and so on but as a function of a field of social relations organized around the replication of value itself. It becomes a node of a *diagram* to be mapped across numerous *functionally* interrelated terms. These terms, related by and within the process of surplus-value production, are otherwise independent and aleatory. Value, around which all social relations objectively reticulate, connects seemingly separate elements, invisibly. But how, precisely, does Picabia advance this notion of a subject dispersed over processes of valorization? By what means can this articulation take place, in advance of language or of the kind of political economic discourse that would come to describe it many decades later?

That device is the diagram. In *Realism, Rationalism, Surrealism: Art between the Wars*, Briony Fer, David Batchelor, and Paul Wood define the diagram as an index of artistic praxis, or facture, and of a temporally unfolding process.[17] It has long been noted with reference to Constructivism and other practices of the early twentieth century that while "the diagrammatic line is drawn from the realm of science and technical drawing . . . the final work has elements of notation. The works do not 'represent the world' if that is taken to be the model used in figurative art, but they contain allusions to the world in which they were produced by the currency of associations, materials, methods."[18] Less elaborated, perhaps, is the degree to which the shift reverberates through the century across historically and geopolitically specific movements to—replacing figuration—render otherwise unfigurable and invisible (because total) shifts in the mediation between the social field and its reception.

Key is a shift in the register within which line is expected to deliver meaning. Replacing contour and mimesis with notation, this transition at the heart of basic visual practice signals a more profound relation to the de- and recomposition of content and meaning at a fundamental level, perhaps not unlike the transition that the image underwent in the wake of technological reproducibility as famously described by Walter Benjamin in "The Work of Art in the Age of Its Technological Reproducibility." This would suggest that abstraction, or what is referred to as "aesthetic abstraction," issues from the abstractions shaping the real movement of history. But I get ahead of myself.

The diagram is often appropriated as a form of cognitive mapping, displacing drawing as it had been understood through the *longue durée* of figurative European art. Drawing had functioned as the cornerstone of that regime of representation, breaking the visual plenum into figure and ground and guaranteeing the integrity of a depicted body against the envelope of space. Drawing has assured the integrity and importance of the figure as an expression of a body in dimensional space by first breaking the visual plenum into figure and ground and then guaranteeing the integrity of a depicted body against the envelope of space. This is to say that line set into service of contouring shape enables pictorial representation at the most fundamental level; furthermore, beginning from *disegno* in the context of the Italian Renaissance, it is the very cornerstone of illusionistic picture making. Its primary function there was to open the flat two-dimensional picture plane onto the semblance of a three-dimensional space, and therefore onto a "realistic," however deceptive this term may be, or perceptually convincing form of representation. Long understood to be the foundation of that normative aesthetic apparatus, the capacity to produce and manipulate linear form had also by the start of the twentieth century come to be a vehicle of expressive capacity, notably in the Viennese and Central European context and its debt to Romanticism. As Molly Nesbit convincingly argues in *Their Common Sense*, the Duchampian ready-made is a response to industrial design and its form of manufacture.[19] Nesbit notes that Duchamp's generation was the first to be taught mandatory drawing-for-design in the French public school system, ostensibly to train engineers and factory workers alike.

Girl Born without a Mother of 1917 and *Young Girl* of 1920 would seem, then, to literalize the condition of being a subject within capitalism as occluded, the glitch to which Rancière attends by understanding capitalist relations as a function of circuitry tracking parallel to circuits of valorization that can only be forged through a diagrammatic logic, a logic capable of figuring a dynamic of relations. Far from reflections on events having come to pass, both works speculate on subjugation *to* capital at the molecular level of the constitution of the self, as the condition for the possibility of subjectivity itself.

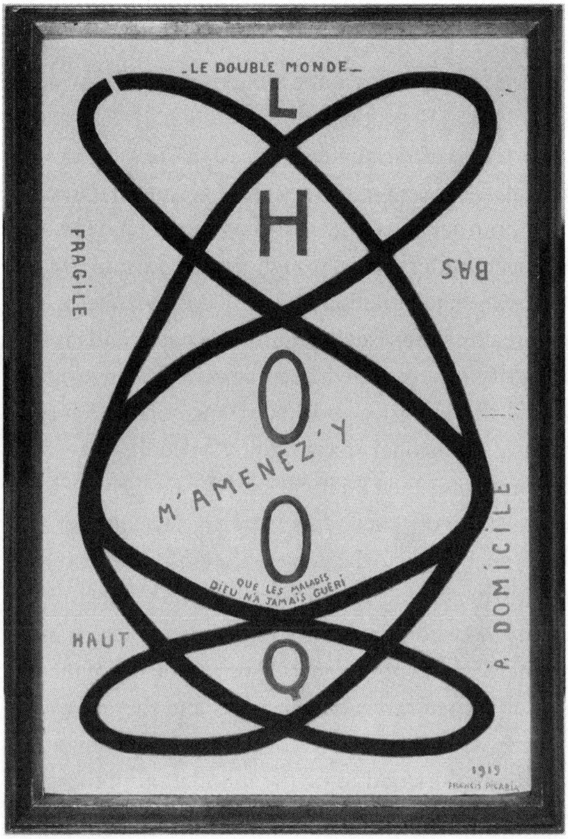

Fig. 2.4. Francis Picabia, *The Double World (L.H.O.O.Q)*, 1919. © CNAC/MNAM, Dist. RMN-Grand Palais / Art Resource, NY.

The diagram acts as an obvious structuring principle in *The Double World (L.H.O.O.Q)* (1919) (figure 2.4), a dialogic response to Duchamp's base materialist work of that title that same year. In Duchamp's version, a reproduction of the *Mona Lisa* is supplemented with a beard and goatee. The letters of the title cross the lower register, or that which would have been the foreground had the stenciled letters not reestablished the inherent flatness of the picture plane. The letters, if spoken swiftly, generate an accidental speech act that would sound, in French, like "she has a hot ass," and thereby interrupts the historical sanctimony of the *Mona Lisa* in the pantheon of Western art with crass humor and a whiff of denigrated and denigrating desire—a classic Dada (low) blow to middle-class values. Picabia's version dispenses with any last remains of anthropomorphic content. Instead, the letters *L.H.O.O.Q.* descend vertically down the plane, surrounded by the thick black line weaving across and between the letters. Again, the words *bas*, *fragile*, *haut*, and *a domicile* appear. It is as though Picabia were charting the subject-to-object relations necessary to any articulation of desire in the movement of the line itself, the line taking on dominance as a recording of movement outpacing the terms among which it moves.

The avant-gardes of the early twentieth century demonstrate no shortage of clairvoyance. Futurism, Dada, and the assorted hybrids generated of their mutual encounters seem to have served as a form of dialectical research and development for the era postdating them, which is to say our current moment. Picabia's are far from the only works eager to exit the increasingly obsolete logic of representation. The number of works that turn away from representational logic and expressive drives toward the operational capacity of the diagram in the context of both the Russian/Soviet and Italian Futurism mark 1915–20 as a generative time in rethinking the very parameters of artistic mark making. We could tendentiously situate these numerous experiments across the historical avant-gardes from Dada to Constructivism and Futurism as so many cultural instances marking the elaboration and development of the purely aesthetic appropriation of the diagram as a heuristic device. But this unfolding of a cultural development is a clear expression of the ways, means, and metrics—the cognitive mapping—of the capitalist mode of production as it integrates itself into forms of everyday life so operative as to be invisible to all but the analytical lens of aesthetic praxis. Reciprocally, that new form of praxis, or the diagram as an artistic medium, affords ways of describing the radical reordering of the world by capital. While it would be impossible to map the one (i.e., the genealogy of the diagram) onto the other (i.e., the historicity of capitalist reintegration of global markets), a pattern common to both inquiries (i.e., aesthetics and the social field) nonetheless emerges. In the absence of any causal correlation, the transformation of line nevertheless marks the progress of capitalist immiseration and the transitional points between moments of progress. It is as though the deterritorialization of line somehow recorded, indexically, the de- and recomposition of (cognitive) mapping in "line" with the process of abstraction through value, itself another name for capitalism.

While Dada, Surrealism, and the Soviet avant-gardes all demonstrated a perfervid attachment to new forms of media and technology, and while all three avant-gardes envisioned a new subject wrought by its forms (much as and in debt to the way in which Marx had tried to describe a historically emergent new class), Picabia's inauguration of the diagram is highly attentive to the position of this new subject in a changing totality reticulated through abstraction. His gesture, as well as Duchamp's deference to it, in turn, suggests the way in which art both prefigures and mediates transformations in the development of *subjectivity* with reference to the productive forces, as well as historically changing social consciousness about those shifts—if not too literal transitions in engineering and production. But the problem of the machine part's entry into the organic condition of human form and experience is most commonly located in discussions of Italian Futurism. In order to distinguish Picabia's project, a discussion of other branches of the avant-garde also oriented to the machine will be helpful.

In *Prosthetic Gods*, Hal Foster reads F. T. Marinetti's "The Founding and Manifesto of Futurism," published in 1909 in the Parisian newspaper *Le Figaro*, arguing that reification, the becoming thing-like of both persons and experience, is the core concern of Italian Futurism, which ushers in a peculiar strain of politically regressive European modernism centered around the incorporation of the human and the machine. In the manifesto, Marinetti describes experiencing a car crash, which he survived only to be reborn as a new and enhanced human. But for Foster, in Marinetti's project, "we [humans] are comic when we appear both automatic and reified, puppets of blind instinct further reduced within modernity to the status of mechanistic things. This kind of troping or turning is also at work in his stoical embrace of the brutality of mechanical life or his conflated sense of war as romance."[20] Through a reading of Sigmund Freud's theory of the death drive, Foster notes the proximity of the machine to inert things. Foster concludes his discussion of the etiology of reification as an expression of the death drive with two questions: "Could it be that Futurism is not as aberrant as it appears? Could it be that the very stake of high modernism at this time involves wagers with reification and death?"[21] A glance across the avant-garde, and specifically at the inauguration of the ready-made and the diagram in Duchamp's and Picabia's Dada works, would support Foster's query, dislodging the fascination with machines from the exclusive property of Marinetti's project, resituating it as a shared condition of the moment at large. And if we locate the human-machine hybrid in the operational mode of a diagram, we might have a different reading of the part machine-subject to which these practices allude and which Foster associates with death—namely, a coming to terms with and a response to a new ontology, a new form of life itself (rather than simply death) brought to bear by a new mode of production requiring new forms of articulation. Picabia's mobilization of the diagram, far from a simple incorporation of the machine into an otherwise traditional subject, suggests a very different understanding of the posthuman, one in which a social totality generated of a new metabolic of production and its attendant manufacture of worker-subjects issue from and take part in a larger matrix of social abstraction. This difference is articulated in the diverse forms and methods by which each artist addresses the machine. Unlike Marinetti, Picabia displaces the traditional forms of both icon and symbol, both picture and word (the cornerstones of mimesis in pictorial representation and poetics, respectively) for the *movement* of the diagram as it charts and inscribes a social dynamic set into place by the mechanisms within which the subject is *subject to* the replication of value and, in turn, comes into being through a kind of cycle or circuit. Again, this otherwise unrepresentable operation is the special affordance of the diagram and its capacity to articulate a dynamic over a fixed identity. The diagram can describe an increasingly unrepresentable social totality structured around valorization in which the human becomes one nodal point among many.

Italian Futurists are frequently associated with fascism, at least in much of the Anglophone discourse.[22] This affiliation is well founded; however, the becoming-machine, or the advent of a post-human-machine hybrid, is drawn into this conclusion. But as I have hoped to show through an exploration of Picabia's diagram, this trope—of the part-machinic and part-human assemblage—might be relocated in any number of aesthetic and political modalities across the avant-garde, from Futurism to Dada, and across the political spectrum with which they are each affiliated. Nevertheless, the association of the machine with fascist politics casts its shadow over other aspects of the avant-garde and is useful to parse in order to further locate the specificity of Picabia's engagement with the machine and its entry into the matrix of the human to generate a new model of anthros, the worker-machine.

I turn in seeming digression to Guillaume Apollinaire, a figure who might be situated as a nexus linking the contradictory tendencies of art practices in the 1910s. His fluid passage across the geopolitically and ideologically discrete branches (French, Italian, American) of the avant-garde has functioned as a source of contention for numerous generations of cultural historians, not least for the way in which it suggests aesthetic and ideological continuity and filiations.[23] His trajectory, in short, challenges the maintenance of easy categories reticulated through clean ideological positions. Apollinaire can be credited for being the first to mobilize the term *avant-garde*, drawn from military jargon and imported into cultural discourse to denote those forms of articulation, pictorial and poetic, that broke from traditional representation and from the signifier's burden of duty to deliver a transparent, organic "reflection" of putative reality. Apollinaire personifies the complex lines of geological and formal affiliation that connect Cubism, Dada, and Italian Futurism. Having moved through the social constellations constituting each, he forged fierce bonds first with Pablo Picasso, who depicts him in *The Family of the Saltimbanques* (1906), an homage to the bohemian urban life afforded by modernity. Apollinaire and Marinetti met sometime between 1906 and 1909. The former subsequently collaborated with the Italian Futurists, with whom he published his renowned calligrams, before finally becoming a kind of muse to Duchamp, who for his part immortalizes the artist in the work *Apollinaire Enameled* (1916). But Marinetti also included Apollinaire's textual experiments with those of the Futurists. Apollinaire's calligrams, the work for which he is perhaps best known in literary histories, were published in 1913 under the title *Antitradition Futuriste Manifeste Synthese*. His name also situates yet another mechanomorphic drawing by Picabia, made in 1918 and titled *Portrait de Guillaume Apollinaire*. This Guillaume Apollinaire is a machine part in two dimensions as indicated by the text comprising the proper name. The lower third of the picture pulls this flatness into relief by offering orthogonal lines, that foundational trope of drawing two dimensions into the illusion of three—that is, of moving from diagrammatic space to representational space and back. Jones interprets this piece, against her own interpretation of Picabia's later mechanomorphs, as a moving portrayal of anthros in confrontation with machines and machine-like structures, not least those that the poet would have encountered in the trenches and on the front lines.[24] Over this mechanomorphic index of Apollinaire's interventions in history and poetry, a text reads: "tu ne mourras pas tout entier," or you won't die all at once. Picabia is making it clear that a state of transformation, a dynamic of metamorphosis in the ontological category of anthros, is at stake.

Apollinaire might also be credited for the kind of preoccupation with machinery that came to articulate itself differently across the branches of the avant-garde. His own contribution to the moment includes an extended poem titled "Futurist Anti-Tradition. Manifesto = Synthesis" (1913), drafted a year after his declaration that the artist wishes nothing other than to be "inhuman." Baker situates Apollinaire's fluidity in the contradictory battle for position characterizing the moment, one defying neat polarities on any register. He notes in particular a conflict within the left in which the avant-garde occasionally found itself implicated. Baker recounts one incident in particular in which the long-standing antagonism between communists and anarchists, both to the far left, surfaced in ways that offer the historian some clues into the complex imbrication of aesthetics and politics.

> The Dadaists came to the club au Faubourg seeking workers. They had been ill-informed. Greeted, to their amazement, by an audience of one thousand people, the Dadaists quickly realized that this mass mostly excluded the working class. There were many socialists, who seemed eager to attack the Dadaists. But there were anarchists there too and the comedy of misunderstandings of this evening saw the debate devolve into a vigorous conflict between the socialists and the anarchists, with the anarchists putting up a brisk defense of the four men [artists] and siding with the Dadaists against socialism.[25]

Notably, it was only with the artists' arrival that those two left-affiliated political cultures could concretely differentiate themselves. The socialists, who were not themselves drawn from the proletariat, were not interested in the estrangement of sensory tactics and effects. They were not open to radically questioning the perceptual, cognitive order through which capital came to replicate itself or through which it might be dismantled. They were there only for a discussion of platforms, positions, and programmatic political strategies. It was not interesting to them that Dada offered a way of decomposing a set of values reticulated through quantification, to profit maximization and instrumental rationality. By contrast, the anarchists, stumbling upon these four eccentric young artists, must have intuited the presence of fellow travelers capable of articulating radical social and political transformation in the aesthetic proposition.

Apollinaire is not the only accomplice of the avant-garde to have traversed a spectrum of political and aesthetic affiliations. Soviet linguist Roman Jakobson, for instance, continued to conjugate Marinetti's exploration of language with that of communist poet Vladimir Mayakovsky, long after both the German and Italian rise to fascism had come to pass.[26] Already in a long essay first published in the August 2, 1919, edition of the Moscow newspaper *Iskusstsvo*, which is to say a full decade after Marinetti's *Founding and Manifesto of Futurism* and two years after the Bolshevik Revolution, Jackobson states that "the overcoming of statics, the discarding of the absolute, is the main thrust of modern times, the order of the day."[27] He develops there a genealogy from Cubism to a shared international avant-garde that he calls "Futurism," a category containing Marinetti as much as Mayakovsky. He locates an operational mode or signifying strategy across the avant-garde while curiously bracketing ideology: "Futurism brings with it practically no new pictorial devices, instead it widely utilizes Cubist methods."[28] Here, he explicitly posits a structural and operative (if not thematic or ideological)

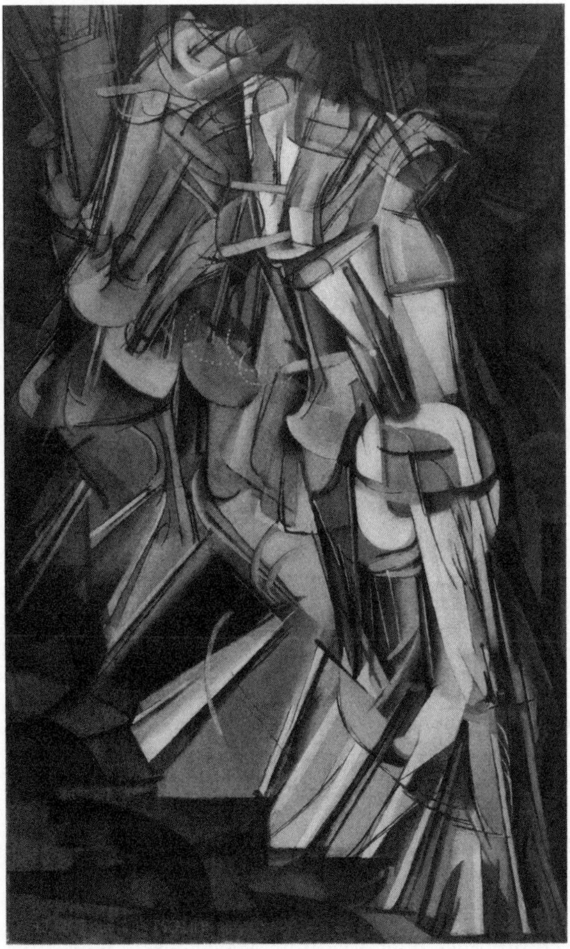

Fig. 2.5. Marcel Duchamp, *Nude Descending a Staircase (No. 2)*, 1912. The Philadelphia Museum of Art / Art Resource, NY.

continuity, an almost technical affiliation, between Dada and Futurism. Duchamp's *Nude Descending a Staircase (No. 2)* of 1912 (figure 2.5), for example, owes its initial reception to this transitional moment.[29]

While aesthetic differences between the movements have surfaced, the question of what differing aesthetic and ideological positions held in common, or why they had any common concerns, has not. And that common inquiry was the question concerning technology.[30] If we pivot from an examination of the political history of ideological affiliation within the avant-garde to that of the emergent economic changes that motivated fundamental shifts at the level of form and signification, another picture begins to form. Despite the profound differences at the level of both formal operation and political affiliation, a shared fixation with a posthuman condition might be situated as the ultimate symptom of a moment in which the worker-subject came already to be understood as machinic, caught between living labor and fixed capital, commodified labor-time and calcified *thing*. Returning to Foster's claim in *Prosthetic Gods* that reification stands at the vanishing point of the avant-garde's inquiry, the question of historically specific *motivation* for the shared concern across the avant-garde strongly suggests a different horizon. Rather than a mere expression of the psychoanalytic notion of the death drive suddenly mysteriously central to artists in the teens and twenties as never before, changes at the level of the social real, of social abstraction itself, subtend the becoming machine of anthros in the avant-gardist imaginary, over and above any sudden need to illustrate the machinations of the unconscious. In other words, the reality that begins to seep into the work is real abstraction itself. Reification is not the function of the death drive; it is the very real historical effect of living labor become fixed capital, already articulated by Picabia's *Girl Born without a Mother*, wherein the worker on the factory floor and the machine converge to form the technology, the assemblage of machine and labor-power, necessary to value production.

If any one trait could be said to define the avant-gardes, it would be the compulsion to reach the furthest horizon of futurity by situating practice prefiguratively, as though that longed-for future could be summoned here and now through practice. This places both American/French Dada and the Italian Futurists out of step with their time, abutting communism on the one hand and fascism on the other, belonging ultimately to neither category and yet anticipating our own present. Above all, they prefigure the cyborg, the part-bio-organic, part-mechanical entity. Donna Haraway, author of "The Cyborg Manifesto," who defines the cyborg as part animal and part technology and a form of life long elaborated past gender binaries and impervious to the demands of labor, has said that "the main trouble with cyborgs, of course, is that they are the illegitimate offspring of militarism and patriarchal capitalism, not to mention state socialism."[31] The cyborg born of this triangulation seems to have had older siblings in both the Italian Futurist and Dada fantasies of crossing man and machine, and crossing ideological lines to arrive at a heightened relationship to capital accumulation. Both poles of the avant-garde might have prefigured the contemporary cyborg. And yet this prefiguration articulated that which had already *come to pass* in the labor-to-capital dynamic as a changed composition within and among workers: the transition of living labor into fixed capital in response to social abstraction.

Again, Haraway, among others, locates the originary matrix of the cyborg in the historical, geopolitical, and cultural arena as the formation of the avant-garde: the experimental state formations of the early twentieth century reorganized around capital.[32] She tracks their ramifications in the technological capitalist formations of the present, which extend into the twenty-first century in this our era of Apple, Amazon, Google, and Facebook. In this regard, her account tracks parallel to Antonio Negri's telos of the twentieth-century worker. Negri historicized this as the shift from the craft and agrarian to the mass worker, followed by the cyborg and information workers.[33] But as is the case in the foundational work of Benjamin and so many others before him, the economic formations beneath political and ideological constructions take second place despite, paradoxically, Benjamin's insistence on the economic metabolic specific to each era as motivating its ideological and political developments: "Since the transformation of the superstructure proceeds far more slowly than that of the base, it has taken more than half a century for the change in the condition of production to be manifested in all areas of culture."[34] In other words, although Benjamin opens his essay on technology and technological reproducibility with an emphasis on material cause, his subsequent discussion turns to ideological developments, losing site of the currents coursing under and across those formations.

Far from the Italian Futurists' political allegiances, and yet tracking parallel with the problem of the technological eclipse of any traditional notion of human will and agency within capitalist social formations, or social synthesis constituted "behind the backs of men" in the indifferent sphere of the market, Picabia turned to the machine part as a way of thinking through the Marxian preoccupation with a new kind of subject: the proletariat.

Jeune Fille (1920), born of the interval between the revolution of 1917 and its immediate compromise under the New Economic Policy (NEP), could be said to personify this condition.[35] Like the ready-made, that first cultural figure to try to mediate the all-consuming "volition" of the interval between the factory floor, currency, and social life—and yet pivoting from the ready-made's object status to think the subject, and elaborating *Universal Prostitution* of some few years previous—it personifies the subsumption of subjectivity in the expanded social field. She, the eponymous "young girl" of the work, takes up the task of describing circuits of subjectivization. The condition of possibility for the reproduction of labor is nonetheless overcoded—sexualized, *fetishized*—to keep the system going while masking the sacrificial economy of the labor bearer at the heart of value production.[36] In other words, the gender identity of the actual worker, the exemplary proletarian, is not in question; the availability of labor-power, for sale, anonymized and abstracted from any concrete identity on the part of any individual worker, is. And that labor-power, or living labor, comes to be congealed in fixed capital—the machinery of production—in a way that allows value to accumulate for the capitalist.

The subject becomes itself a technology in the self-replication of capital. While Seurat explored the model worker in relation to anonymity, interchangeability, and indifference in the promulgation of abstraction—joining aesthetic abstraction to social abstraction to correlate form and content—by 1915, the very presentation of the human form no longer advanced the degree to which social abstraction had reconfigured the world within which the human lived. What Benjamin had called the "empty" homogeneous time of capital—where life comes to be worth what the value-form can procure after having absorbed living beings' socially necessary labor-time, now turned to "dead labor" congealed in the commodity form or set in fixed capital as equipment and technology—had forged a new kind of being. The transubstantiation of life demanded by capital not only evacuates the primacy of concrete experience but reconfigures it as metricized abstraction.

My argument, then, posits Picabia's mechanomorph, diagrammatically articulated as a function of relational circuits in a machinery of production, as an avatar of the cyborg understood as the becoming technology of the worker-subject. Here, I am not arguing that Picabia's work functioned as research and development in the engineering and design of machinery in any literal sense. I am, however, suggesting that it prefigures a new worker-*subject*. This subject is characterized by a primary split between the labor bearer's social subjectivity and that of their value-productive capacity. The subject thus split and reconstituted to be saleable brings this labor-power, which has already dominated the individual's development in preparation, to an abstract market as an anonymous purveyor of that labor-value. In other words, the work locates, identifies, and diagnoses a subject reconstituted to accommodate changes in the technical composition of capital and its circuitry. Political economists of labor only later located at an equally molecular level the change if not challenge to "man" by the emergence of the worker as a new form of life that in turn changed the technical composition of labor in the labor-to-capital dynamic crossing the century. Negri's telos of modern labor may or may not be accurate; however, his understanding of the changing nature of anthros in relation to the circuitry of value is one that Picabia recognized early. If anything, Picabia's mechanomorphs might presage what workerist theorist Mario Tronti called, in 1962, "the social factory" by way of describing not the way in which everyday life mimics industrial rationalism and machine production but how collective social relations and individuals come to be reorganized in relation to any given regime of value. In capitalism the sale of anonymous and abstract labor-power is the precondition to the existence of the infamous abode of production itself.[37] This sense of a reconstituted social being and collective composition of work could not have been available through representation. It required an acknowledgment of the shifting nature of the subject and of what it could express or what could be articulated about it when it arrives, as though a kind of being. Picabia's peculiar form of *personifying* dead labor as a new ontology—labor made inert as invested in the machinery and technology of production itself—is picked up by subsequent generations of artists to elaborate the degree to which abstraction expands far beyond the factory floor and into the social field, saturating all social relations irrespective of any particular, individual, or concrete relationship to the site of production.

What follows will pick up more recent returns to Picabia's modality of query by which to probe contemporary capitalist labor dynamics. Among the only twenty-first-century practitioners to pick up on Picabia's personification of capitalist abstraction, artist collective Claire Fontaine defines their understanding of abstraction as a function of "exchangism." They explicitly cite Alfred Sohn-Rethel's theorization of a market unconscious offering a sole, if invisible, form of unity in an otherwise seemingly fragmented and separated social order, and point specifically to the asymmetrical indifference of the act of transaction in the market for which every object is destined and around which every subjective experience revolves, as the source of a seemingly unfigurable totality: "These social relations are imperceptible abstraction."[38] They develop the problem by noting that one seemingly isolated procedure—the market valorization of value in the moment of exchange—could determine all social relations elsewhere, off market site: "One could even go so far as to formulate the hypothesis that, just as the value-form contaminates the whole realm of objects, including those that aren't commodities, in the same way this value form injects exchange value into behaviors, colonizes or infects *all* human behaviours including the most spontaneous, emotional and disinterested ones."[39] Here, "exchangism," or the market transaction where goods and labor-time are valorized, comes to determine any and all social relations that *seem* independent of the market.

The space and time of a transaction negate both the space and time of production as well as the contextual situation in which those involved in any given transaction otherwise exist. They equally nullify intention because they are motivated by an autonomous logic: that of price, profit, and circulation.[40] It is indifferent even to production and consumption other than as these affect the relation between value and price. The impersonal vectors of the market determine that which happens on the market, offsetting contingencies. No one determines the cost of any particular resource outside the machinations of the market and its balance sheet.

Key here is the way in which this imperceptible procedure that defies its own thought—caught in a circular logic where the subject is its own blind spot and where abstraction happens "behind his back"—comes to operate as the only form of social synthesis made possible by the way in which capital totalizes social relations equally imperceptibly. And this is why it is of note to artists, as a question of what is visible, perceptible, able to be conveyed: "the paradox is that commercial exchange is in reality a social tie created by an activity that negates it. Because the use of money authorizes every owner of commodities to abstractly (but concretely) pursue his own personal interests, without obstructions, without even thinking about his place in society."[41] They attribute to Sohn-Rethel a conceptual way into this "absurdity" wherein collective self-interest is negated by unconscious individual self-interest that ultimately also negates the subject. The market totalizes, creating not so much a political unconscious as an economic one that silently tethers all of life to its interests, autonomously of human conscious or will.

How, then, might the way in which this personification of the laborer as the very technology of the transition from living to dead labor-made-technology, step away from the assembly line and enter the social field in order to articulate it, to personify it, *as* a social field in and of itself?

3

The Future of the Futurists

The Young-Girl: En/gendering Real Abstraction

In the organic composition of capital, "variable capital" denotes the regime of the worker's subjection as so much potential surplus value in relation to the principal framework of already existing fixed capital. For surplus to be extracted from variable capital, the human bearer of labor-power must enter into increasingly mimetic relationships with fixed capital, as though the subject were looking forward to that moment when their capacity could be estranged from them and realized as value. Their survival depends on that primary estrangement. And with automation comes the progressive increase in the proportion of constant capital; a new kind of subjugation to subsumption develops at the level of the worker's social subjectivity in keeping with the acceleration of the forces of production. The subject becomes increasingly "machinic" in order to functionally operate in proportion to the efficiency of the technical subsumption of variable capital, or labor, itself. This framework becomes an ontology and expands to all of society. It could also be said that a small amount of subjectification took us away from machinic enslavement, but a large amount brings us back to it.[1] Gender has historically occupied a contradictory relationship to the extraction of surplus value from its individual bearer. Posited as natural and external to the whole problem of the organic composition of capital, which is to say labor, it turns out to have been fundamental to the matrix of value. Without gender, capital could not have saturated the social field as invisibly or as seamlessly. Gender is the pivot that enables the renaturalization of capital, its becoming "real."

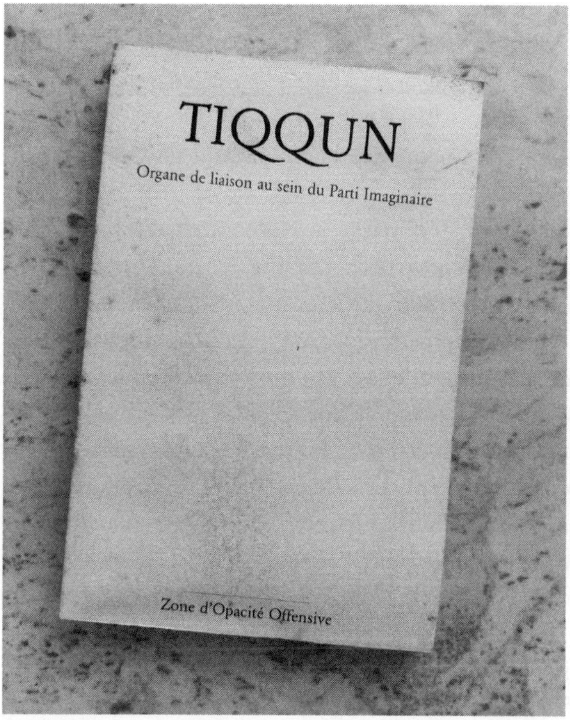

Fig. 3.1. Cover of *Tiqqun*, October 2001. Dépot légal: Octobre 2001. Distribution: Belles-Lettres, ISBN 2-913372-11-2. Courtesy of Claire Fontaine.

Preliminary Materials for a Theory of the Young-Girl is a DIY user's guide to gender de-reification, or rather, de-reification as the abolition of gender. It is not for the faint of heart, as evidenced by its reception. Published as part of the contents of the first issue of the magazine *Tiqqun* (figure 3.1), this genreless text, more montage in response to concrete abstraction than anything else, opens with a conceptual manual for the reader to help steer the journey through its textual and stylistic territory. The language there describes itself as a "vision machine." This text-as-instrument is therefore intended to afford the good reader a way to sense the "total war"—what the writers call the encroachment of capital into every last recess of experiential life and beyond, even the unconscious—in a way so molecular and immersive as to be intangible, a "molecular diffusion of constraint into everyday life."[2] They state baldly that "in reality, the Young-Girl is simply the *model citizen* as redefined by consumer society since World War I, in explicit response to the revolutionary menace."[3] The Young-Girl is a form of "civil" warfare by other means. This means she is a form of seduction of and by the commodity fetish in the most paradoxically puritanical, instrumental, and rationalized sense. "She" is the personification of the product that must arouse desire to keep the cycle of circulation moving and to fuel its most crucial moment of all: the transaction. She is the way that capital "wins," so to speak, and most effective because it is libidinal, unconscious, and parasitically operative in the register of desire.

The authors of this text hope to describe in words what Picabia figured as a form of life, as the model citizen of capital, the *Mechanomorph*, dated to 1920. Neither Tiqqun's writers, nor Picabia, nor for that matter Marx, can exactly "represent" this phenomenon. It is here anthropomorphized as the Young-Girl in hopes that the reader accustomed to personification and character development, the most elemental forms of narrative, might grasp the configuration of subjectivity, social totality, and the autonomous metabolic of value. They anthropomorphize value—"the anthropomorphosis of Capital is a *fait accompli*"—in order to acknowledge the autonomy of the value-form, which has accrued more rights under the formal law as property than many persons do.[4] The authors write: "At the beginning of the 1920s, capitalism realized that it could no longer maintain itself as the exploitation of human labor if it did not also colonize everything that is beyond the strict sphere of production."[5]

Tiqqun derives the Young-Girl as much from Picabia's Dada experiments as from Marcel Proust's character Albertine in *Remembrances of Things Past*. Albertine is the object of the narrator's obsessive desire. He constitutes an entire world around his purely imagined and unrealized relationship to the fetish, here anthropomorphized in the character of Albertine, not least because her own agency, her own desire, is woefully and explicitly beside the point. It is enough for this figure to stay in the role of the fetish to motivate an entire matrix of emotions and actions, all of them speculative, in remembered aspiration. For the narrator never technically possesses Albertine. His desire for her does, however, dispossess him. And yet it is clear that she is all but inert at the level of her own consciousness and drives.

Albertine's status as active or passive, subject or object, is as indeterminate as her sexual identity or gender. As Tiqqun writes, "The tomboy comes to impose herself as a modernity more stunning than all the stars and starlets that so rapidly invaded the globalized imaginary. Albertine, encountered on the seawall of a resort town, arrives to infuse her casual and pansexual vitality into the crumbling universe of Marcel Proust's *In Search of Lost Time* . . . a new figure of authority is born and she outclasses them all."[6] The writers choose their words with economy in calling the object of desire a "figure of authority." It signals a gear shift from the authority of language and of legal, political space to that of the unformalized, atmospheric, and atomic circulation of desire, which in turn set the real circuits of value into motion.

Authority of course may still be located as ever in personages of state and institutional power; the negative space among these figures is nonetheless thoroughly colonized by an abstraction compelling them into motion through a metabolic of self-replication reticulated to quantified value. When Tiqqun writes that "every Young-Girl is an automatic, standard converter of existence into market value," she is understood less as anthropomorphic and more as a machine part, a converter.[7] This language summons Picabia's "Young-Girl," which suggested the birth of a new subject position at odds with itself, set into a contradictory tension between labor bearer and individual.

The having-become-personage-of-capital's transformative circuitry is a done deal not so much as a result of the legal protection of property over persons in legal juridical discourse, nor the accension of the market itself at an objective social level, but rather the existential, psychological, and libidinal way the subject formed within capital relates to, imagines, and therefore reconstitutes themselves as value. Others have called this existential outlook a form of possessive individualism insofar as identity itself is predicated on the logic of property relations.[8] For Tiqqun, the subject's compulsion to organize the self in identification with goods and services in order to successfully integrate into the replicative logic of production works against the best interests of the subject. The person who bears labor capacity betrays the self in order to assure the valorization of that capacity. The subject's remaining and actual tendency to experiential freedom is short-circuited by the compulsion to recognize oneself only in preconstituted objects that are themselves *guaranteed* valorization, in anticipation of and identification with the transactional circulation of one's own labor-power. The totality of the self is then subsumed under that labor-bearing component that seeks maximum valorization in the misrecognized interest of the person whose personhood still stands in any remaining excess to value.

The Young-Girl is index of the way in which, given capital's saturation into everyday life, the reverse has happened. The totality of the person is organized around a limited labor-bearing operation—setting the self into a constant civil war at the level of self-replication. But that subject has canceled its ultimate best interests in full identification with value itself in seeking self-valorization within the narrowing constraints of its regime, which has, in turn and through time, become naturalized.[9] Competition compelled by the labor market drives the dominance of the self that is most fully attuned to itself in relation to the anonymity and contingency of a labor market. As Sohn-Rethel formulated it in "The Formal Characteristics of Second Nature":

> When Marx says that, from the standpoint of competition, everything appears inverted, it must be noted that the basic form of competition is, precisely, exchange. Because of the inevitable inversion of our consciousness within this society, consciousness of this inversion necessarily remains bound up with critique; practice necessarily requires theory. It is only possible to harm oneself with a blade missing its handle, and so it is in the case of practice without theory. How can we explain socialization by way of alienation?[10]

One way of explaining it would be to set any number of the fragments of its ubiquitous self-evidence in mass culture into a mimetically exacerbated, intensified, exaggerated, yet estranged framework. In the Young-Girl piece, much of the typography in which words appear on the page, paper or digital, mimics the typographic visual field of popular advertising and editorial content intended for those populations understood to be susceptible to product propaganda. Taken together, these pieces of mass language and mass spectacle become not only its empirical evidence but also its own theory; the auto-theory of the commodity. In other words, the evidence—language taken from women's magazines, a euphemism for the language of capital unleashed on the social reproducer reimagined as ideal consumer—becomes its own theory of the contemporary subject or would-be subject whose subjectivity is replaced by placeholders for value. The self is replicated as unconsciously and as autonomously of human interest as the anonymous circuits of consumption and production that in turn reproduces it.

The pages of *Preliminary Materials for a Theory of the Young-Girl* are preliminary insofar as they are the regurgitated pieces of the total field, accumulated in sarcastic dependence to an indifferent capital. I will return to this difficult tone and affective gloss. That fragmentation is articulated by the nature of the speech, which is aphoristic, hasty, yet strangely familiar, as though from a generically universal technical guide or manual. And they are also preliminary in that this abstract totality in which the subject is both embedded and yet to which they are blind only offers itself as fragmentary.

And one way of dismantling this socialization-as-commodity—that which passes for socialization—is to shock the reader who may well be any form of Young-Girl, the consumer, and ever hopeful producer whose self-organization is consciously or otherwise reticulated to marketing its most basic capacities in order to "live." The language is provocative and confrontational yet cold, analytical, as though it were calculated to precipitate a specific result: discomfort. It provokes an un- or antisociality to try to isolate a cause for the already existing yet invisible social forces of capital. The relentless description of the Young-Girl becomes unbearable, driving the reader to disgust. It operates as a form of "negging," a method of purposely antagonizing someone as a means to get a desired result from them, such as greater intimacy on the part of the nagging suitor or the drive to action on the part of the reader-subject who retains enough agency in the face of atomized capital to want to do something to redeem or protect itself, but who can articulate this capacity only negatively and dialectically. The writing is therefore an instrument, designed to draw out a response. It is a user's guide, not a form of entertainment or philosophy. It is an exhortation to lucid vision—a "vision machine"—if not direct action.

Francis Picabia's *Portrait d'une Jeune Fille Americaine dans L'Etat de Nudite* (*Portrait of a Young American Girl in the State of Nudity*) (figure 3.2), made in 1915, had offered one such portrait. Given portraiture's historical commitment to the human countenance, this mimetically exacting representation of a mechanical tool seems to describe a new kind of subject, one caught between acting as agent and therefore rising to the occasion. This occasion is articulated in the framework of the portrait. Its historical power was to present its content as an exceptional human. This genre, portraiture, functioned historically as a sacrosanct temple to the subject, an honor now structurally bestowed at the level of form on a common utilitarian object simply through portraiture's tendency to anthropomorphize. Its historical power was to present its content as an exceptional human. Here, Picabia's sitter is but a utilitarian implement. The perverse portrait insinuates pure instrumentality as the limit of this object's "identity." A strange hybrid, an impossible ontology, *Young American Girl in the State of Nudity* describes a condition, a socially produced ontology, that cannot be identified, much less represented, within the traditional parameters of either historical and classical identity, much less its representation in conventional portraiture. It might rather be understood to demonstrate a *process* of both object production and concomitant subject formation as the artist conceived it.[11]

Chapter 2 argued that artists during the period known as the avant-garde were eager to articulate the becoming-equipment, indeed the becoming-technology, of the anonymous workers' abstracted labor-time. They hoped to figure the transformation from living to dead labor, from working life to the ossification of the worker in relation to value. *Girl Born without a Mother* by

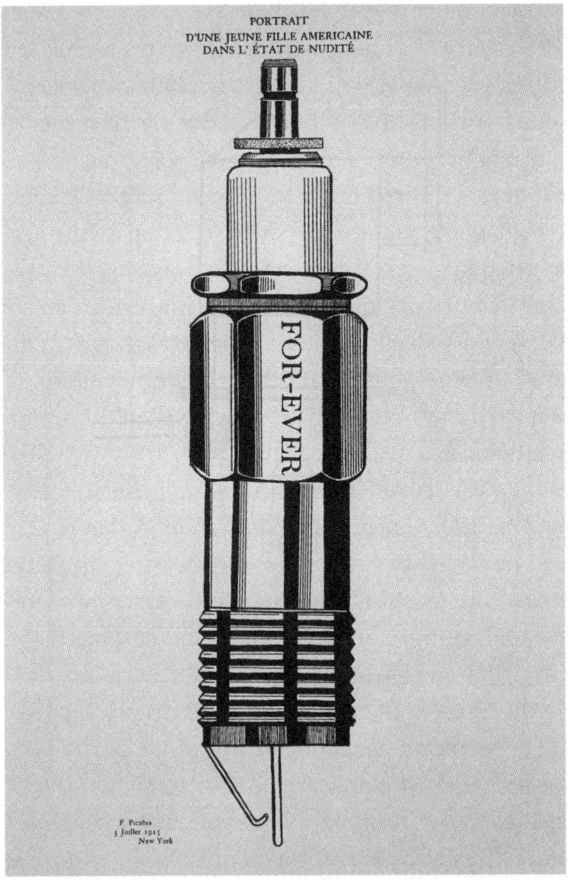

Fig. 3.2. Francis Picabia, *Portrait d'une Jeune Fille Americaine dans L'Etat de Nudite* (*Portrait of a Young American Girl in the State of Nudity*), 1915. © RMN-Grand Palais / Art Resource, NY.

Picabia is a way to designate the impossible-to-depict: the becoming fixed capital of living labor. The "girl" born of machine parts is herself a machine. She works on and yet also *is* the assembly line, enveloped in a matrix of gold. She articulates the *anthropotechnical* aspect of capital in which the worker is congealed in both the commodity *and* in the fixed capital that becomes the very technology of production. At the same time, reciprocally, she re/marks the way the logic of the commodity and its formative technology is internalized as a technology of the self.[12] This is to say that the subject is organized and organizes itself around the demands set by production such that the circuitry of value moves well past the site of production, the factory floor, and into the social field. The subjects are as (unconsciously) oriented to the transactional judgment set by the market as the thing they anonymously takes part in manufacturing. It is as though the commodity and its maker

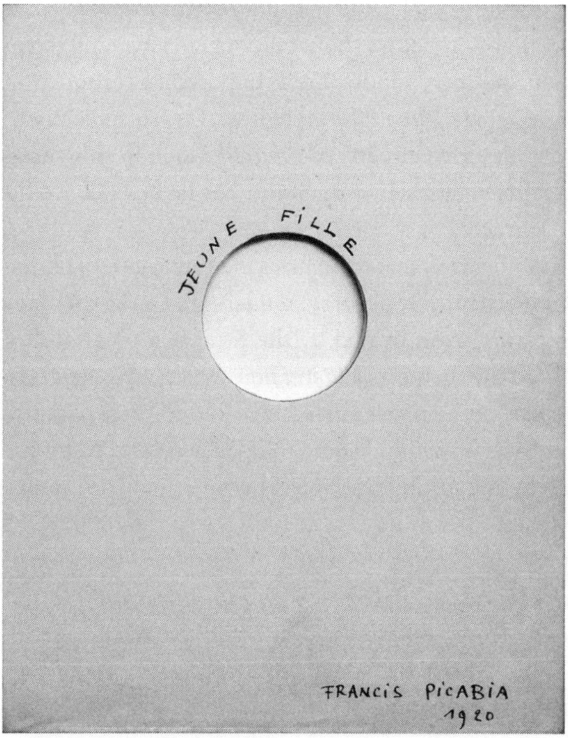

Fig. 3.3. Francis Picabia, *Jeune Fille* (*Young Girl*), 1920. Ink on paper with circle cut out, 11 × 8¾ inches (28.0 × 22.3 cm). Private collection, Courtesy of Galerie 1900–2000, Paris-New York.

stepped away from the factory floor to merge as a hybrid being, a cyborg, connected to circuits of value however distant from the site of the market or of production itself. Caught in the interstice between production and consumption, this figure expresses the movement among and between both terms. That movement, or process, constitutes the subjects just as it contributes to making the objects that the subjects then consume. A tautology emerges. It structures the social field populated by this new creature, who is fragmented and strewn over value's routes, from bearer of labor capacity to consumer. It were as though the individual were made up of stations in the course of value's self-replicative path. As such, having de- and recomposed the self, capital enters into mimesis with it: "Though capitalism has long since escaped the walls of the factory, it is the rise of the Young-Girl that signals the market's hegemony over the social . . . She is the 'total acculturation' of the self. . . . That is, the Young-Girl's production is *self-production*: hard-won conformity. The Young-Girl is the 'anthropomorphosis of Capital.'"[13] Forty-two years after Picabia's *Mechanomorph*, in 1962, Marxist theorist

Mario Tronti coined the phrase "social factory" to address the *expanded field* generated by capital subsumption across the totality of society.[14] The term designates how circulation and consumption are as important as production to cycles of valorization. Picabia's *Jeune Fille* prefigures this "social factory." The Young-Girl's task is to describe circuits of *subjectification* in this social factory. But like the social factory itself, a theory of her emergence would take almost a century to surface.

Picabia made more than one work that thematizes the young girl. Explored in chapter 2, the first is a mechanically accurate rendering of a car part presented in no uncertain terms, as indicated by the title, as a portrait of a human person. He revisited the theme as a *literal* hole, or negative space, in a collage. The negative space of the paper affixed to a second piece of paper that becomes its ground casts a shadow where the paper refuses to lie flat against its support, thereby remarking the hole as a hole, as literal rather than depicted negative space.

As discussed in the previous chapter, the model of the subject summoned by Picabia—in *The Double World* (1919), *Universal Prostitution* (1916–17), and *Girl Born without a Mother* (1917)—is strewn over a network of social relations and, more specifically, nodes in a mode of production. This would suggest that the negative space or literal hole in the visual field is part of a series that limns something of the ontology of the subject in the circuitry of value, a placeholder in a process that might best be expressed by the diagram. Picabia's *Jeune Fille* understood as either a literal or depicted hole—sliding from concrete to abstract through a process of representation—thus elaborates the constellation of work explored in chapter 2, a series that clearly seemed to be struggling to understand the effects of seismic change in the fabrication of objects on the formation of *subjects*, of persons reconstituted by the commodity form to which they poured not only labor-time but time away from capital, in moments of consumerist self-replication. Picabia's extraordinary epiphanic supplement to his friend Marcel Duchamp's ready-mades was to recognize that any query into the object—the putative ready-made—was already beside the point, or at best only a part of the point. For Picabia, ready-made things are symbiotically linked to ready-made, or made to be ready, *subjects*. *Jeune Fille* describes, then as now, the way the subject is the necessary *medium* of capitalist valorization. In short, if in modernity, objects are ready-mades, subjects are in turn made to be ready to assume their purpose in the cycle of market valorization.

This reiterated trope of the *Jeune Fille* (as portrait of a machine part, and as hole) indicates that the problem—the Young-Girl as emblem of depersonalized, abstract, reified labor-power briefly delivered by a worker-subject who remains faceless—exceeded already by 1920 any specific medium or support that might best articulate it. While the figure, such as in Seurat's *The Models*, remains bounded by a pictorial delivery, Picabia's struggle with and choice to jettison it indicates anxious ambivalence about what *form* the phenomenon might best take. Ahead of its formalization—not unlike Marx's prostitute summoned to indicate a new social form—the Young-Girl as the very figure of a subject reconstituted by processes of reification to which they un/consciously contribute came to motivate yet another kind of conveyance at the close of the century. Just as abstraction itself, resonating from the non-site and non-time of transactional exchange, casts its shadow over the totality of social relations, reforging an unconscious synthesis, the social factory too enveloped and saturated an ever wider social formation. The figure of the Young-Girl stepped out of the picture plane and into other media to suggest the degree to which she, or it, had already come to qualify the social forms of everyday life.

I return to the textual reiteration of the Young-Girl with which this chapter began. By the close of the previous century, in 1999, a small group of artists, students, and activists forming a collective briefly known as Tiqqun revisited Picabia's trope in the form of a publication. *Preliminary Materials for a Theory of the Young-Girl* was written by an artist among the collective who parted ways with Tiqqun shortly after its brief run and formed another collective, the artist group Claire Fontaine. The latter went on to formulate the becoming "readymade" of the artist-subject in texts such as "Readymade Artist and Human Strike."[15] As I will explore toward the close of the chapter, the Young-Girl is the obverse of the ready-made, or the ready-made imagined as a subject. By similarly configuring even the artist as a kind of ready-made person, the writer of the text extends the condition of subject formation under capital to even the most privileged among persons, the exemplary artist and deliverer of the last traces of auratic collective meaning.

The collective Tiqqun, whose name derives from a messianic Jewish term for healing and redemption, published two volumes of writing in 1999 and 2001. Issue 1 included a piece titled "Preliminary Materials for a Theory of the Young-Girl" later republished as a book under that same title. The text assumes and speaks through a masked and fictional character, the eponymous Young-Girl, qualified by an embittered and yet far-from-authentic voice that replicates the demands of a capitalist consumer-subject in need of ready-made subjectivities in order to guarantee its own social reproduction within a social ecology all but subsumed into the interest of capital. This figure, which the authors explicitly cite as ungendered, articulates a dynamic about how the subject is made to be, and actively makes itself be, "consumable" in mimetic inscription of the commodity form so that it can "earn" the right to consume, via direct or indirect market mediation. This is to say that the figure could be either a worker and direct value producer or a consumer, just as they could be of any gender. Indeterminacy here reflects the mobile dynamic of valorization itself, mediated by a market. This circular dynamic between production and circulation maintains the circuits necessary to the social law of value in operation.[16] In other words, the work explores the tautology implicit in reification: the compulsion to offer one's objectified labor-power for sale as an estranged, abstracted, and anonymous thing—in short, the compulsion to *prostitute*—in the sole interest of one's own daily self-reproduction. The obverse is the need to have purchasing capacity to survive. It expresses the orbital logic of the subject whose subjectivity as such is "made to be ready" to become an abstracted, anonymous thing and to take its place along the circuitry of valorization as described in chapter 2.

The Young-Girl performs what Foster calls "mimetic exacerbation" of the subtle misogynist aggressions of everyday life to which young persons are tacitly expected to become inured in order to survive (or become employable) among social relations in the regime of the "second nature" of capitalist abstraction.[17] Tiqqun tells us that this Young-Girl is the standard "model" citizen of empire, the perfect consumer whose consumption therefore guarantees valorization and through it the continuity of cycles of production and accumulation, again, an intersection in a set of operations that can only be expressed diagrammatically, if at all. But she also stands for the social sadism that is fully naturalized under those conditions. The process of naturalization becomes the very object of inquiry. And that very process is invisible because it is saturated; it is everywhere and therefore nowhere. Tiqqun is describing the very technologies of the self that are demanded of the subject by capital, thus generating "selves" that nonetheless cannot identify themselves *as* objects of capital. Clint Burnham, the Marxist Lacanian analyst, locates a summary of the problem in Tiqqun's language, "The Young-Girl is the ultimate slavery through which empire has obtained its slaves' silence."[18]

Burnham discusses Tiqqun's difficult and dialectical prose poem in its historical context, which ranges from the early twentieth-century manifesto or prose poem à la James Joyce or Apollinaire to twentieth- and early twenty-first-century forms of politicized international punk culture reticulated to utopian anti-state communism, which he sees as exemplified by the Russian art and music collective Pussy Riot. As a practicing clinical analyst,

Burnham categorizes Tiqqun, Pussy Riot, and a few other rare instances as examples of "The Pussy Supposed to Know," a variation on Jacques Lacan's fictive Subject supposed to know.[19] In other words, far from the doubly victimized female subject position implied by some readers, the mimetic exacerbation with which much art, according to Foster, amplifies and thereby not only draws attention to but *compels* the reader or listener into accessing consciousness of the violence of the everyday appeals to none other than they who should be most shocked. This subject has the most to lose or to gain through dismantling the technologies of the self that render one a reified thing, in which the "heart and ass" are divorced in total abstraction. It does this by way of escaping bland didactic *reflection*.

In *Preliminary Materials for a Theory of the Young-Girl*, in contrast to most others, Tiqqun used many of the graphic and rhetorical devices constitutive of the avant-garde moment of 1910–30 internationally and across media. It was as though both Picabia's figure and the kind of typographical choices he and his comrades used—across print, collage, watercolor, and numerous other media in relation to abstraction, on the one hand, and political economy on the other—had lain dormant for many decades, waiting to be understood and reposed as a question or problem about what it means to be an agent with any vestige of autonomy, critical or otherwise, within capitalist social formations.

Much of this exploration takes on the problem of sexual fetishization, or the kind of market reification that would lend itself to gender assignation and commodified eros, or soft porn. If anything, Tiqqun's "theory" of the eponymous "girl" begins to afford a lens, belated by a century and a half, into why Marx might have picked up the eccentric and technically erroneous metaphor of *prostitution* to qualify the sale of labor-power and the forms of social abstraction to which it gives rise. Tiqqun's Young-Girl has internalized the outer limits of misogyny, irrespective of whether she be male or female or any other gender, to make herself into the ultimate commodity. Here, the commodity forged of the sale of labor-power is figured as the sale of sexuality, or a received and estranged petrified sexuality understood through the framework of the commodity. Again, one way of understanding the device through which Tiqqun formalizes the commodity of labor-power would be the rhetorical device identified by Hal Foster as mimetic exacerbation. But now, that which is being exaggerated for emphasis is the relation between labor, commodity, and the subjectivizing and subjugating summoning of desire. Eros is posited as an entry into value's circuits more than as a vital drive. In this text, the dominant logic by which market formations operate is ratcheted and heightened to demonstrate the violence inscribed in sexuality that passes for erotic provocation or even normative in everyday life.[20] It was as though all the social mores that should have found themselves offended by Picabia's figure of the reified worker, or Marx's "prostitute," finally surfaced in the elaborated qualification of this social formation who, finally, might describe any and every one within capital who operates under the compulsion to organize their own subject formation in the interest of being employed.

From the vantage of a leftist politics scattered over geopolitical sites of conflict in the opening years of the twenty-first century, few "events" of a purely cultural nature—*Tiqqun* was, after all, a short-lived publication—have galvanized such a fraught examination of what a radically left, anti-capitalist feminism might be as much as a handful of responses to Tiqqun's *Preliminary Materials for a Theory of the Young-Girl*.[21] In other words, the critical outcry against this work offers the best index into the missed encounters between the elaboration of capital over the century and the cultural forms that have tried to figure the totality of capitalist social relations, which are already unrepresentable.

The remainder of this chapter explores the reception of *Preliminary Materials for a Theory of the Young-Girl* alongside the text as a belated reception of the work explored in chapter 2, Picabia's "Young-Girl," itself a belated expression of the subject-worker—the recomposed subject of capital in both productive and reproductive roles located at any point along the pathways of value who must organize the social self around a transaction, or Marx's "universal prostitute." To review, here so-called prostitution is far from a form of self-determination, a choice to bring one's flesh to market, but rather the function of a structural determination reticulated through the mute compulsions of the market, which acts as a crucible of exchangism that forges, as though alchemically, subject positions in its own interest. I explore Tiqqun's *Preliminary Materials for a Theory of the Young-Girl* and *The Cybernetic Hypothesis*, which reflexively continue where the avant-garde left off in its study of abstraction, reification, and the way that concrete, living labor becomes fixed capital, inscribed in technology—the becoming technology of the human. *Preliminary Materials for a Theory of the Young-Girl* resumes an attempt to find ways to figure the entwinement of subjectivization, value, and technology that constitutes real abstraction. Finally, Tiqqun's appropriation and elaboration of the early twentieth-century avant-garde turns to an examination of how the avant-garde had prefigured its future: "The multitude not only uses machines to produce, but also becomes increasingly machinic itself, as the means of production are increasingly integrated into the minds and bodies of the multitude."[22] The cyborg toward which Picabia's *Jeune Fille* had reached and which Donna Haraway had theorized passes over into a barely allegorized description of the mass subject, of anybody and everybody, plugged in to networks of consumerist value. While the issue of consumerist valorization is by now self-evident enough, the way it inscribes the subject as cyborg has yet to be discussed.

The text is situational and interpellative insofar as the readers are invited via so many tricks and strategies of advertising to identify with this objectified being or person whom they identify with objects. The text *performs* reification. Yet this very performance of reification forecloses specific identification insofar as it is too generic. The reader is offended insofar as they both fail to recognize themselves and yet recognize themselves overmuch in the description of a generic condition. This language of performative reification describes the "self-" inscription of the worker-subject into technology as though it were a matter of sovereign free will. As Burnham notes: "The universality of the Young-Girl, then, is the universality of the non-All," which is also the logic of the signifier that inheres in the internet, a genericism so utterly common and generic that no one can recognize their own specific parameters in it and yet, because of its anodyne, nonthreatening genericism, into which they will happily register themselves/ourselves.[23]

The *Young-Girl* describes the very point of a technology of the self that is at once seemingly particular and for all that totally impersonal. Picabia's other iterations of the *Jeune Fille* made the point fairly clear: the subject is the hole in the picture in relation to the totality of the picture in which she or he is seemingly absent, thereby revealing the totality of the social field as such. Likewise, abstracted from concrete labor as abstract labor, the workers' labor-time is fully absorbed into a structure of fixed capital with which they at once overidentify—it is naturalized—but in which they fail to locate their specific experience.

This system, or network of systems, is not *one*. As raised in the context of the diagram in the previous chapter, capitalism cannot be identified or located in any one person, place, or thing. As such, the nature of its sovereignty is diametrically opposed to the way sovereignty was once located in a unitary person or institution. Capital, by contrast, is dispersed, scattered, and yet multisystemic. It operates among terms linked along the chain of production, circulation, and supply; its metabolic is "representable" only through schematic and nonmimetic forms of articulation, most of which are noncorrelative, as statisticians remind us.[24] Unlike for the social sciences, the personification of subsumption in the expanded social field does not claim to *define* the process of valorization but only to attempt to *describe* how it might affect the entire sociocultural field while remaining outside that field as an artwork that ultimately remains denotatively opaque throughout its allegorical descriptive capacity.

The Young-Girl of the eponymous theory, like Picabia's "Young-Girl," is a presentation of a marker or space holder with which any and every one might identify themselves in the interest of fulfilling the demands made by capital, as though being a "model" subject might win maximum survival value. As such, it is an agent of nonagency who acts nonetheless as the necessary condition for the production and consumption of the commodity that, in turn, keeps value itself continuously in motion by being "present" to it but also by continually evacuating themselves. The ontological status of the commodity as a repository of value in transit rather than as a necessary use-value per se is mirrored in a subject formation that is necessary to circuitry but not necessary to fulfill the necessary conditions of being a self, replete with the interiority that might threaten to rupture supply chains. In any case, she is born of machinery, like Picabia's *Girl Born without a Mother*, discussed at length in chapter 2. This Girl, followed by the repeated Young-Girl, situated alongside the ready-made, is the first cultural signifier to figure the all-consuming "volition" of the gap diagrammed by Rancière in *Reading Capital*, elaborated in chapter 2. To review, this gap, diagrammatically accessible but impossible to identify and locate in any one person, place, or thing, marks the movement among production via labor, consumption, and circulation in the symbolic form of money—currency that translates labor into value in the abstract transactional space of exchange.

But it is also an allegory of *technology*. The figure of the Young-Girl, like Picabia's *Jeune Fille* some eighty years previous, is constitutively bound up with the historicity of technologies, of the collective and of the collective-self that are co-emergent with capitalism's acceleration. Cognitively mappable only through diagrams and data imaging, capital increased, according to Tiqqun, with the introduction of technocratic surveillance designed to minimize contingency. Similar to the managerial class born of the factories of the nineteenth century and expected to ensure maximized surplus-value extraction with minimal labor (through which so-called Taylorist efficiency was enforced), by the mid-twentieth century, daily contingencies were to be managed so as to maximize surplus value.

In the segment of *Grundrisse* known as "The Fragment on Machines," Marx imagined that in "the future," which is to say the era spanning the late nineteenth century to our twenty-first-century present and beyond, in which individual and collective labor capacity is congealed in the forms of equipment and technology that maximize the extraction of surplus value by making the labor process more efficient and diminishing the amount of "living labor," is proportional to the fixed capital necessary for profit maximization. Here, Marx discusses the movement from concrete to abstract labor, the "general social knowledge" that became the direct force of production both at the level of generalized labor but also in the way that generalized knowledge is objectified in machinery. Automation, as Marx argues, allows for the productivity gains that, in turn, make automation and updates on fixed capital possible, a circular logic in which the worker is threatened, if not with obsolescence (after all, only labor generates value), with a shrinking capacity to replicate daily life. Dispossessed, the worker finds himself to have become an object of gratuitous excess to the circuitry to which he contributed and which constituted him and into which he expended his time. The result is a brokered kind of "solution" in which the worker must assimilate to machines, internalizing their operative economy and becoming appended to them rather than the other way around.[25] This is the source of the cyborg, long before the advent of modern warfare as Marinetti and the Futurists imagined it.

The shift into which the Young-Girl steps is again that posed by the problem of the "social factory," or the way that, against the tendency of the rate of profit to fall, capitalist valorization becomes the work of the totality of the social field. The problem of value extraction moves increasingly from production to consumption and is measured ever more perfervidly in a cybernetically monitored world. The subject under capital takes on the double responsibility of generating surplus at the level of production but also at the site of consumption. Again, the key "moment" is that of transaction, in which production and consumption conjoin. But this means that consumption is monitored, policed, measured, and managed with the same metricized efficiency as production. Into this accelerated set of circuits, now compounded by surveillance technology, the Young-Girl finds her "meaning" or function.

In *The Cybernetic Hypothesis*, also republished as a book, Tiqqun studies the extreme and essential transformation of the mass subject with the advent of information technologies.[26] As they write, "Information cybernetics founds a new politics of subjects based on communication, on transparency to oneself and to others."[27] By the 1960s, Norbert Wiener had begun to conceptualize a socio-cybernetics with a larger scope. A new model of the subject carefully mediated by institutions such as the hospital, the school, and the courtroom comes to adjudicate as the specter of the factory diminishes. In place of the factory, cybernetics affords power a chance to keep count and to look over the distribution, organization, and reproduction of labor-power-bearing persons. Tiqqun's account notes that "the contemporary history of the economic discourse should be considered from the angle of this rise of the problem of information. From the crisis of 1929 to 1949, the attention of economists focused on the questions of anticipation, of uncertainty connected with demand, of an adjustment between production and consumption, of projection of economic activity."[28] In other words, production coerces consumption by generating new forms not only of advertising and financing but also of predicting and managing consumer behavior.

Philip Mirowski's *Machine Dreams: Economics Becomes a Cyborg Science* delivers an exhaustive account of the entwinement of computational mathematics, including game theory and set theory with predictive and above all prescriptive economics in the United States (and Europe) after World War II, funded by the American military. Mirowski, a historian of economics and technology, uncovers the history of the adoption of advanced mathematics, including probability, by the American military's intelligence apparatus in the interest of devising predictions against enemy operatives. However, by 1949, the same modeling techniques were turned on domestic populations to attempt to predict mass behavior in order to surveil the domestic consumer base. Mirowski's book traces the development of modeling that later gave rise to templates for the elaboration of algorithms in the sphere of marketing and consumer management. By the century's close, those same instruments had become utterly saturated in an expanded social field in the interest of corporations. In short, Tronti's "social factory," something of a metaphor meant to explain the interrelated web of circulation, consumption, and production far from the factory floor, had become absolutely literalized.

Tiqqun also discusses how set theory entered economics, as much as economics entered set theory, as Mirowski argues, by way of Wiener's explanation of the feedback loop. However, having argued for its systemic coherence, Wiener did not fully grasp various aspects of subjectivity formation along the axes of capitalist re/productive cycles. Moving mathematical models of probability and causality into the social register through economic behavioralist "sciences" required some forms of translation, "a conditioning that is also a precondition for the existence on a market."[29] The gathering of cybernetically oriented statistics began as descriptive and then "switched over" to modulate the behavior of the consumer and producer, with or without their necessarily much less conscious or purposive "choice."

In the United States and elsewhere, part of this "switch over" from modeling to prescriptive forms of consumer encouragement via advertising and product positioning was readily adopted at the level of industrial design and object manufacture. Product design manifestly embraced an expanding labor market in order to capture the energy of a suddenly expansive productivism at the level of consumption. If newly advancing wage earners could also purchase at the same accelerated rate as their economic advancement, they could fuel the economy twice over through this purchasing power. Capitalists saw new horizons of profit in this burgeoning consumerism. The new freedom to buy more things encouraged newly mobile classes to express that status through more sophisticated consumer habits, which, in turn, encouraged the proliferation of ever more differentiated goods.

For instance, the Italian economist Ruggero Cominotti, who also consulted for Italian design firms like Olivetti, encouraged companies to run increasingly more exhaustive marketing surveys. He contended that advanced production would fuel equally advanced consumption in a manifest reversal of the traditional assumption that consumption drives production through demand. He also went so far as to argue that design and manufacture could cause new models of subject formation, through interpellation and advertising.

> Design becomes important to the extent that it is the principal instrument for renewing not only the outward form but also the functions of the products, and for establishing relations with users. Anyone who can read the signs can see in the products of the respective firms how each of them intends to contribute to changing the physical and human environment, and the pace with which it is prepared to improve this environment by means of products that offer a harmonious balance between function and appearance and winning consumer acceptance.[30]

Cominotti goes on to make the case that design modernizes and practically civilizes those who consume it, that design "encourages the urbanization of the masses expelled from agriculture."[31] Subjectivity itself is designed and produced by that which it consumes, whether it technically needs it or not.

Again, labor-power-bearing subjects, subjugated to circuits that are only schematically representable, "switched over" to being of *double* utility by midcentury: first as producers of value and then as consumers setting value into circuits far beyond either the sites of its production or of its consumption. But Cominotti's point is much more subtle: object consumption makes people as much as people make things. The nature of identity, behavior, and comportment could be sculpted through consumption.

An uncanny coincidence is the way that the historical conjuncture of World War II and its immediate aftermath, the moment when military intelligence was applied to the domestic population in the interest of augmenting profit, saw the genre of the pin-up of young women proliferate exponentially as never before. While assorted machinery associated with transport had long been assigned female names (ostensibly as a form of protection), the 1940s and 1950s was when images of young girls were distributed as never before, above all to men in the service, who often affixed these images to airplanes and other assorted large-scale machinery of warfare. The image of the Young-Girl itself "exploded," disseminated both abroad to those in service and at home, a phenomenon that only continued to swell into the 1950s and the eventual beginning of a "niche" market in popular soft pornography, evidenced by the rise of moguls such as Hugh Hefner.

The prototypical work of Earl Moran, which many claim to be the source of what later became the calcified parameters of the genre, was quite rigid about the formal and technical aspects of the pin-up. Moran stipulated that "the perfect woman is five feet seven inches tall in her shoes, or five feet four inches in her bare feet. She must weigh between 112 and 115 pounds. Her waist must be 24 to 25 inches, her hips from 35 to 36 inches, and her bust from 34 to 35 inches. The color of her hair doesn't matter, although blondes do photograph best."[32] In addition to very narrowly circumscribed bodies, Moran developed a typology of facial expressions and gestures that operate more or less paradigmatically, influencing the kinds of motions and countenances—everything from the look of fake surprise to inclusion of common props, many of them indications of modernity like telephones and radios—that continue to be popular, including the kinds of body language one encounters in the modern "selfie" or self-portrait. His work has come to signal the era, the same historical period that Tiqqun, Mirowski, and others identify as the moment when advanced mathematics began to formulate algorithms and other heightened strategies for consumer development and, in short, officiated the marriage of economics and technology.

But Picabia had already prefigured the Young-Girl's meteoric rise to prominence in common culture and had already begun to associate this trope with technology. Likewise, long before Cominotti or any of the thousands of newly minted executives tasked with profit maximization for their respective companies, Marx had already investigated the necessity of each moment in the circulation of value to every other moment in *Grundrisse*, where he describes the mutually reenforcing circuits of production and consumption almost as a series of feedback loops building on each moment along the circuit. Marx argues that production does not simply fulfill basic use-values but is historically motivated by the specificity of demands that are also produced by a cyclical structure of reciprocal determination.[33] In this regard, Cominotti's designs are nothing new.

What is new by the 1950s is the way that cybernetics imagines the subject as a *machine* that might be molded and sculpted into the correct consumer habits, as though it too were an object of design. Mirowski points out that economists began to think of individuals and group dynamics as complex machines in which computing equilibria might be established. The triangulation of consumer surveillance, modeling, and, ultimately, the rise of algorithms engineered to affect consumer choices tightened the movement of the circuit. The image of the Young-Girl becomes the very figure of the conjuncture in which it emerges, although the point is not that this figure is a metonymic stand-in but rather that she personifies a new kind of compulsory subject formation. Tiqqun's understanding of technology is attuned to the specificity of this radically new becoming-cyborg of the individual in keeping with the postwar aspiration to make of each person a perfect production-consumption-machine:

> For in fact the cybernetic hypothesis calls for a radically new structuring of the individual or collective subject, in the direction of a hollowing out. It dismisses interiority as a myth and along with it the entire psychology of the 19th century, including psychoanalysis. It's no longer a matter of separating the subject from their traditional external ties as the liberal hypothesis had demanded, but of reconstructing the social bond by stripping the subject of any substance. Everyone must become an envelope without flesh and blood, the best possible conductor of social communication, the locus of an endless recursive loop that rids itself of kinks.[34]

This kind of double utility to capital, once as producer of surplus value and/or the labor-power to produce it, and again as consumer realizing value in the impersonal space of the market, which, in turn, requires the wages to do so and thus compels labor, is difficult to grasp if only because of the way the ideology of the free sovereign individual lubricates both moments, obscuring how compulsion itself is a process along a circuit. Each moment implies every other moment. But the contradiction whereby individuality is canceled in the name of individuality seems to demand of the subject ever *greater performances of individuality* in order to somehow outpace the social formations that make the subject a generic part-object in a larger network of value. Put otherwise, the *Jeune-Fille* is the agent of nonagency, the condition for the commodity that keeps the system going by continually evacuating herself—which is what the machinery wants of her.

To recap: the Young-Girl internalizes the unconscious compulsion or social synthesis organized around value in order to constitute her "self" so that she can take part in the necessary circuits that structure her lifeworld and which she is expected to replicate. She is thus a node in a network of machinery and a social metabolic in which she has no specific stake outside of guaranteeing her own "value," understood exclusively as the internalization of the aggregate of consumerist "choices." Her interior life or the substance of her thoughts, insofar as these are permitted to exist in a second nature formed by real abstraction, is not at issue. In this regard, she is the expression of the circuitry of production, reproduction, circulation, and consumption of objects through which subjects are objectified. What is offensive is the dawning realization that this form of pure exteriority has displaced the traditional notion of the subject as replete with psychological and emotional depth. In short, it is an affront to the model of the subject that would insist on a free and sovereign form of self-realization. The producing and consuming monads within capitalism may believe themselves to be entirely free of technologically mediated and ultimately economistic motivations. However, they cannot possibly be transparent to their own structural determinations, which certainly operate unconsciously insofar as the realization of value itself constitutes a social unconscious.

I turn now to a discussion of *Preliminary Materials for a Theory of the Young-Girl*'s reception before resituating it as a singularly rare acknowledgment of the posthuman subject necessitated by capital.[35]

Two notable feminist responses, by poet Ariana Reines (who translated the pamphlet into English) and Nina Power, symptomatize the gender aporia at the heart of the problem of coming to terms with a totalizing problem that presents itself in gendered terms. Of course, we might pause and ask, again with a century and a half of belated hindsight, why Marx's initial expression of new forms of abstract labor should also have to have been gendered. In the preface to her translation, Reines describes her translation process thus: "So I've already said that translating this book made me sick. . . . I don't know why I've been hesitant to say this publicly."[36] And yet she does "say," in fact write, a vivid description of her immediate affective reaction of illness while working with and on the text. This colorful expression of disgust does not confront its source: misogyny as that which is structured into circuits of value realization via consumption, abstracted from the particulars of persons, places, or context, or the fact that capitalism is already indifferent to those particulars. She does not note the degree to which the Young-Girl operates as a figure for an abstracted phenomenon. On the register of poetics tracking parallel to Picabia's forms of symbolization (the icon, the diagram, the collage), *Preliminary Materials for a Theory of the Young-Girl* uses language to expand on the mechanomorph, to situate it as a subject position and develop its "interior" monologue, its "thoughts" and "feelings," which are shown to be already ready-made. Some such phrases include "in their divorce, the Young-Girl's heart and ass have become two empty abstractions."[37] How else might the condition of the split subject, divided between its experience of itself as a social being attached to others and an object compelled to sell its labor-time, its "ass," be expressed? The text expands on Picabia's "girl," no less. Was *Portrait d'une Jeune Fille Americaine dans L'Etat de Nudite* any less brutal in its presentation of a Young-Girl as a tool?

The text is an extended collage poem appropriating the textual, typographic, and conceptual apparatus of futurism as a study of the becoming machinic object of the human in order to conscientiously provoke the very illness Reines purports to experience. It is a semifictional essay-poem imposing on the reader a heightened and intensified account of what it is to experience the self as a thing among other disposable things in a harsh social landscape where most collective affect is evaporated by separation, anomie, instrumental reason, and above all the law of value. The readers cannot identify themselves here because to do so is already foreclosed by the ideological scrim of everyday life. The text operates as a description of the objective conditions that the readers, interpellated by the very experience of reading this or any text as a free, self-determined consciousness, cannot see or afford to bear. The object does not recognize itself as such, caught in the forms of appearance offered it. The Young-Girl personifies an absent totality with which the readers cannot bear to identify, however much it might describe each one of us.

To the question posed most succinctly by Fredric Jameson in *The Political Unconscious: Narrative as a Socially Symbolic Act* and again in *Postmodernism, or, The Cultural Logic of Late Capitalism* of *why* "totality" is both the horizon of cultural mediation and the rock against which it is inevitably shipwrecked, or why this inaccessible totality is acknowledged as having been invisible and ultimately absolutely unrepresentable all along, one reply might be that any attempt to grasp (much less present) the enormous complexity of life within global capital would exceed the consciousness of any one subject position situated within it.[38] Again, contingency cancels any total "view." This answer may or may not be especially satisfying, but it is one attempt to address why "realism" as a direct presentation of social reality is ultimately foreclosed within modernity if not within traditional culture. Capital itself stands in excess to any access to its own reality, making the social field invisible to any subject position inscribed within it. As Alberto Toscano and Jeff Kinkle note in *Cartographies of the Absolute*, any attempts at social realism become partial perspectives of the social, which, as illustrations from a contingent perspective, belies the point of realism. A circular logic results, ending in aporia or worse, the formation of particularist ideology: "Ideology [is] the subject's imaginary representation of their relation to the real."[39] Any figuration claiming to realism as such becomes a conditional imaginary, fetishized and, therefore, merely symptomatic of the impossibility of totality. The fragment resurfaces as the perceived "truth" of the situation, which becomes in and of itself a theory to account for the subject's limited relation to a restricted totality.

Jameson relies on Louis Althusser's Marxian-Lacanian understanding of subject formation and of the individual's partial relation to the social and the economic mediated by language.[40] Althusser read culture, and art in particular, as a path into the question of subjective misrecognition and misidentification. Althusser's dependence on the Lacanian understanding of the signifier in relation to a foreclosed real, which Althusser conceived specifically as the social-economic field, in turn afforded Jameson the theoretical apparatus through which to read culture as an etiology, or a repository of symptoms and clues, of an "absent cause" that could not be figured directly. Jameson in turn elaborated a theory of hermeneutics, that of effectively replacing a "reflective" understanding of art with one wherein culture is the complex mediation of withdrawn causality issuing from a social field yet imperceptible within it.

But again, for both, the problem of unrepresentability remains on the side of the subject who, caught in a labyrinth of misprision, somewhere among the (social) real, imaginary, and symbolic, at once interpellated into social formations and yet misidentified, is pathetically tasked with trying to tie a signifier onto an opaque political-economic reality in partial and structurally problematic ways. In the "blind field" of everyday life, the subject may as well be blindfolded, groping to "read" the signs and sequences of the social order that in turn constitutes "the real."[41] Much of the discourse of the past several decades that attempts to forge any convincing account of the relationship between the subject and the putative "real" passes through the theory of the subject offered by Lacan and relies therefore on a model of the unconscious also posed by him. While for Althusser, and therefore Jameson after him, this real is itself inscribed in the social-political field, it is nonetheless illegible as a totality because it is sifted through the contingency of the subject's partial purchase on the world outside of them. Reines's reading of an allegory of capital presented in gendered terms misses the theory of capital for the gendered terms in which it is presented. To this missed encounter, I add only the continued inquiry into the universal prostitute of Marx's original allegory of the newly constituted worker, posed as a function of structural terms and compulsions to self-reproduction that exceed the parameters of any theory of self-determination, which would include the framework to which Reines seems to adhere, believing there to be a space outside the subject formations reticulated to value and to forms of social synthesis that are equally organized around it.

In her 2013 review "She's Just Not That into You," philosopher Nina Power, who takes the trope to be a transparent representation of a girl or woman rather than a personification of capital irrespective of fixed gender, wrote that "*Theory of the Young-Girl* is a text that *both* critically parodies yet uncritically regenerates the misogyny that resonates at the heart of a culture that celebrates youth and beauty above all else while simultaneously denigrating the bearers—young women, overwhelmingly—of these purportedly desirable characteristics. Locating in the tautology descriptive of labor-power's inscription into commodified life a missed critical vantage, Power seems to believe that there is an external location from which to judge those fully constituted by the abstract social logic that the work tries to describe through what she calls "parody." Perhaps what Power chooses to overlook in the mimetically performed narcissism of the fictionalized voice is that men, other genders, and subject positions irreducible to gender are also caught in a point of sale in a market that demands and attributes to them those characteristics in order to compel the very transactions that all subject positions, historically marginalized or otherwise, must replicate for the purposes of their own daily self-reproduction.

Both writers miss the forest for some superficially offensive trees. *Preliminary Materials for a Theory of the Young-Girl* is not a case study on the ethics of representation, much less a bid for a representational politics. It is a description of real abstraction configured as a subject and of how the modern subject internalizes an unconscious social synthesis set by the transactional logic of the market. How might a figure as common, omnipresent, anonymous, and ubiquitous as Marx's universal prostitute, the worker compelled to work and yet made to seem as though she were taking her time to market freely, possibly be presented other than through the mimetic exacerbation that could precipitate what is fully naturalized in everyday life? How might it finally *appear* as the product of coercive violence that it is? How can the subject, reified and scattered among nodal points in circuits of valorization, possibly recognize herself as such when the appearance of social forms predicated on free will and self-determination preclude it? A negative-dialectically derived feminism that owes as much to Autonomia—above all to Mario Tronti, who theorized "the social factory"—as to a constellation of Italian Marxist feminists including Leopoldina Fortunati, and as much to Carla Lonzi's radical negativity derived from Adorno's concept of authenticity as Michel Foucault's critique of power and Guy Debord's rage against spectacle, Tiqqun's figure of the Young-Girl is a way to finally discuss gender from a materialist perspective, as a function of social formations rather than as sex or even as social construction. But this address takes the form of a *performance*, not so much of identity as such but of capital's social forms: "The Young-Girl's love affairs are work, and like all work they have become precarious."[42]

It is no doubt shocking to implicate "love" as "work" in the pleats of the social factory. Love or some approximation of it, especially within the fantasy of the consumer who purchases, conjugated with work and with remuneration for work is no doubt the property of "prostitution" or sex work. In *What Is Sexual Capital*, historians Dana Kaplan and Eva Illouz try to locate a kind of pith or essence that might be said to properly qualify emotional and erotic life. However, like the library of materialist feminists who precede them and on whom they elaborate, the matter of sexuality and affect is shown again and again, through sociological case studies, to be already both a form of labor-power and an ideological apparatus by which to lubricate the circuits that compose the social factory *as* a social factory. In other words, circuits of valorization saturate the spaces that once were exterior to the factory floor under the rubric of that which is held to be essentially extrinsic to capital: love. But the authors go a step further and perform a kind of archaeology of the subject in which selfhood is organized around the notion of affective bonds, understood to be the foundation of social formation, even as these very bonds are themselves nodal in the reproduction of labor-power, the primary point made by autonomist feminists of the 1970s but also in the formation of a self. That "self" is produced through the notion

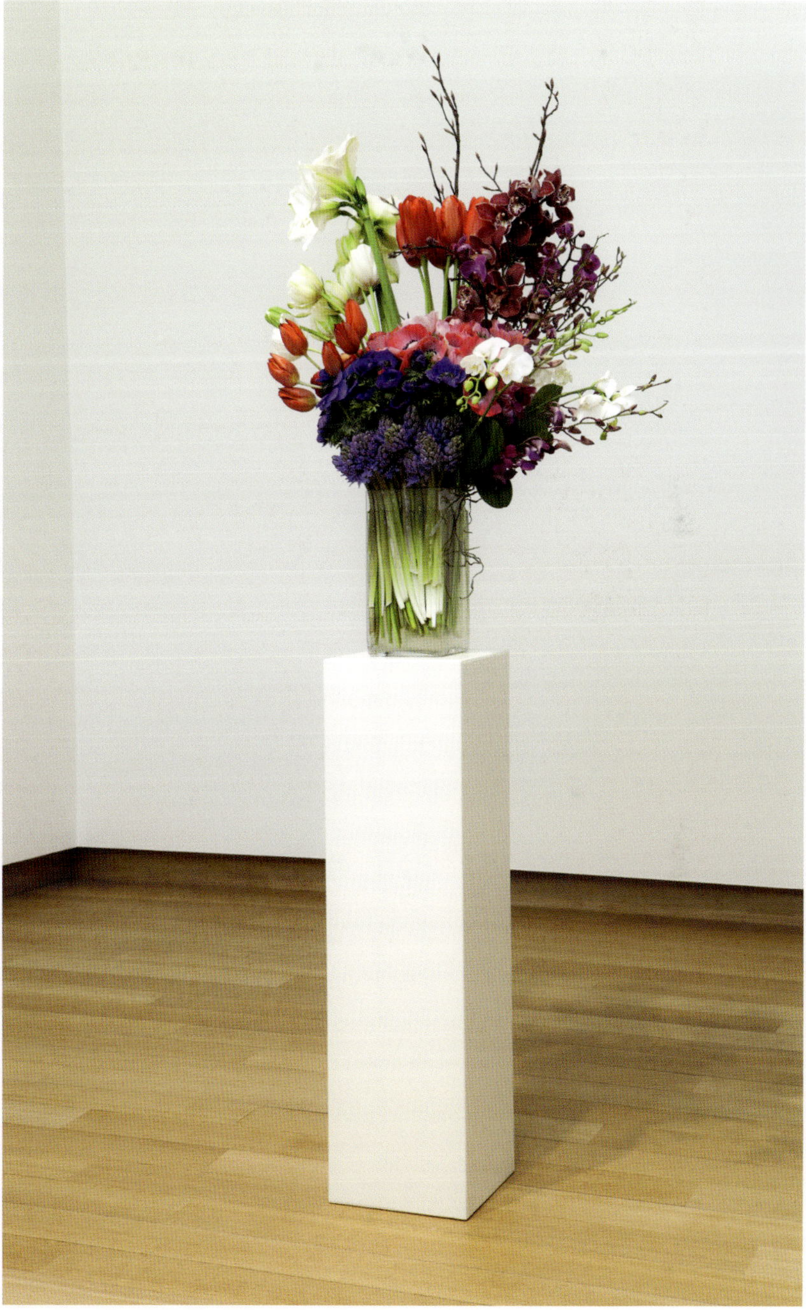

P1 Willem de Rooij and Jeroen de Rijke, *Bouquet II*, 2003. © Schenking / Gifted by Carol Greene, Greene Naftali Gallery, New York, NY (US).

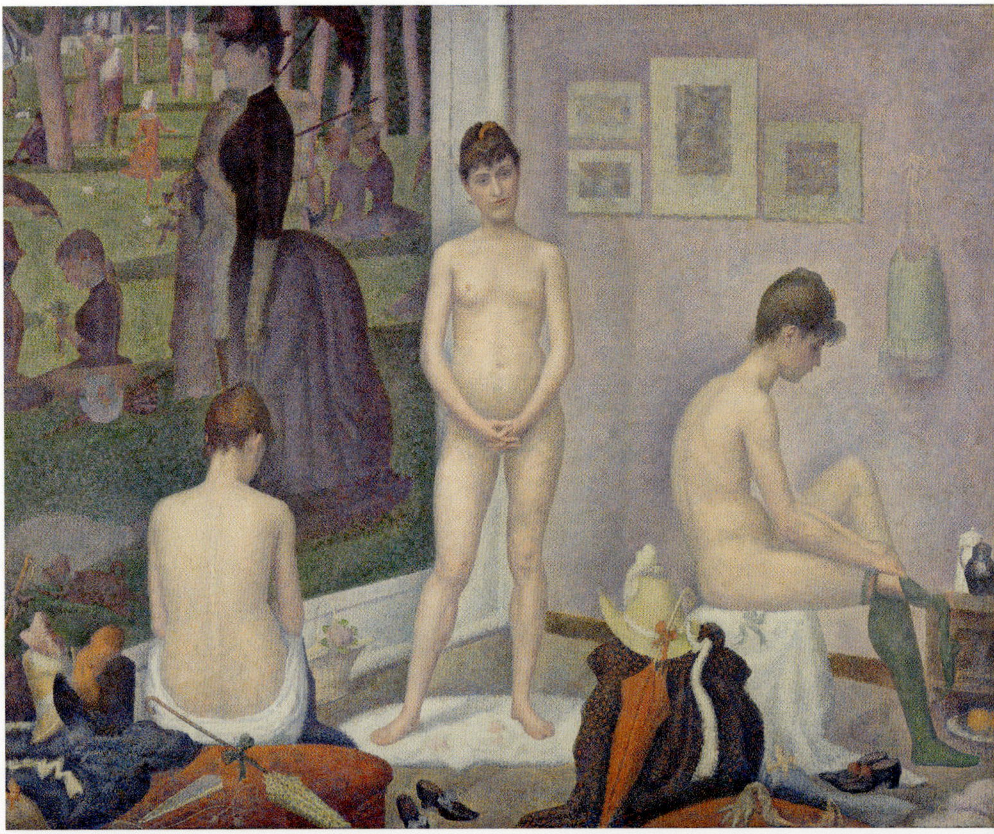

P2 Georges Seurat, *The Models*, 1888. © The Barnes Foundation, Philadelphia, PA.

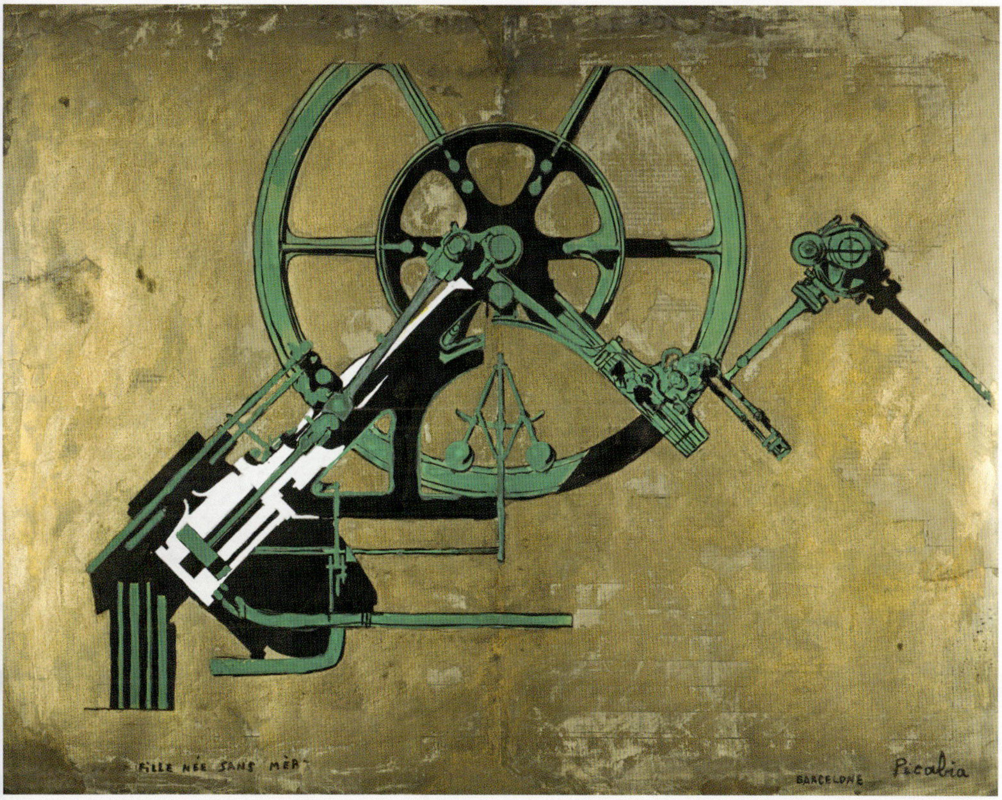

P3 Francis Picabia, *Fille née sans mère* (*Girl Born without a Mother*), ca. 1917. Gouache and metallic paint on printed paper. 50 × 65 cm (framed 90.8 × 75.9 × 3.8 cm). National Galleries of Scotland. Purchased 1990.

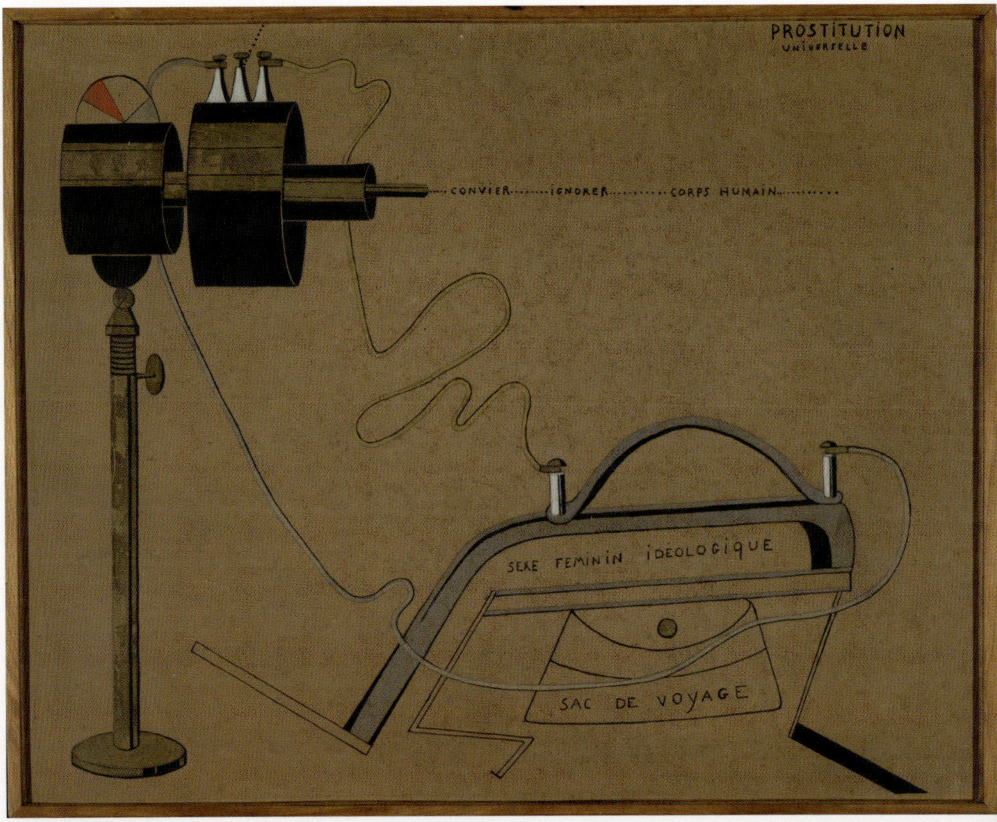

P4 Francis Picabia, *Universal Prostitution*, 1916–17. © Yale University Art Gallery. Gift of Collection Societe Anonyme.

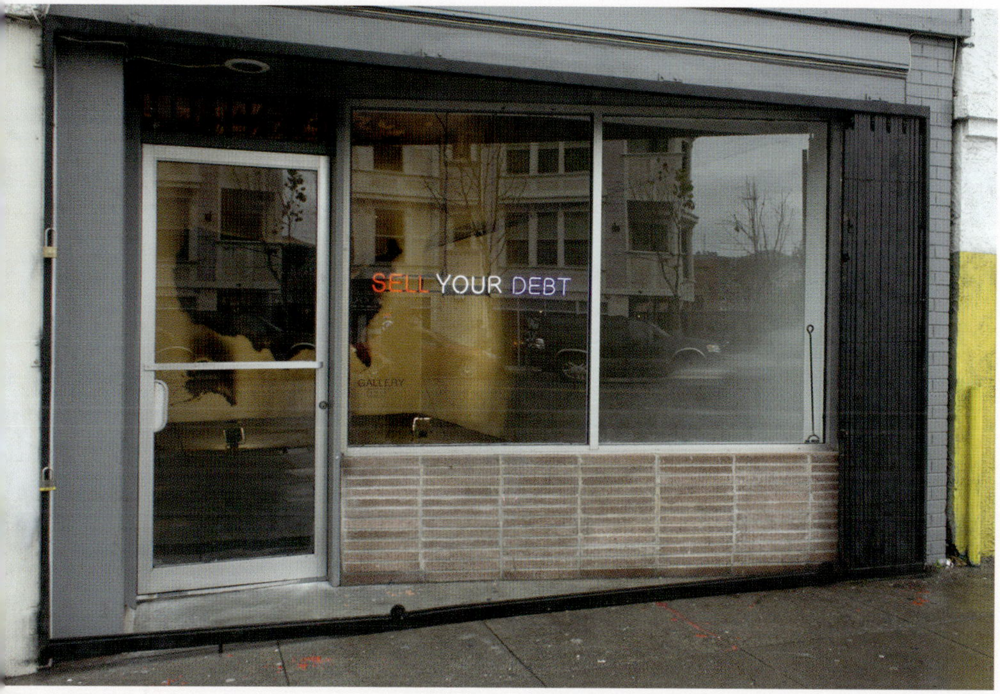

P5 Claire Fontaine, *Untitled* (*Sell Your Debt*), 2012. Installation view, Claire Fontaine, *Sell Your Debt*, Queen's Nails, San Francisco, US 23.01–23.2.2013. Courtesy of Claire Fontaine.

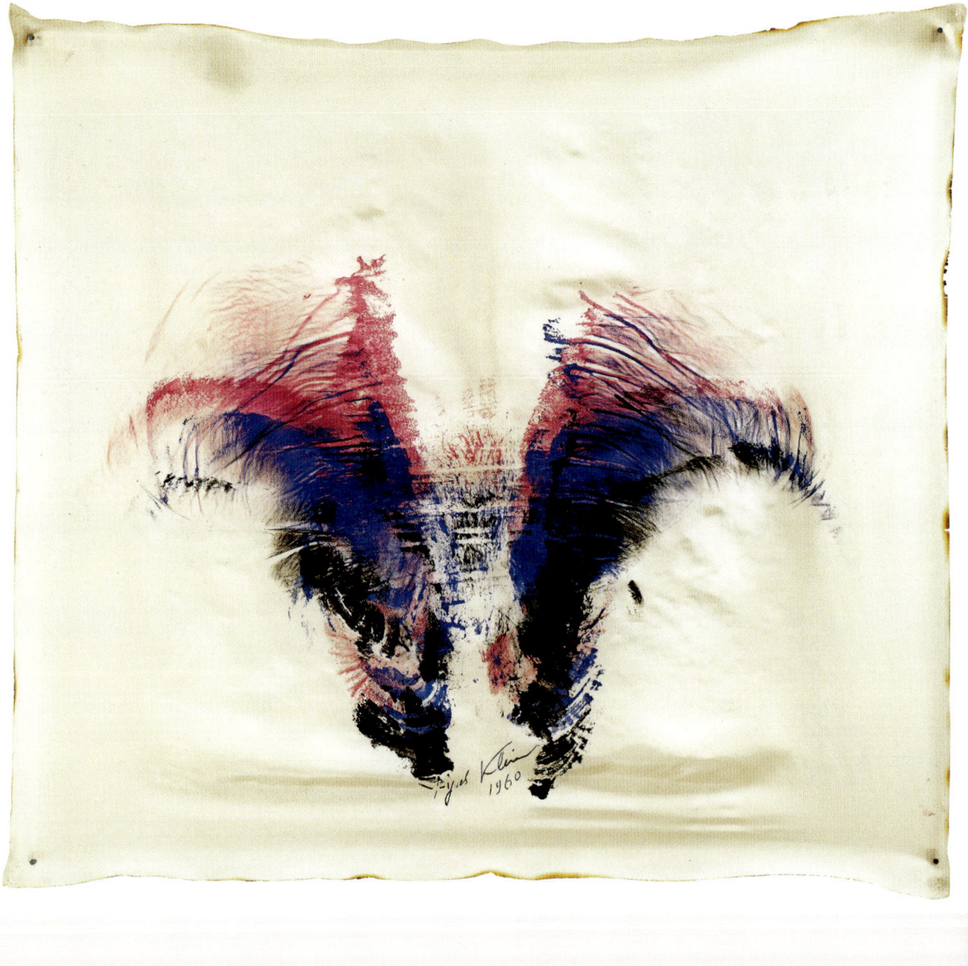

P6 Yves Klein, *Untitled* (*Shroud Anthropometry*), 1960. © The Estate of Yves Klein c/o ADAGP, Paris.

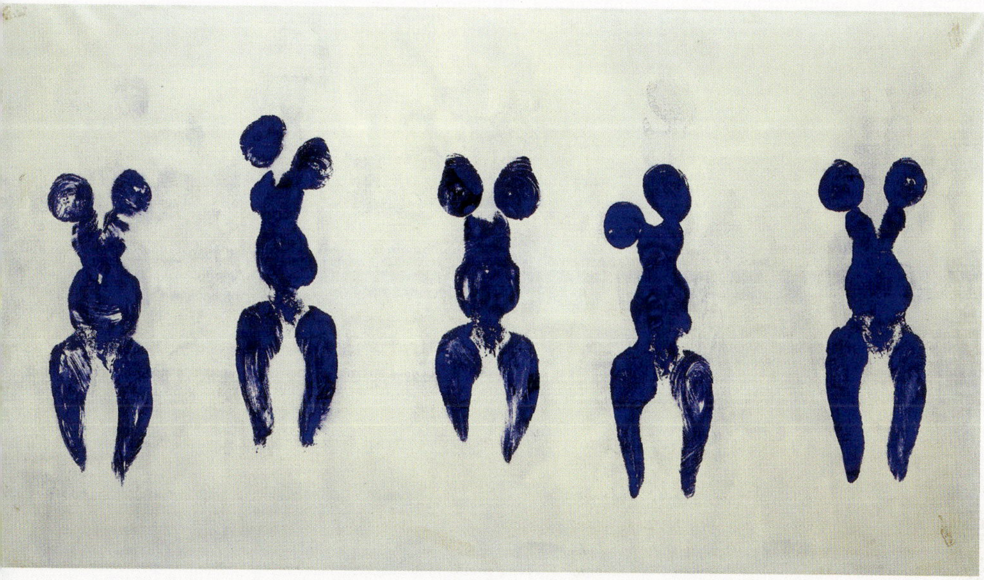

P7 Yves Klein, *Anthropométrie de l'époque bleue* (ANT 82), 1960. © Banque d'Images, ADAGP / Art Resource, NY.

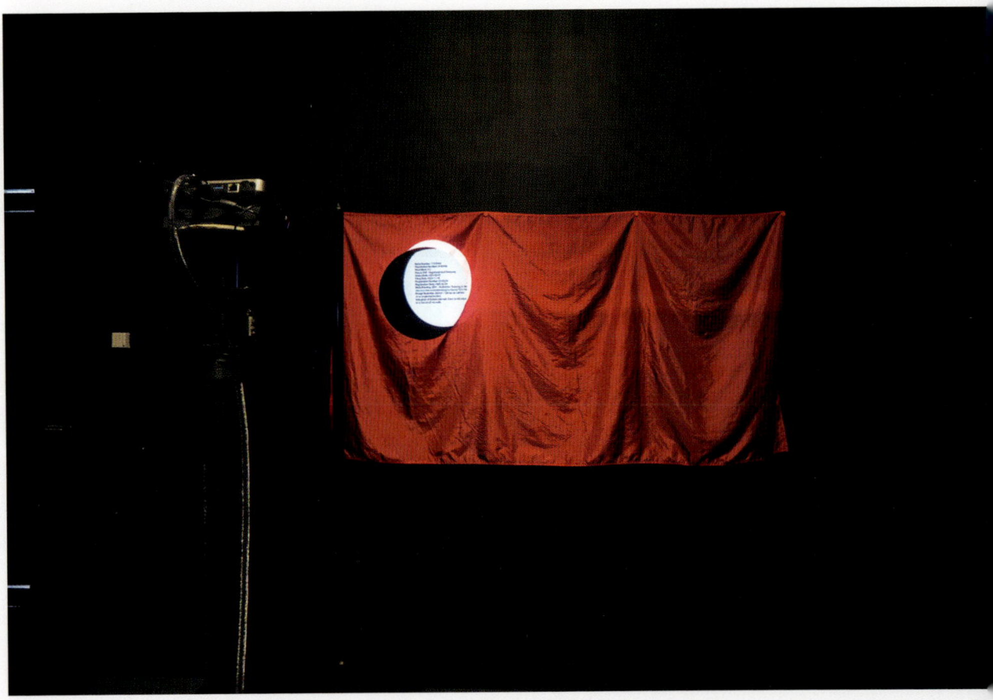

P8 Hannah Black, *Flag*, 2022. Denier nylon, still-image projection, 70 × 45 inches, detail from *The Meaning of Life*, 2021. Image courtesy of the artist and the Art Gallery of York University, Toronto.

that its feelings, the "innermost" recesses of its affective experience, should also augment its value, its social credit, and that its very formation should be oriented to this capacity for social credit. Within these social formations, love is bound up with access to value. And love becomes work. But Kaplan and Illouz's discussion of the sociological character of contemporary eros is already personified in the Young-Girl.

While critics of Tiqqun mistake the analysis for its object, what interests me is the belatedness of the offense, finally surfacing a century after the saturation of the operations allegorized by the Young-Girl into the social field such that those operations can now only be seen framed as "art." The *Young-Girl* and a "theory" *about* her a century later places her in an imaginary and invisible matrix between subject and object, between worker-consumer, commodity, and the "living currency" for which she stands as a nicely packaged figure of capitalist totality insofar as those totalizations happen in every interstice, at every limit, above all in the private recesses where desire replicates order and order replicates desire. She gives us the neat "total package" of the way that forms of subsumption ramify in everyday life to violently replace older forms of subjectivity yet remains all the more invisible precisely because it saturates everything everywhere.

Part of what is deemed offensive about the Young-Girl is the presumption that the description of a being devoid of interiority should qualify an already marginalized subject position: women. However, taken as part of Tiqqun's whole body of work, this condition of eviscerated interiority is explored as part of the very etiology of the subject that they identify as part of the "cybernetic turn." The processes they trace are shown to be "stripping the subject of any substance" regardless of the positionality of that subject along the aporetic axes of gender and race. As such, the Young-Girl is the subjective dimension of the ready-made, a relationship investigated in chapter 2 in the argument that Picabia moved the insights first advanced by Duchamp at the level of the object into the question of the subject.

Tiqqun's early formation had developed under the influence if not outright mentorship of philosopher Giorgio Agamben. Among the many significant discussions in Agamben's extensive oeuvre, many of which can be heard influentially coursing through much of Tiqqun's writing, one stands out for its immediate relevance: his understanding of the ready-made. In *Man without Content*, a riff on the title of Robert Musil's novel *The Man without Qualities*, Agamben raises a crisis of interiority signaled by modern art. He summons Walter Benjamin's Angel of History, the figure elaborated in "On the Concept of History," in which the angel turns around to find that history configured as linear time has generated a long trail of wreckage and catastrophic misfortune mistaken for progress but is nonetheless compelled by the winds of Time to push forward in spite of this history of disaster and human suffering. For Agamben, who takes as his primary examples the poetry of Arthur Rimbaud and Antonin Artaud and the artwork of Marcel Duchamp, modern art is signal for the way it inscribes the consciousness that must face the situation but does so not only through affirmation and assimilation but also through forms of withdrawal and evacuation.[43] The artwork registers the heaping ruins of traditional judgment, which presupposed a subject capable of a transcendental vantage, by turning the creative principle inside out. As Agamben writes:

> More and more frequently, contemporary art presents us with productions before which it is no longer possible to resort to the traditional mechanism of aesthetic judgments, and for which the antagonistic polarity of art/non-art appears totally inadequate. In front of the ready-made, for instance, in which the otherness of the formal-creative principle has been replaced by the alienation of the non-artistic object that is inserted into the sphere of art, critical judgment is, so to speak, immediately confronted with itself, or, to be more precise, with its image in reverse: what it is supposed to trace back to non-art is already itself non-art.[44]

Far from dismissive or derisive, for Agamben this is precisely the ready-made's special salience. While not exactly "reflective" in any traditional correlative sense, it marks the sensitivity of the gesture to the reality of social formations in perpetual crisis in which the subject does not recover in any simple sense. While the aesthetic judgment that had functioned as part of the faculties of the subject of the Enlightenment, indeed constitutive of the subject as such, are no longer possible in a social field of instrumental contingency, a new form of apprehension takes its place: art criticism. However, this latter form of criticism is itself an index of the withdrawal of art itself as an expression of autonomy. Agamben's discussion might be one explanation for why theories of art become more numerous than new forms of art. His analysis hinges on the ready-made, that which philosophers and art historians alike refer to as the theoretical object of the twentieth century:

> Contemporary art, in its most recent tendencies, has further advanced this process and has by now produced that "reciprocal readymade" Duchamp was thinking of when he suggested the use of a Rembrandt as an ironing board. The extreme object centeredness of contemporary art,

> through its holes, stains, slits, and non-pictorial materials, tends to identify the work of art with the non-artistic product. Thus, becoming aware of its shadow, art immediately receives in itself its own negation, and bridging the gap that used to separate it from criticism, itself becomes the logos of art and its shadow, that is, critical reflection on art.[45]

Here, the work of art becomes a way to *think* the traditional artwork, insofar as the traditional work of art is a function of creativity and therefore extinct in the wake of social abstraction, anonymous production, and the generalized labor that penetrates even the artwork, which we might call, in homage to John Roberts's work, a "labor theory of culture." And yet thinking through this extinction offers a road map through the otherwise foreclosed future of art and locates a new horizon.

Claire Fontaine refreshes this by now exhausted and endlessly reiterated fact of art making in capitalism by forcing the issue of the ready-made's entry into the ontology of the subject, by posing the artist, rather than the object, as a ready-made *subject*, a subject position generated of the reified relationship of objects and subjects in a matrix of social abstraction in which any form of autonomy necessary to creation is foreclosed. Nonetheless, the very acknowledgment of this condition clears a space to allow for the recrudescence of a kind of creative capacity, but under the pressure and duress of market compulsions and behaviors.[46] The *ready-made artist* is not qualified by any special genius or distance from the market. Already a "ready-made" subject, they take their contingent consciousness of the situation to find interstices of interruption and capacity. The Young-Girl is a pendant and precursor to this figure, fully preconstituted by a kind of market subsumption in which any pretense to creative privilege is already entitled if not obscene, and surely mythical. A structural difference, of course, is that unlike the Young-Girl, the ready-made artist through constant critical reflection on the withdrawn utopian conditions of art seeks some form of "redemption." This search for interstices in which to de-reify reification and to create freedom where none exists circles back to the name Tiqqun, or "redemption."

And at the same time there is something specific about *feminist* claims on the part of a theory of the Young-Girl. Why would its theory seem to duplicate a specifically misogynist tone and why, above all, would it hold this particular subject position, whatever its actual gender, accountable for its own unconscious misery?

From the vantage of materialist Marxian feminism aware of the double burden—at once socially replicative and productive, at once mediated and *renaturalized* with relation to the circulation of value—the provocation to feminism is urgent. The necessity of shifting a lens away from the fetish of identity and onto the social totality in which the Young-Girl takes her instrumental part is itself part of the project. Women-identified and women-assigned bearers of labor and consumerist value realization cannot begin to dismantle the structural determination in which they are implicated and to which they contribute unconsciously by focusing on the isolated representation of women in capital. In this regard, Tiqqun continues the avant-gardist project of shock, irritation, and affront.

Insofar as the Young-Girl personifies the circuitry by which the subject is reconstituted, "she" stages how capital is not *in* crisis, it *is* the crisis: the reification of human life under the second nature constitutive of a new ontology, this mysterious *Gattungswesen* of which Marx writes in the *Economic and Philosophic Manuscripts of 1844*. The voice that both identifies and disidentifies with the object-subject of desire, and likewise does and does not identify with a transcendental feminist critical subject, certainly expresses the contradiction of what it is to even be "included" as subjects within a blind field of capitalist social formations made opaque by that second nature.

Ultimately, in *all* historical iterations, *Jeune-Fille* and the Young-Girl are inscriptions of the subject constituted by value and not the other way around. Women, objects of the earliest form of exchange, whose exchange as such marks the shift to patriarchy, and whose mediation thereby defines it, are the oldest form of property. As agents of production and consumption, they become the first form of mediation, of *currency*. Exchange structures forged on the presumption of women-as-property and living currency guarantee lines of filiation, organizing a chaotic field of bodies into kith and kin, into social relations.[47]

And here is the missed premise: the feminist point informing Tiqqun is not that women need to achieve equality in the systems of validity and value. The actually existing conditions that it behooves women, *Jeune Fille* identifiable or otherwise, to break at this unbearable limit is the entire abstract system of value that currently makes patriarchy concretely possible insofar as patriarchy depends on it for its own reproduction. But how can this be possible if the networks determinative of this subject formation are part of the social unconscious? It would take the *shock*—that foremost affective strategy of the avant-gardes—of awakening at the level of perception and sensation (as well as of political consciousness) to do anything about that which cannot be addressed by the politics of representation.

4

The [Young-Girl] Worker as Equipment

Yves Klein's Living Paintbrushes

> It is not that ideologically produced illusions veil material relations but rather that things produced by capitalist society—commodities in their very graphicness—veil social relations.
> —Sami Khatib, "'Sensuous Supra-Sensuous'"

The relationship between living and dead labor continued to haunt and vex post–World War II art's return to the avant-garde, however unconsciously. This took the form of an attempt, often reactionary, to try to reverse the material currents of history whereby purchased labor-time inscribed in objects, and in equipment and technology, formed a second nature displacing the immediacy of social relations. The search for an articulation of embodied vitalism nonetheless dialectically evidences the creeping social abstraction that informs the naive attempt to resist it. As ever, the paid labor-time of women operates as a site where the dynamics of real abstraction make themselves most apparent. In February 1960, the midcentury French Pop artist Yves Klein began tasking models to become "living paintbrushes" in order to make his *Anthropometries* (figure 4.1). He directed a naked woman to cover her body in blue paint—a pigment he titled International Klein Blue (IKB), for which he attempted to receive a patent, denied him by the government—and then press herself onto a receptive surface on the ground. With every movement, the blue imprint of her body conceives seemingly expressive "gestural" marks over the surface. Yet those expressive gestural marks were not understood as any index of her interiority, as, for instance, the gestural marks of the New York School painters had been understood. Klein controlled or purported to have full command of the model's movements by directing her. Only a few weeks after having arrived at this new process, Klein held a demonstration of his new working method to an audience of one hundred selected by the owner of the Galerie Internationale d'Art Contemporain.

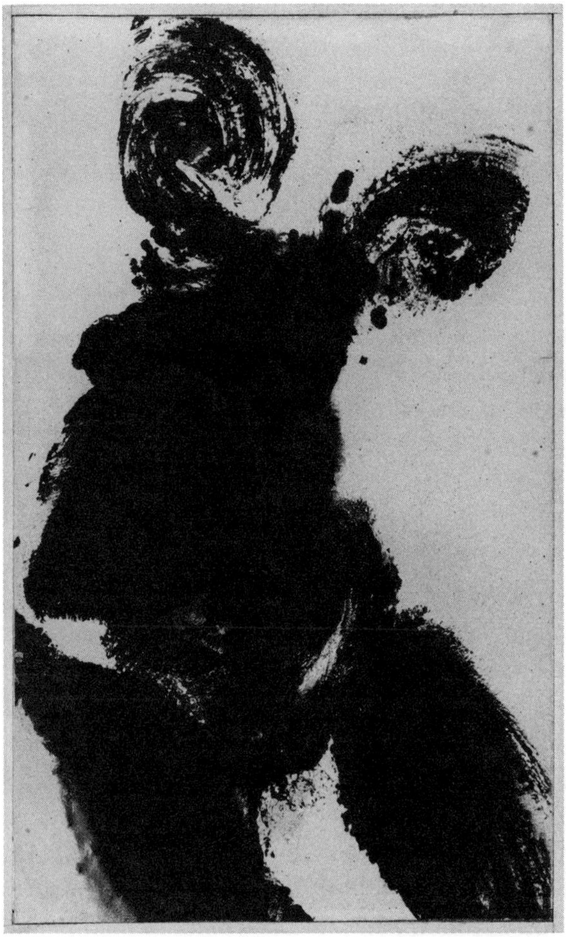

Fig. 4.1. Yves Klein, *Anthropometries*, 1962. © 2025 Museum Associates / LACMA. Licensed by Art Resource, NY.

At 10:00 p.m. on March 9, 1960, a hand-picked audience composed mostly from the Right Bank filled into the gallery and sat on gilded chairs around large white sheets of paper. A small group of violinists and cellists took their place across from the audience and began to play music.

Klein entered in his tuxedo and a Maltese cross acquired from his participation with a Saint Sebastien Brotherhood and began to conduct affairs. The air of cultish activity married to the exclusivity of the audience and its formal attire testify to Klein's dearest wish to invest his work with the very aura that his own strategies violently exsanguinated. The small orchestra nonetheless played a "monotone symphony" of droning tones while three women walked in with a bucket of blue paint each and began covering themselves with the color pigment and then pressed against white paper as the artist directed their actions.[1] He wore white gloves.

In the performances of the works' making, Klein situates himself explicitly as a different kind of subject-position vis-à-vis the artwork: that of manager, however much this ultimately banal managerial position was veiled by Klein's hope of conveying some sense of genius. He is fully clothed, indeed dressed in formal wear to emphasize the margin of separation from the actual maker of the work, the worker women. Already set apart, the artist insists on absolute detachment. Detachment and the evacuation of psychological or affective expression came to be a common feature of advanced art of the 1960s in response to the exaggerated emphasis on the myth of the exemplary artist at its height in the era of the New York School. Jackson Pollock stands for that paradigm. Klein's process is almost diametrically opposed insofar as the artist's distance from the means of making the work becomes a performance of his purported "genius" standing over and above the physical act of making the work. Of course, in the belated lines of reception structuring the cross-Atlantic transmission of culture, Pollock's model of painting as a vehicle for immediacy and presence continued to dominate a European cultural imaginary, as evidenced by Klein's closest friends and allies in the European art world at the time, such as Lucio Fontana, who founded his postwar practice on a negative dialectical dialogue with the Pollockian gesture.[2]

By contrast, Klein makes it abundantly clear that he does not want the traces of making, his making, to be linked to his own body, or any indices of his own somatic register to be folded into the work. He outsources those matters. As such, he complicates the degree to which art at midcentury found itself preoccupied with mark making, the gesture and the grapheme. Fundamentally, what distinguishes Klein's *Anthropometries* is the basic fact that the body whose movements result in the work is conceived as a "living brush." Far from the expression of any kind of interiority, it is the tool and implement come alive under the agency of a manager.

This complicates the implications of the mark. Klein appeared to imagine that he was able to gather the energetic forces of the body while at the same time evacuating its density. Here, the very vitality the artist seeks is absorbed in the fully reified means by which he attempts to access it. If anything, Klein mimics the role of the manager who directs the worker, but in this case the real social relations between "artist" and paid model are overwritten by the social mystification around art.

The audience received Klein's work as amusing if mildly shocking—with the exception of one viewer who claimed to have experienced a religious and sacred quality in the presentation.[3] Klein thereafter hired the photographer Harry Shunk to photograph and film his *Anthropometries*. He insisted that they conveyed his quest for artistic and spiritual purity.

Throughout the *durée* of his efforts, Klein remained persistent about wanting to mobilize the "life force" and the universal energy of the living body. He employed only female models and signed the *Anthropometries* as finished works. Yet these tended to emphasize the female corporeality of the models—the thighs, stomach, and breasts in a general roundness of the bodily imprint. They thereby open onto a kind of lyrical sensuality and a nostalgia for the European tradition of the nude. Despite his use of young women's bodies, he nonetheless understood the personified vigor he set into motion to be universal, unspecific to any particular embodied subject position. Yet he also pronounced his intention to have that hoped-for vitality to be subsumed under the answerable masterful authority of the artist, which he visualized himself to be. For Klein the imprint as the indexical trace of the body occupies a privileged eidetic presence that channels authorial presence.

In a 1960 text titled "Truth Becomes Reality," Klein expounded on his arrival at this formal solution as a way to dispense with traditional studio instruments such as brushes and toward a form of pigment delivery that could satisfy his desire for the elemental, primordial, and embodied vitality he sought.[4] He describes how he first used house-paint rollers (à la Alexander Rodchenko in 1920) to maintain physical and emotional distance from the canvas and to avoid expressive interiority and "psychology" of any kind. Finding this process empty and unconvincing, he then turned to the women he had hired as models. Notably, the women in his employ were not there to pose—Klein never engaged in any kind of mimetic or representational work that would require a model. As he reports, they were paid to be there to prevent depressive solitude. Klein paid women to arrive at his studio, undress, and spend the duration of their shift naked as a form of "company."

It may be possible that Klein knew of another instance of an artwork that had replaced the representation of the body with its indexical demonstration. Marcel Duchamp's *Female Fig Leaf* (1950) presents a plaster cast of a woman's genitals. Duchamp did not realize this work as a bronze cast until 1961, however, a year after Klein's *Anthropometries*. This interpretation of female form in negative spatial terms renders it as opaque, impenetrable, and understood as a kind of irreducible material thickness. Whether or not he was aware of Duchamp's plaster *Female Fig Leaf*, the works evidence almost diametrically opposed impressions of the substance of the body. Where one forecloses access, the other translates the thickness of the body to a kind of

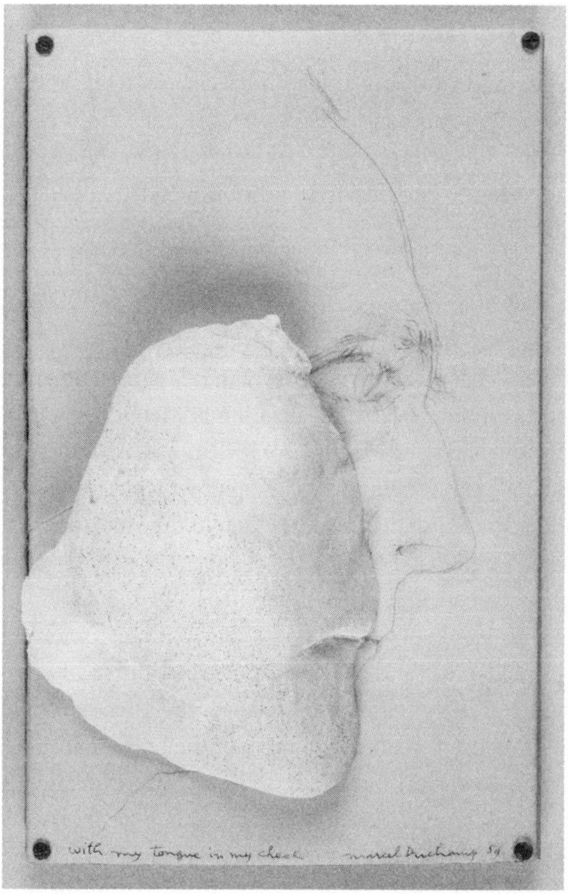

Fig. 4.2. Marcel Duchamp, *With My Tongue in My Cheek*, 1959. © CNAC/MNAM, Dist. RMN-Grand Palais / Art Resource, NY.

transparent and generic notation, however lyrical. However, Duchamp did complete *With My Tongue in My Cheek* (figure 4.2), a piece that sets off traditional representational notion, such as contour, against the indexical cast of the artist's own face, in 1959.

It is less likely that Klein would have been aware of a superficially similar work—on the surface uncannily similar to Klein's *Anthropometries* owing to the direct indexical imprint of body parts on exposed blueprint paper—made by Robert Rauschenberg and his then-wife Susan Weil, *Female Figure* (1951). An imprint generated photographically—light on photosensitized paper—the work insists on the anonymity of the process and trace. By contrast, in his white gloves and dictatorial post, refusing the implication of his own body in the process of "making," Klein preserves the artist's traditional identity as the site of masterful authorial intention and a privileged transcendental consciousness.

Klein states that the decision to have the women convey their bodies as indices occurred to him in a moment of listlessness in the studio as he sought a way to contain the same "presence" they generated in the studio, for which they were paid, into the work itself. In other words, they need not serve their historical role of offering a form of assistance to the artist's capacity to depict his understanding of sensuous bodies in space but are there as workers in potentia, paid to offer company. This came to be understood as part of what it was to be an artist, regardless of the obsolescence of modeling or depicting verisimilitude. What does this suggest of the classical genre and how does it at once pose a reaction and a radicalization of Manet's *Olympia*, that foundational gesture formative of modernism? Klein asked women to cover themselves in paint and press their bodies to a pigment-receptive surface as a way of channeling the company they provided in the studio.

He declared the body to be "all-powerful, and it does not think."[5] This sense of charged physical presence void of thought or the mind's labor, namely, intellectual labor, not only evokes Alfred Sohn-Rethel's discussion of the division between intellectual and manual labor constitutive of capitalist social relations. It also doubly reifies and collapses the already reified body of the worker and of women. Klein's emphasis on the body that "does not think" turned out, with historical hindsight, to be the most erroneous component of Klein's strategic nongesture for the models. In an interview with the BBC in October 2016, one of Klein's models, Elena Palumbo-Mosca, decided to correct the record. She stated that, despite Klein's language, the women hired to work in the studio who later came to be applicators of paint did indeed engage in difficult intellectual labor. Palumbo-Mosca stated, "I was not a paintbrush because, in spite of it all, I did use my brain."[6] Whatever Palumbo-Mosca meant by this, her statement once again draws attention to the absurdist, unreflexive reification at the heart of Klein's project.

And yet Elena Palumbo-Mosca's remarks beg a sustained analysis of the division of labor along intellectual and manual lines, a division heightened and collapsed in a human asked to become a tool for the delivery of the work once understood to be both a representation of her and an indication of the artist capacity. With that in mind as a guiding principle for the elaboration of the avant-gardist *Jeune Fille* into the mid- and late twentieth century, the following pages think though the contradictions unleashed in Klein's project. In order to try to understand the strange contradiction at the heart of Klein's search for "vitality" at the very moment that he takes up the fully reified labor-power of a Young-Girl made instrument, I mobilize Pierre Klowsowski's notion of "living currency," coined to describe the particular investment in women as bearers of value but also as infinitely exchangeable, a general equivalent anterior to and formative of money itself. This will also entail a reading of Luce Irigaray's "Women on the Market," in which she explores the originary source of value as such: again, women.

The problem of the commodity form crosses Klein's oeuvre, as the following chapter will explore. But the "living paintbrushes" that made the work for which he is best known, the *Anthropometries*, evidence a new threshold of the problem set that this book is investigating: the becoming commodity of the subject-worker whose labor-power valorized in transactional exchange signals the heightened real abstraction of everyday life. Here, Francis Picabia's *Jeune Fille* seems to step out of the frame, before the theory of her offered by Tiqqun, to convey something of the abstraction driving the worker into a post- or nonhuman condition as techne, the technology necessary to producing an object.

Klein locates a vanishing point where reification becomes a doubly gendering operation. As such, he returns to the problems of a gendered division of labor at the heart of modernist art as Georges Seurat had done, this time uncritically. At the same time, the artist continued to insist on the spiritual and transcendental significance of this work, evidenced already in "Truth Becomes Reality." In order to trace Klein's at once pioneering and yet utterly inevitably obvious strategy toward the sale of women's sexualized labor-time, I will probe the artist's equally pioneering way of conjugating the artwork with the commodity, in advance of American Pop art, where this convergence is more commonly located. In a brief detour into biography, I also explore the fact that Klein married one of his "paintbrushes," Rotraut Klein-Moquay.

Five years earlier, in 1955, Yves Klein had attempted to procure a trademark on the blue pigment used in European art for centuries. That particular blue that Klein identified as his property and invention carries already something of the material and transcendental contradiction that the artist continued to ratchet throughout his career. Associated with the blue of the ethereal heavens since at least Giotto's Scrovegni Chapel in Padua, this distinctive shade comprised the signature blue of the Virgin Mary's robes in much Italian painting crossing the thirteenth through sixteenth centuries. Klein's most vociferous supporter, the art critic Pierre Restany, took this color to denote the ultimate spiritualism and purity of the artist's work. At the same time, as Michael Baxandall has revealed, the pigment sourced in present-day

Palestine was exceptionally expensive, equal only to gold, and acted as a marker of a patron's wealth.[7] This specific color was quite literally worth its weight in gold. It represents money. Klein had hoped to rebrand this shade of blue as International Klein Blue, or IKB. The abbreviation operates more like a commercial brand. Klein referred to his IKB exclusively in English. A brand name in a foreign language (English) operates on the home language (French) in a special way that acknowledges the ceding of a locally specific culture to market-determined international culture. Klein's act of brand-naming a pigment for the first time in painting's history can be understood as a response to the international proliferation of brand-named American products. Andy Warhol, six years later, channeled the same developments in mass culture by situating iconic brand names—Campbell's, Coca-Cola, Marilyn Monroe—as a way of pressuring painting and its pretension to transcendental status. And yet the latter never devised a logo nor attempted to procure legal rights to any specific object. But if Klein's serialized and object-like panels in a chromatic idiom he hoped would operate as a marker for his own brand prefigure some of the key strategies of Pop within the decade, they also belatedly rehearse aspects of that first luxury commodity for which a patent was indeed conferred: Chanel perfume.

Klein first exhibited the IKB-covered *Propositions Monochromes* (figure 4.3) in January 1957 at the Galleria Apollinaire, Milan. This event, in turn, presaged the dissolution of painting and its recalibration as a serial object central to Warhol's exhibition of paintings of Campbell's soup cans at the Ferus Gallery in Los Angeles in 1962; like Klein, Warhol took the panels off the wall and set them into new forms of display. This exhibition has come to stand as the genesis of the category of Pop. There, the soup completed the circuit from the supermarket shelf, to the private terrain of the artist's body, back onto the shelf, this time that of the art gallery. The Ferus Gallery show made no attempt to conceal the fact that painting had indeed become an *object*. Rather than framing and mounting the canvases on the wall in accordance with every traditional practice of pictorial display, Warhol placed the pictures of Campbell's soup on shelf-like ledges. This small and singular gesture not only challenged the status of painting but also transformed the gallery into a shop, or rather dissolved the operative fiction that the gallery was ever anything *but* a glorified shop. Warhol marked the gallery as a commercial site for the procurement of luxury goods rather than a sacrosanct space of disinterested beauty, in and of itself a prosaic observation brilliantly staged by Claes Oldenburg at the Store on East Seventh Street in late 1961. But Klein set into mutual relation the canvas and the brand-named object

Fig. 4.3. Yves Klein, *Untitled Blue Monochrome*, 1957. © The Estate of Yves Klein c/o ADAGP, Paris.

of mass consumption. This suggests Klein's market-oriented logic was grounded in the formal properties of the monochrome *prior* to the reference to any specific brand names or commercial logos, a notion to which Warhol himself nods in an interview in which he cites the French painter's mode of display.[8] Indeed, Klein attained international recognition for the blue object-like panels comprising the *Propositions Monochromes*. The instant success of the work in the aftermath of the Milan show motivated Restany to coin the phrase "Nouveau Realism" to describe the work, thereby inaugurating a category that later included a number of French artists who resisted any last trace of painting as a "window" onto higher virtual worlds, despite the manifest incongruity between the designation and the spiritual purity that the critic continued to perfervidly assert as Klein's work's import.

For at the same time that Klein prefigured the blatant reification of painting as serialized if not completely generic objects openly avowed by American

Pop, he continued to aver a long-obsolete language positing art as a vehicle for transcendental presence. Klein appears to have known that what the European public wanted most to see was painting as a site of elemental yet transcendental experience, going so far as to title some of his works *Zone of Immaterial Sensibility* (1962), even as historical and international economic forces were placing remnants of European "culture" under tremendous pressure. And the language around the work succeeded in establishing its reception; in 1957 in Milan, only one critic vocalized skepticism about the pretense to transcendental immateriality of the seemingly arbitrarily priced identical panels. The critic Marco Valescchi couched his analysis in the observation that the panels recalled the radical empiricism and reductive materialism of strands of the Soviet avant-garde more that the spiritual aura of Quattrocento masters such as Giotto, despite Restany's persistent claim that these set the key in which Klein's work was to be interpreted.

The paradox that Klein mobilized may be a result of his own ignorance of the productivist register he participated in. Unlike Warhol, Klein never had the hands-on experience of working in commercial design or in constructing window displays for department stores. He skipped the many steps that culminated in Warhol's importation of mass culture into art. Klein preferred to simply insert art into a market logic with a much more efficient nominalism. He had once declared, for instance, that the color of the sky along the French Riviera should be patented and that he should hold the patent. Going one step further than Warhol in advance, he fashioned and attempted to establish the brand from his own proper name, a gesture the American Pop artist never advanced.

The most striking transposition visited on painting in Klein's work was the structural logic of serial repetition. The seemingly blank canvas understood as a modernist trope also permitted the kind of repetition articulated in the commodity. But to say that seriality is isomorphic with the commodity is a cliché and fails to understand either. I am not hinging the present argument on any such pseudomorphic collapse between fungible objects and artworks engaging seriality as an aesthetic and phenomenological problem. I am interested, rather, in how a creeping awareness of reification in a different register altogether, that of the subject itself as constituted in and through labor-time, came to suggest the very possibility or impossibility of making art at all. In order to frame this problem succinctly, I will describe Klein's *Anthropometries* and how they were made, before turning to how Klein returns to and reiterates any understanding of anthropomorphic form at that particular moment in the history of art, when it was being at once resuscitated and resisted.

Klein at once prefigured and short-circuited Pop, moving swiftly from a flirtation with the most obvious traits of the commodity—the brand, the serialized endlessness, the modality of display—to an outright obsession with money. A handful of pieces that Klein made in 1960–61 demonstrate a preoccupation with the artwork as a vehicle of monetary value. One such piece from 1961, *Box with Gold Bars*, sets Klein's eponymous blue into equivalence with gold bars, the kind once stored in bank vaults to secure paper money. By covering the top interior of the oval box into which the bars are set with IKB, thereby forming two registers, each occupied with what comes to be understood as two expressions of the same substance, a kind of equivalence emerges between the gold and the blue. A year previous, in 1960, Klein completed a retort to the avant-garde monochrome that had declared the end of painting in favor of a new proletarian project. Klein's "spin" on Rodchenko's monochrome *Triptych: Pure Red, Pure Yellow, Pure Blue* of 1920 replaces those primary colors with "Monopink, Monogold and Monoblue." While the latter is of course IKB, the pink insinuates a new kind of postwar commercialism while the gold, standing in for yellow, could not be more denotative. Indeed, the gold need not symbolize. It operates directly as money. The artist made a similar monochromatic piece, affixing gold leaf to the surface that same year. Klein need not conjugate art with commercial value any more symbolically when the artwork itself is an instantiation of money, outpacing any price it could be said to have or profit it might fetch. For all his deployment of immaterial spiritualism, Klein evidences a thorough understanding of the totalizing determinations of the market.

Klein sets a similar problem into motion with the *Anthropometries* realized in the same year as his fascination with gold. Consciously or otherwise, Klein's next step suggests that he was motivated by the same question that had driven Seurat: the need to picture the transition from living to dead labor and from the studio to the posthumous work. In both cases, this transition presents itself through the problem of gendered labor.

Anthropometries demonstrate a keen sense not only of the collapse of object and subject in the phenomenon of the living paintbrush but also the imbrication of the problem of value embodied by women twice over: as bearers of labor and/or the reproduction of living labor but also as the origin of wealth as such, as explored in chapter 1. Klein's turn from seriality to new forms meant to summon vitality and life in art—and art in life—simply laid bare, despite Klein's intentions, the doubly hidden abode of production congealed in the commodity, the labor-time of anonymous gendered labor folded into the work. It operates finally as a demonstration of living labor become dead labor, sanctified as abstract art, rather than evoking "life" or vitality in art. I ask why the artist turned to nude models as bearers of mark making, of aesthetic value rendering massive profits at (art) market. "Truth Becomes Reality" is a straightforward descriptive title insofar as it described in mystified terms the renaturalization of a so-called reality through the engineering of malleable social relations to lubricate value. Here, reification enters an existential phase, surpassing finally and fully the domain of objects, or living labor congealed in objects, to openly reframe human beings as realized things, the very social condition Picabia had predicted.

Klein's relationship to the women who made the *Anthropometries* was, with one key exception, purely transactional. As in all forms of exchange, daily social relations are suspended or reordered for the purpose of facilitating the economic transaction. He paid them for their presence in his studio. What motivated the transaction, in turn, was notably Klein's declared loneliness in the studio. In "Chelsea Hotel Manifesto," Klein concedes that what motivated him to seek the presence of models was simply that he was lonely in his recently moved studio and that he wanted a little company: "I therefore hired models as other painters do, but unlike the others, I merely wanted to work in their company rather than have them pose for me. . . . It was a way of preventing the danger of secluding myself in the overly spiritual spheres of creation, thus rupturing the most basic common sense, repeatedly affirmed by our incarnate condition."[9] Once again, the contradiction at the heart of Klein's project asserts itself: transcendental purity in distinction to embodiment, which he deems as somehow compromised. He misses the mediation of the market, which makes his choice all the more symptomatic. But again, what is key is the way in which Klein's breakthrough hinged on what to do with the models, and more fundamentally, their reason for being in the studio at all. Seclusion, alienation, loneliness, and the need for human company drove Klein to the point of purchasing socially mediated labor-time. In short, social abstraction as such resulted in a set of circumstances that are in turn fully articulated in the *Anthropometries*, which are the indices of labor-time born of an intensive need for contact.

The origin of the work in social abstraction is strangely felt in the aesthetic abstraction that results from it. Klein made it quite clear that "the shape of the body, it's strange colors hovering between life and death, hold no interest for me. Only the essential, pure, effective climate of the flesh is valid."[10] Configured as a tool, the body is appropriated into abstraction in the moment of exchange at the same moment that Klein hopes to deny material abstraction in the name of the transcendental tenets on which he continues to insist. That Klein misses the actual abstract conditions underpinning his choice is already indicative of the nature of abstraction that happens "behind the backs of men." As Sami Khatib states in the essay "'Sensuous, Supra Sensuous,'" "whereas at first sight economic value as exchange value seemed to entertain an autonomy . . . we can now specify that this autonomy is underpinned by another relation, expressing an asymmetry: the asymmetry of economic exploitation and surplus value-extraction, structurally implied by the act of selling and buying labor-power."[11]

Klein misses the mediation precisely because the exchangism forging the social synthesis rendering the women available to him is so saturated as to be invisible, everywhere and nowhere in particular. That the social contact he craves would be at once enabled and canceled by a more entrenched separation and abstraction, ultimately expressed in the reification of the women he hired despite his intentions, structures both the paradox of Klein's project and the paradox of the social field.

Sohn-Rethel's singular contribution to any understanding of social relations is that commodity abstraction is not subjective or a property of thought. It is precisely its objectivity that causes it to be missed: "It is not reducible to the intellectual faculties of the Kantian transcendental subject . . . and yet a real process of exchange takes on the form of thought, that is an abstraction."[12] In other words, precisely Klein's attempt at being a subject free of material determination entrenches him all the more in material conditions he cannot *see*.

Klein's obliviousness to the material social relations undergirding his praxis makes it all the more of a vehicle by which to understand those conditions—in hindsight. These "libidinal economies" are transparent to economics only within the opacity of the aesthetic object refracting the invisible social conditions of its manufacture as much as of its bid for dialectical resistance. Khatib attends to the aesthetic mediation of capitalist mediation: "These various forms, by which value and meaning are produced, are precisely what I would call the aesthetics of real abstraction, that is to say that the value for of the commodity is homologously structured in accordance with certain aesthetic forms of signification—like symbol and allegory."[13]

This unwitting, unconscious allegory might be best conveyed by reference to another of the artist's paradoxical works. Klein's *Yves Peintures* (1954) are a singular instance of the gap between the operative logic of the work and the claims Klein wished to make about them. The artist made a luxurious, sumptuous, and opulent catalog of paintings in which he "reproduced" the putative originals by cutting out pieces of colored paper and fixing them into a book, alongside the place and year of art making. However, the "originals" being reproduced were in fact never made and did not exist. Klein unconsciously attempts to make of the ready-made an object potent with "authenticity," even to the point of differentiating each color block by reference to the site of its making, as though summoning the very definition of the aura as a "web of time and space."[14] This fictional web evocative of auratic presence makes of the fictional object something precious. That authenticity might be marked by price or preciousness defines reification in art as such. Klein's impossible and maniacal desire to invest the ready-made with the very forms of authenticity antithetical to it and which it had attempted to eradicate symptomatizes the contradiction. And yet, again, the very gap between the demystifying capacity of the ready-made and Klein's wish to reinvest it with presence and magic articulates the conditions within which Klein found himself.

The ready-made addresses the condition of the work of art in the age of formal subsumption, the defining characteristic of which is the production of objects *for* a capitalist market. Within a total social system organized to generate surplus value, objects come to be designed to produce *desires* as much as to satisfy existing demands for basic use-value.[15] For if, as Lukács notes, "the universality of the commodity form is responsible both objectively and subjectively for the abstraction of the human labor incorporated in commodities," the Duchampian ready-made's anti-aesthetic register acknowledges the degree to which technical manufacture and fragmented, autonomous labor had eclipsed original creation.[16] But from there, matters grow more complicated. This formal subsumption, in which objects are made for a market rather than made for the satisfaction of needs or desires and incidentally placed on the market to realize those ends, does not entail any automatic democratization of object relations. As discussed in the previous chapter, designer and industrially manufactured goods for the home were assumed to have a democratizing function in the United States—to level class, as it were—whereas in Europe, the same market formed by similar goods concomitantly created deeper vertical striations marking class distinctions, thereby keeping those divisions visibly in place, if not augmenting them. Again, object consumption became a way of de-marketing class and class aspiration.

This heightened "disproportion [is] not as important or so difficult to grasp as within practical social relations themselves."[17] As all object experience came to be determined by the advent of the commodity and in turn to inform social relations mediated by objects, all social relations came to be routed through this particular form. Discussed in the previous chapter, the concept of the "social factory" articulated a description of the phenomenon of real subsumption in the broadest terms, in social relations far from the scene of production itself on the factory floor; it meant that the separated and reified categories of culture, politics, economy, and everyday life (public versus private) no longer obtained in their separation.

Klein's attempt to package authenticity through the hybrid monochrome–ready-made at once internalizes and reverses the insights afforded by the Duchampian ready-made. *Traveler's Folding Item* (1916), in particular, affords a pithy object lesson in mystification and opacity. There, Duchamp places a typewriter under its vinyl protective sheath, over which the brand name, Underwood, is embossed. The protective veil confers a mysterious quality to a familiar object that has its trademark inscribed on it. The simultaneity of its named identification, which renders what is underneath the cover fully transparent, and obscuring vinyl envelope causes a sense of uneasy dissonance, as though the object were engaging in a strange form of cognitive striptease. Similarly, if somewhat more evasive, Klein's *Yves Peintures* seem to point to something else, something concealed, when in fact the entirety of the work is right there on the page. While the notion of a catalog makes a false claim about work that does not exist outside the pages of the book, those pages nonetheless deliver the totality of the work such that the gesture of pointing to an elsewhere or an underneath becomes unnecessary. Both works collapse the artwork into a reproduction while concurrently insinuating that there must be a difference between what is before one and the "real" work out of view. Both defer and displace while also insisting that "what you see is what you get." Maurizio Lazzarato has explored Duchamp's strange hybrid object not only as an analysis of the work of art in the age of commodity subsumption but also as that which "precognized" a shift from a blue-collar to a white-collar or managerial job market.[18] "The *subjective* impoverishment of artists and technicians (but also publics)," Lazzarato explains, "develop according to two logics that appear contradictory at times: first, industry incorporates and 'de-potentiates' the critique of the division between art and non-art initially raised by the avant-garde movements while, second, reestablishing this distinction."[19]

In "Yves Klein, or the Dead Dealer," Thierry de Duve makes the case that Klein's work illuminates not only the failure of the avant-gardes but also the congruence of economics and aesthetics, or capital and art. Klein becomes the petit bourgeois who enacts the degree to which money has replaced God, the transcendental experience, and any form of alterity in the European imaginary. Klein's aspiration is to make of inert manufactured matter something intensely alive and of the intensely living a dead tool. "Yves Klein, or the Dead Dealer" traces not only the historical conditions pressing Klein's every gesture into an inevitable mimicry of the commodity form but also the strange conjunction of reification in stark contradiction to a stated intense desire to evade that very reification and to deliver absolute authenticity. This primary contradiction is the very signature of Klein's oeuvre. But why is the nude, dislodged from its place in representation to become a medium, a choice vehicle to deliver this contradiction in which the petit bourgeois replaces, in de Duve's terms, God with money?

Pierre Klossowski, fellow traveler to the Surrealists, and to Dada artists including Francis Picabia, asks, "Could we not say that economic norms comprise a substructure derived from affects . . . and if there were a final infrastructure, would it not be constituted by the behaviour of our affects and impulses?"[20] Klossowski bases this query on his historicization of the shift in labor across early modernity (the seventeenth century) into the twentieth century. He cites Charles Fourier and the Marquis de Sade as early analyses of the biopolitical conjuncture of (anonymous) labor and the metropolis, auguring Marx's value-theory:

> Prior to Fourier's utopia and its proto-refutation, Sade had developed a form of communal life based on the violation of the physical and emotional propriety of persons. He did so in the name of the universality of the voluptuous sensation and as a postulate arising from his full-fledged atheism. With the disappearance of the moral god, who had been the guarantor of the self as responsible for and identical to itself, everyone now belongs to everyone else in the form of goods. But what appears in Fourier as the FREE moral expropriation of persons in accordance with a differential law of affinities gives way, in Sade, to a principle of UNIVERSAL PROSTITUTION. Slaves are not inert objects deprived of self-esteem but living beings that have been reduced to the status of an object. Their attraction lies in the fact that they can be humiliated in their dignity and integrity, that is, in their ability to possess their own good, to possess themselves. In Sade it is the destruction of this integrity that produces the erotic emotion. The quality of this prostitution is produced by bidding up the price of subjects in inverse proportion of their emotional degradation.[21]

For Klossowski, secularization and the resulting diminishment of any taboo on secular sexuality *prefigure labor as such*. In a prescient observation that portends many current theorists of twenty-first-century capital, notably Michel Feher, the availability of surplus bodies constituting a labor force is entwined with the desire on the part of the cognitive and emotional drives coursing through these bodies to seek affirmation and praise as much as remuneration. "Erotic emotion" is enjoyed by the master of the slave but comes to inform the slaves' complicity with their servitude. Klossowski does not broach the specificity of the gendered body in the passage quoted here. I will return to Klossowski's discussion of the dialectical advances of industrialization, which inform the collective desire to relocate charged intensity in both the laboring body and in the instrument used by the labor-bearing body as performed by Klein's living paintbrushes.

First, I would like to return to Klossowski's astonishing words: "With the disappearance of the moral god, who had been the guarantor of the self as responsible for and identical to itself, everyone now belongs to everyone else in the form of goods. But what appears in Fourier as the FREE moral expropriation of persons in accordance with a differential law of affinities gives way, in Sade, to a principle of UNIVERSAL PROSTITUTION." The author does not cite Marx explicitly, yet, as Daniel W. Smith argues, "living currency is meant to be a challenge to traditional Marxism since for Klossowski the infrastructure is not economic but impulsive, and phantasms play a generative role equivalent to that played by labor in Marx."[22] While the analogy is oversimplifying and untenable from a "scientific Marxist" perspective, or at any rate in Smith's interpretation, it does account for the prescience of Klossowski's theory of affect within capital as well as the viability of his thesis about bodies as an early operative analog to currency. By extension, this phenomenology of agency and object, of female-gendered objects of desire and capital accumulation available to an agent of accumulation, erupts violently in mid-twentieth-century art and theory. Klossowski offers a theory of labor and a necessarily concomitant labor theory of gender in supplement to Engels's *Origin of the Family, Private Property and the State*.

As I mentioned previously, the models for Klein's "living paintbrushes" were with one exception anonymous women hired to work. One of the models was Klein's wife, Rotraut. This "exception" binds Klein's professional studio practice to the private sphere of his intimate life, thereby dissolving the boundary thought to guarantee bourgeois social reproduction. Klein introduces at once into the home and into the studio a fully automated luxury object, a perfected bearer of social labor-power, able to generate the material side of his studio praxis and of his family replication. Klein accomplishes a model of abstraction distributed across the spaces of production and reproduction, across professional and "personal" borders.

The only *Anthropometries* in which Klein includes himself is a marriage portrait of himself and Rotraut, an impression of his body adjacent to hers, doubled. Presumably marriage has contractually guaranteed a reciprocal state of property to the midcentury modern Western wife. While actual coinage, metal-based printed money, has been dated to roughly the fifth or sixth century BCE, for both Engels and Klossowski, the ownership of women signals the passage from first a matrilineal society to an agricultural one dependent on animal husbandry and crop cycles; this in turn is exchanged for an industrial society in which gender doubly determined a division of labor and therefore of human value. Women are devalued. And yet they operate more than ever as vehicles for the measure of value insofar as they reproduce labor-power. As such, doubly devalued yet doubly useful, their exchange and circulation prefigure a later abstracted money form. Currency is intimately entwined with a gendered division of labor and therefore the categories of gender themselves. The logic of capitalist accumulation and circulation *produces* gender as such. This circuit is first identified and explored by Picabia (and later, Tiqqun), although it has come to be a cornerstone of Marxian economic history.[23] This analysis of the origin of gender proves useful to traditional Marxism insofar as it solves a problem at once marginal and at the heart of the problem of value and social relations. Women continue to operate as a nexus mediating the relation between the two.

Michel Foucault also seemed to have immediately recognized the significance of Klossowski's thesis and stated as much, in a letter dated to winter 1970:

> Dear Pierre,
>
> I should have written to you as soon as I first read *Living Currency*. It knocked the wind out of me, of course, but still I could have responded. Now, after having reread it several times, I know that it is the greatest book of our time. . . . But there it is, now it has been said, and indeed it is so great a book that everything else recedes and counts only half as much anymore. This is what we should have been thinking about: desire, value and the simulacrum—the triangle that dominates us and has constituted us for many years of our history.[24]

In this regard, he offers a gloss on the fundamental point made by Engels:

> In an old unpublished manuscript, written by Marx and myself in 1846 [the reference here is to *German Ideology*, published after Engels's death], I find the words: "The first division of labor is that between man and woman for the propagation of children." And today I can add: The first-class opposition that appears in history coincides with the development of the antagonism between man and woman in monogamous marriage, and the first-class oppression coincides with that of the female sex by the male. Monogamous marriage was a great historical step forward; nevertheless, together with slavery and private wealth, it opens the period that has lasted until today in which every step forward is also relatively a step backward, in which prosperity and development for some is won through the misery and frustration of others. It is the cellular form of civilized society, in which the nature of the oppositions and contradictions fully active in that society can be already studied.[25]

Engels locates the division of labor in the division of *gendered* labor. While he grants that the legal and juridical framework of modern civilized societies spins the appearance of free will and rights ideologically, women nonetheless operate as *living currency*, thereby contradicting that ideology.

Klein made much of his wedding to Rotraut; the ceremony was recorded and presented as a work in a spectacular display predating the media-saturating celebrity cultures of the later twentieth century (figure 4.4). Marriage itself becomes an artwork insofar as it is a vehicle and guarantor of value, sealing the deal in the triangulation between value, simulacrum (the image), and desire, to echo Foucault's triad of key terms.

Philosopher and psychoanalyst Luce Irigaray offers a key discussion of the entrenched gender dynamics of economic development that speaks to Klein's *Anthropometries* with an uncanny relevance. In "Women on the Market," she advances a more specific reading of originary mediation in which women personify and embody the secularization of wealth in a manner uncannily consistent through the history first of early market exchange through to the elaboration of the capitalist mode of production and into real subsumption, where objects are not placed on a market but conceived for that market.

Irigaray elaborates a similar analysis of the trajectory of capitalism and its dependence on the extraction of value-productive labor from working bodies and socially reproductive bodies by noting the foundational centrality of gender to its matrix. She founds her analysis in structuralism, specifically Claude Lévi-Strauss's kinship analysis in his major theoretical statement, "The Elementary Structures of Kinship" (1947), which formed the basis for

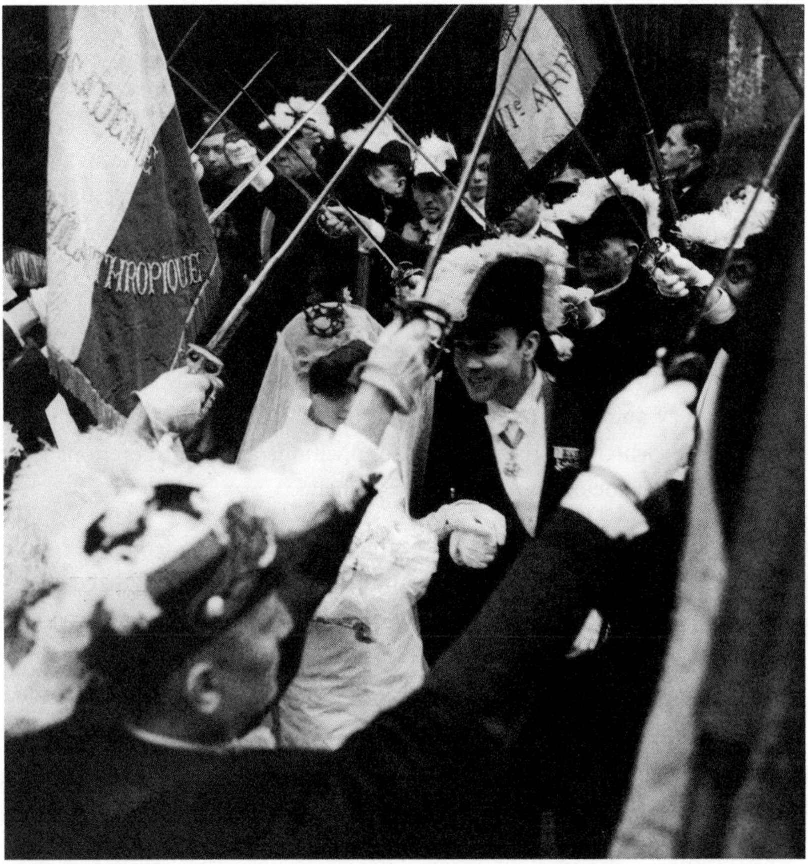

Fig. 4.4. Yves Klein and Rotraut Moquay wedding. Photographer unknown.

his magnum opus *Savage Mind* (1962) and subsequent writings. Irigaray begins "Women on the Market" with a familiar enough generalization: "The society we know, our own culture, is based upon the exchange of women. Without the exchange of women, we are told, we would fall back into the anarchy of the natural world, the randomness of the animal kingdom. The passage into the social order, into the symbolic order, into order as such, is assured by the fact that men, or groups of men, circulate women among themselves, according to a rule known as the incest taboo."[26] This opening claim bolsters Freud's argument in "Totem and Taboo" that order and law are established among men as a way to negotiate access to women. What falls out of that argument, which she is quick to reinsert, is the way in which this foundational form of society organized by deference to the father among warring and perhaps patricidal brothers generates a structuring principle that organizes not only a social field but the subtending metabolic or economy with which it replicates itself and which affords its mediation to and with nature.

> A fortiori: why are men not objects of exchange among women? It is because women's bodies—through their use, consumption, and circulation—provide for the condition making social life and culture possible, although they remain an unknown "infrastructure" of the elaboration of that social life and culture. The exploitation of the matter that has been sexualized female is so integral a part of our sociocultural horizon that there is no way to interpret it except within this horizon. . . . The work force is thus always assumed to be masculine, and "products" are objects to be used, objects of transaction among men alone."[27]

Irigaray explains how and why it is that the condition of "objectification" has come to be renaturalized to the point of becoming not only invisible but also immutable over millennia. The transactional logic of the market, the very signature of abstraction, is the lynchpin in the motivation of an economic horizon determinative of sociocultural norms replicated over time to become second nature. Irigaray explores claims about the passage from nature to culture so dear to hegemonic anthropological analysis in which only the role of women remains fundamentally unchanged to generate a social order that is fundamentally, as she calls it, a homosexual monopoly insofar as the ontological category "human" seems only to pertain to men: "In this new matrix of History, in which man begets man as his own likeness, wives, daughters, and sisters have value only in that they serve as the possibility of, and potential benefit in, relations among men."[28] Women form an infrastructure, mediated by and mediating social relations in endless replication of a primitive agreement whose specific origins are incomprehensible. Again, in a second nature eclipsing "nature," a transactional logic gains precedence and erases any trace of its telos. Here, heterosexuality is simply a symbolic form wherein "heterosexuality has been up to now just an alibi for the smooth workings of man's relations with himself, of relations among men."[29] She calls this social mediation a new matrix of history in which women move along an axis of objects while men conduct commerce along the axis of subject positions; the social gender binary is not the result of sex as such for her but a function of this productivist system of categorizing bodies by assigned use-value.

Irigaray reads Marx's labor theory of value through Lévi-Strauss's analysis of kinship structures. For her, Marx's analysis of the commodity in the famous passages on the commodity fetish in *Capital*, volume 1, section 1, part 4, pertain first and foremost to women, that is, to a subject position that precedes the development of the commodity form.[30] In this, her work corroborates that of Sohn-Rethel, who sees the market and transactional space it necessitates as a predecessor to value-productive commodity manufacture: "Marx's analysis of commodities as the elementary form of capitalist wealth can thus be understood as an interpretation of the status of woman in so-called patriarchal societies." Marx's understanding of the commodity fetish is, in short and unbeknownst to Marx, a theory of gender. This account of gender locates the logic of "commodity" fetishism in social relations that precede the capitalist mode of production. In a mesmerizing passage, Irigaray observes:

> Woman's price is not determined by the "properties" of her body—although her body constitutes the material support of that price. But when women are exchanged, woman's body must be treated as an abstraction. The exchange operation cannot take place in terms of some intrinsic, immanent value of the commodity. It can only come about when two objects—two women are in a relation of equality with a third term that is neither the one nor the other. It is thus not as "women" that they are exchanged, but as women reduced to some common feature—their current price in gold. . . . Since these qualities are abandoned in the long run to the needs of the consumer.[31]

Rotraut is exceptional in Klein's work, and yet set into equivalence in the way in which her presence is conjugated with the generic models and the way that the results themselves de-differentiate bodies. In this regard, the way in which bodies are differentiated or de-differentiated along these axes of intimacy and anonymity in *Anthropometries* is diametrically opposed to Seurat's *The Models*, in which, as discussed in chapter 1, the artist goes to great pains at the level of composition to demarcate familiarity from the relative obscurity of the concrete laborer who in her anonymity stands for generalized, faceless abstract labor.

The actual origins of Klein's paradigmatic gesture are transactional; the substance, or content, to which he aspired and named as a known quotient of "vitality" were made possible by the paid time of the models whom he sought out of a sense of isolation and loneliness in the studio. The results were interesting enough to repeat with Rotraut, while the social relations leading up to the transactional encounter are suspended and deferred, out of sight and mind in order to present the artwork that nonetheless presents the body as transparent and interchangeable. In a sense, it dematerializes the nude in order to rematerialize it along the axes of labor-time articulated in abstract, notational form, not unlike currency. Klein had the Midas touch—the alchemical capacity to invert the actual composition of the object by mystifications that summed a European reactionary response to structural subsumption. That which Picabia had identified in etiological terms comes to be affirmed in Klein's work: the complete reification of abstract labor-power and concomitant abstraction of its bearer herself.

That persons are remade to be *things* is the meaning of real subsumption. At this structural conjuncture, self-reflectively or otherwise, Klein begins a mode of conceptual inquiry where thought itself becomes determined by the *mode of production* making it possible, which also comes to transform the ontological condition of all categories: people become abstract commodities, et cetera, insofar as their abstract labor-power can be coercively extracted without much concern for their concrete properties as humans. The artist, as de Duve noticed, becomes the petit bourgeois manager, there to direct and cull value from the de-differentiated worker.

The displacement from manual skill to managerial outsourcing is also germane to *Anthropometries*. In the photographs that Klein commissioned Harry Shunk to take on the occasion of the first gallery performance of the *Anthropometries*, Klein dramatized his distance from the process of mark making by wearing white gloves. He directed the models, or living paintbrushes, from a distance. In this regard, he demonstrated his remove from concrete craft, any contact with the traditional instruments of Western painting, from brush and paint to model, while doubling down on a sense of administrative control.

Klein evaluated the results of the *Anthropometries* experiments as follows: "I have painted with living brushes—in other words, the nude bodies of live models smothered in paint. These living brushes are under the constant direction of my commands, such as 'a little to the right; over to the left now; to the right again, etc.' By maintaining myself at a definite and obligatory distance from the painting, I am able to resolve the problem of detachment."[32] In this notion of exteriority from the process of physically making the work, Klein wanted to "attain a definite and constant distance between myself and the painting during the moment of creation."[33]

> Many art critics claimed that via this method of painting I was in fact merely reenacting the technique of what has been called "action painting." I would like now to make it clear that my endeavor is opposed to "action" painting in that I am actually completely detached from the physical work during its creation. Personally, never would I want to . . . become a living brush. But on the contrary, I would rather put on my tuxedo and wear white gloves. I would not even think of dirtying my hands with paint. Detached and distant, the work of art must complete itself before my eyes and under my command. Thus, as soon as the work is realized, I stand there—present at the ceremony, spotless, calm, relaxed and worthy of it, and ready to receive it as it is born into the tangible world.[34]

It is precisely this physicality that Klein wanted to transcend, ironically, through the very genre that historically signaled most affinity for the material and the embodied (from Titian and Giorgione on): the nude. And yet he shifted the corporeal register of the trace to a hypereroticized mobilization of the index in which he is himself absent. Klein's work does as much and prefigures a new labor-form that would become increasingly normative in the decades to come.

And by the 1950s, the index was beginning to be a new kind of lingua franca. It afforded Klein the chance to revisit a classical French trope by new means. But Klein's split tendency, to take up traditional and classical tropes while packaging himself as original, were equally driven by transitions in a broader social economic field. As such, Klein's oeuvre stands as almost completely transparent to a postwar economic and libidinal economic landscape described in chapter 3, of the constant surveillance of the worker and consumer to ensure the circuits of value extraction ran smoothly and elegantly, a perfect Sadean mise-en-scène.

5

Surplus Bodies

Santiago Sierra's Exploitive Remuneration

In June 2001, Spanish artist Santiago Sierra collected 133 men to take part in his project for the Spanish Pavilion at the 49th Venice Biennale. Sierra's "action," titled *133 Persons Paid to Have Their Hair Dyed Blonde* (figure 5.1), took place on the opening day of this auspicious art world event. The criteria in selecting the men were as follows: they were to originate from Africa, Asia, or the Middle East and have dark hair. The participants were immigrants and refugees, legal or otherwise. Sierra directed the 133 men to an area in the Arsenale where he bleached their hair, producing a visibly artificial appearance, in effect marking each person as though with a yellow highlighter. The self-assigned role of the artist was to collect, direct, and manage these persons within the spatial parameters of the Arsenale only, in the institutionalized framework of the art exhibition, in front of an audience watching the transformation.

The yellow-headed 133 persons then dispersed, returning to their everyday activities: predominantly illegal street vending on and around Piazza San Marco, a form of survival and daily self-replication now endangering these specific men, rendering them vulnerable to the police and carceral state apparatus threatening to either detain or deport them. This defenselessness before the law doubles back to requalify the at first superficially generous proposition by the artist to offer the men money for very little time and effort; for it very rapidly becomes clear that the men are paid to risk their lives, that this seeming generosity for little time is in fact a meager sum in exchange for a gamble with formal freedom. They were compensated

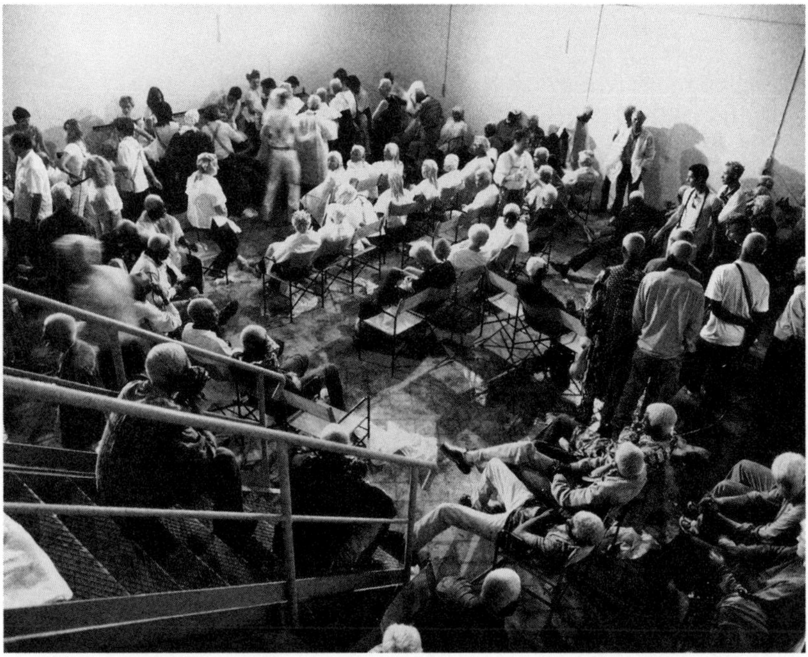

Fig. 5.1. Santiago Sierra, *133 Persons Paid to Have Their Hair Dyed Blonde*, 2001. © Santiago Sierra / VEGAP, Madrid / CARCC, Ottawa, 2024.

nominally to be made exponentially more vulnerable, because now exaggeratedly visible, to the police. The paid volunteers took no part in determining the unfolding of events, nor did they become actors in a production. *Acting*, understood as either the delivery of dramatic content elaborated within the framework of theater, situated in the fact-bearing framework of documentary practices and reenactments, or framed as explorations of agency as in Actionism or neo-avant-gardist task performance, was demonstrably irrelevant to the situation. The realization of any form of agency on the part of the "volunteers" was not only irrelevant but was shown to be structurally unattainable. They had no role in driving a narrative forward or delivering content. This was not that kind of "performance."

The question might be posed as much of Marx as of Sierra, of Andrea Fraser, Hito Steyerl, or countless others from Manet on. Why must the allegorical function operate by means of recourse to paid subjugation, specifically a nonsocially reproductive often sexual act? This chapter argues that Santiago Sierra marshals the genre of performance art, a genre already saturated in the contradictions of exploitive remuneration and the shifting nature of labor in the exponential rise of the service sector as argued in the previous chapter, in order to query the particular strategies of a racialized dynamic nested within the labor-capital relationship and the equally racialized extraction of labor-power from surplus populations, or those formally unemployable and often racialized demographics held in reserve for their labor-power.

Here, a tacitly political dimension supports the extraction of surplus from labor-power. Labor-power is mediated by forms of governance that adjudicate the mediation of the sale of labor-power. Governance—we may call this "the state" for shorthand with full acknowledgment that the state apparatus operates differently across context while maintaining basic functions in all, including the mediation of labor—must first ascertain that some of its demographic composition is "free" to sell its labor-power, a freedom predicated on the unfreedom of others, often women, whose labor is renaturalized. This is the insight of voices among the Italian feminist movement of the 1970s, articulated most succinctly by Mariarosa Dalla Costa and Selma James in *The Power of Women and the Subversion of the Community*: "The unfree patriarch was transformed into the 'free' wage earner, and upon the contradictory experience of the sexes and the generations was built a more profound estrangement and therefore a more subversive relation."[1] Here, any given labor pool is divided into those mediated and those unmediated by a wage.

This form of mediation is then rationalized by deference to categories of identity that retroactively legitimate a division of labor and that in turn become axes not only of gender assignation but also of racialization and racial categories reticulated to value or its lack.[2] Turning around in logic, it is then rearticulated in the social field as a matter of political "freedom," among the rights and freedoms enjoyed by the citizen, the right to work and to have the fruits of one's labor-power assigned value on a market. Yet the phrase "right to valorization" is already a contradiction until forms of governance denaturalize it. For as Marx noted, man is the proprietor of his own labor-power. And yet we see everywhere forms of enclosure and determination on the part of the state that disarticulate this proprietorial relation with the self, substituting for it the will of the state. To what extent have art practices prefigured this condition, in warning, in indifference, or in what Hal Foster refers to as the "mimetic exacerbation" of artist to the hegemon in which he works?[3]

While the central problem of the piece at Venice, featured among the highlighted heads, was visibility itself (and who or what constitutes visibility *as a person* in a social regime founded on the uneven value of labor-power within a state-sanctioned international division of labor), the prefigurative *function* of this spectacular demonstration offered within the parameters of cultural and aesthetic (rather than political) praxis needs to be specified. Now that the global and systemic structure of capital has changed dramatically over the long down turn from 1973 to 2008 and its ramifications, including the location of cheaper labor-power in peripheral states and capital's flight from its former core to extract it, the lines of mediation between capital and culture must also be remapped. To pose my argument as a question, given that the economic reconfiguration on which culture depends has changed drastically: Why are there so few accounts of the restructured global relationship of capital and labor, what of the emergence of a new composition of a *global* underclass (in the absence of proletarians forged in common geopolitical and historical frameworks) in writing about art and social justice?[4]

The artist may be one of the last subject-positions within capitalism to determine their own production under the sign of "creativity" and to be held at an oblique angle to value-productive labor; they are dialectically "free" to be creative. But in the aftermath of art no longer constrained by any medium, beginning with performative practices since 1973 as Marina Vishmidt argues, if not 1915 or 1888, when artists began to be summoned to fulfill a "creative capacity," they have tended to deliver on this expectation of creativity and originality by indexing the very impossibility of meeting this expectation, given the degree to which forms of reification have migrated from the domain of the object to that of the subject, to the artist-subject.[5]

Sierra's work starkly demonstrates openly invisible labor relations in a heightened state-to-market relationship in which immigration is at once necessary and xenophobically restricted, compounded by the adjudication of the value of labor-power along racialized lines. This attenuated observation of how bodies are assigned value by the state and market, the central concern afforded by Sierra's project, supersedes a number of impasses within the discourse of intersectionality, as I will show, but from the perspective of aesthetic praxis, a mode of inquiry radically other to social science. As such, Sierra's aesthetic query performs and prefigures the mutually constitutive operations of proletarianization and racialization, or rather the way in which race is doubly coded by capitalist ideology to maximize the efficiency with which the extraction of labor-power is accomplished and valorized.[6] At the same time that his aesthetic project demonstrates the ways in which the state apparatus engineers market un/mediated wages, it equally reveals the vacuity of ethical claims to democratic equality irrespective of race and ethnicity. Sierra highlights the symbiotic bond between classic forms of social reproduction in the state's production of a proletarian reserve on the one hand, and on the other hand growing racialized surplus populations in the equally changing dynamic between the once capitalist core and its "periphery." While the contradiction between the primacy of race and class may not express itself in the social political register, that contradiction is doubly necessary to capital; it assists capital by coercively driving down the value of labor drawn from deracinated migrant and refugee populations, or equally racialized surplus reserves, and buying them back at a price point cheaper than their racially validated competition.

While Marxist analysis on the one hand and postcolonial and identity-oriented frameworks on the other hand operate in the other's blind spot, resulting in a failure to delineate the way in which capital extracts labor-power from those it most denigrates and devalues on a symbolic register, the kind of cultural enactment of the contradictory conjuncture mobilized by Sierra crystallizes, with rare lucidity, the entwinement of both. Where discourse has failed, art practices such as Sierra's, by contrast, have paid attention. They address the way in which the ideological apparatus operates to obfuscate and displace the particular way in which capital enacts a means of material exploitation through which to procure labor more cheaply, having denigrated its source, while distracting a viewing population ensnared by the liberal ideologies that rationalize daily social replication.

What emerges from Sierra's cruel praxis is a paradox at the core of labor under the current stage of capitalism. Paradoxically, forms of oppression that limit access to social wealth (the wage, for instance) are symbolically mobilized as a means by which to extract labor-power more cheaply and coerce it more seamlessly. The most oppressed demographics are exploited in ways that are markedly different from those proletarianized demographics drawn from the settler colonial state, which continued to arbitrate the circulation of value and labor-power from core to periphery and back in the aftermath of decolonization. The gap between state oppression and market exploitation becomes a way to facilitate the extraction of cheaper labor-power, by first designating those deemed excessive to the social price of the social package, and thereby "surplus." But again, as explored in previous chapters, the abstract transaction is once again the pivot by which to at once occlude and opportunistically manipulate this contradiction between an ideological formation that deems some bodies to be surplus while materially doubling down on an extractive logic.

First Sierra's work forefronts the importance of the transaction. The moment of transaction, in turn, is yet again the arena within which abstraction, understood in this context as dehumanization, takes place, under the guise of the most civil and natural forms of engagement. To emphasize, the logic of the action rested on the suspension of agency of any kind on the part of these 133 persons, emphasizing the marked bodies' susceptibility to structure and to the law. This displacement of causality from agency to structure is denoted by criteria set to the lowest denominator of physical characteristics fixed to racial and ethnic alterity. Any subjective or interpretation of the circumstances was denied by a demonstration of the objective social relations determining the scenario, a demonstration played out over the bodies of these men, bodies that in turn signified, generically, the "Global South" as a source of devalued labor.

Sierra's way of isolating a transactional logic made specific by its reliance on devalued racialized bodies heightens an open secret. While the state builds and manages its reserves, the individuals who constitute it are contingent for survival on the state's mediation of labor.[7] Sierra exaggerates and mimics this asymmetrical relationship between himself and his "volunteers."[8] The act of remuneration in this instance becomes Sierra's very medium, a way to probe the paradox of abstraction itself insofar as it is invisibly stamped out over human flesh in the market-as-social-field that silently regulates everyday life, forming limits to perception itself. Put more ambitiously, Sierra highlights at once the market on which labor-power is abstracted and the way in which this form of abstraction marks bodies as excessive to social order. In this disavowed political-aesthetic order organized around the transaction, the opposition between proletarianization and criminalization is revealed to be a tenuous one bearing on the contingencies of capital's particular needs. The men's abandonment by a regime that distinguishes the disposable (illegal) from the useful (legal) paradoxically presents them as a peculiar kind of fetish, a fetishized form of labor-power disarticulated from the legal and juridical status that would establish their status first and foremost as *human*. Sierra queries Marx's "man" as proprietor of his labor-power. In the social dynamic resting on labor whose bearer is at once "free" in juridical terms to sell but obliged or compelled to place himself on the market in material terms, or in which the individual bearer is set against his own interests, the state becomes an arbitrator of an otherwise almost indistinguishable line between criminal "prostitution" and the basic and universal sale of labor. The "freedom" to set one's time on a market in the interest of daily self-replication is shown to be structural to both categories. By posing the question as such, Sierra's paradigmatic work above all dramatizes the central shift salient to art making at the close of the twentieth century.

The primary feature of Sierra's *133 Persons Paid to Have Their Hair Dyed Blonde* is that it does not traffic in the exchange of commodity goods. It traffics in people. And this ontological shift from things to persons re/marks the conditions of reification marked first by performance art practices, while heightening both its brutality and its contradiction. This is to say that it rehearses the violence of reification by dramatizing its terms. Beyond rehearsal and demonstration, however, the transition from things to *persons* (a word that comprises the title) tells us something about the internal historicity of capital itself. Contemporary capitalism has outgrown its industrial phase, moving from recursive cycles of commodity production that enable the growth of money via labor (the MCM′ cycle of valorization described in *Capital*) in the global core, to one in which surplus-value production is outsourced to the Global South. Revenues, meanwhile, circulate in the Global North in the form of remunerations for services, speculation, or the financial manipulation of equity and debt, what some have called "financialization." This symptom of global economic transition merely exposes the fact that labor-power is the ultimate form of the commodity, congealed in every other commodity to multiply value. This is to say that the disarticulation of the traditional commodity form born from the site of surplus-value production to the objectification of (biopolitical) personhood exposes anew the value-form's autonomy, or rather its indifference, to human life. For again, Sierra isolates one variable: the exchange of human capacity. Sohn-Rethel reminds us "it is the action of exchange and the action alone that is abstract. The consciousness and the action of people part company in exchange and go different ways. . . . One could say that the abstractness of their action is beyond realization by the actors because their very consciousness stands in the way."[9] Sierra locates this un/consciousness as a collective structural condition, a cruelty everywhere and nowhere in particular, part of the social synthesis of everyday life with or without the framing device that is "art."

But a question remains, one that forms a secondary inquiry of this book: how did this "thingishness" move from actual things, objects mediating social relations, to the becoming thingish of all personhood and experiential life? In culture, performance art has ascended over the past several decades as a central category. Performance, unlike object-media-based forms, requires a minimum of one *person* to act as the support for the delivery of content. Although it is set into circulation to denote any number of art practices involving human actors and agents, very few entail performance in the sense of theater or expression.[10] Most of these practices explore the human as a nonagent, a cipher to structure, motivating the queer feminist artist

Yvonne Rainer's term *exploitive voluntarism*.[11] The term *voluntarism*, applied by Rainer to Marina Abramovic's work, which stands at the historical origins of the genre and which often involves the inclusion of bodies reduced to their exposed physical presence, as explored in the previous chapter, negates the very possibility of real agency, capitulating to coercive structural determinations necessary to daily self-replication (survival) under capitalism. In Rainer's explanation: "Ms. Abramovic is so wedded to her original vision that she—and by extension, the Museum director and curators—doesn't see the egregious associations for the performers, who, though willing, will be exploited nonetheless. Their desperate voluntarism says something about the generally exploitative conditions of the art world."[12]

And that exploitive art world, in turn, becomes an index of the growing ubiquity of exploitive voluntarism in the greater social totality. However accurate Rainer's critical analysis and intervention into the business-as-usual of the art world, it nonetheless falls somewhere between blaming the message about the structural nature of labor on the messenger, Abramovic, and mistaking the forest for the trees. Abramovic's strategies of drawing on bodies and minds who are remunerated only by the supposedly "creative agency of the event" are transparent to new modalities of often informal work, casually denominated by a variety of ill-fitting terms such as *service industry* or *gig economy* as the industrial cycle of accumulation in North America (1949–73) in which commodity production was central gave way to a service economy in the era of outsourcing and cheaper labor extracted for commodity production elsewhere. As Vishmidt has recently argued, "post-object art forms such as performance forecast a shift to self-performance as the evaluative prism for all labor."[13] She continues to draw a much larger conclusion from contemporary performance-based artwork, seeing in the genre the articulation of the totality of the current labor-to-capital relationship: "The blurring between service sector and its appearance in the institution of art either in representational or in performative ways, but also on the reliance of that institution, and the broader dimensions of the 'creative industries' is, however edgy its appearance, utterly reflective in the most vulgar sense."[14]

This vulgarity does not qualify the cultural mediation but rather the expanding saturation of exchangism structuring social relations across sectors, ages, genders, and labor pools. Vishmidt concludes, "As has been observed in recent curatorial and art critical interventions, the figure of the artist as a service provider rather than as a maker of things is seen to coincide with the transitions from goods to services in economic primacy in the west."[15]

The social synthesis reiterated in the transactional moment, a kind of economic and biopolitical social contract, however much an "open secret," is shown to function as a shared condition that nonetheless distinguishes surplus populations from those whose lives are deemed necessary enough to capital to be replicated, to be let to live. Art in the neoliberal age, it turns out, is the most vivid index of this fault line that at once joins and differentiates surplus from replicable bodies. The charm of Venice and the sophistication of the 49th Biennale could not prevent poverty, uneven global economic conditions, and the legal juridical uncertainties of exclusion and biopolitical control from literally erupting into view in a way at once incidental, banal, and utterly spectacular.

Before turning once more to the conjuncture of complicitous and antagonistic conditions that enable Sierra's transactional strategy, the composition of the work's audience demands its own scrutiny. A demographic of educated, liberal viewers who congregate every two years in Venice was put in the position of having to confront a social reality principle, with which they dealt through a common suspension and deferral to ethics and their failure in contemporary life. A critic for *Le Monde*, among others, described Sierra's work in general, and his plan at the 2001 Venice Biennale in particular, as the result of an "unpitying cynicism." One may have noted that the messenger was being blamed for the message, or better, for merely remarking a message that is always already in the tourists' faces besmirching the picture. Meanwhile, various social agencies called his use of refugees inhumane despite the fact that the artist worked with refugee organizations.[16] An admittedly minuscule fraction of that putative public, those who have contributed to the discourse on Sierra's project, is polarized between those who see him as exploitive and those who see him continuing the sixties legacy of negative critique, the unmasking of false consciousness determined by capitalist ideology, indeed capitalism understood *as* an ideology (rather than a structural metabolic). Claire Bishop, in her well-known essay "Antagonism and Relational Aesthetics," concludes: "It is worth bearing in mind that since the late 1970s, older avant-garde rhetoric of opposition and transformation have been frequently replaced by strategies of complicity. What matters is not the complicity but how we receive it. If Tiravanija's work is experienced in a major key, then Sierra's is most definitely minor": minor, but complicit nonetheless. Bishop argues that Sierra's work differs from relational aesthetics on the basis of its rejection of "open-endedness." At the same time, she notes that while it marks delimited institutional contexts such as immigration or illegal commerce, it also acknowledges the porousness of these boundaries.[17]

The majority of Biennale visitors reacted with shock and disdain for what they perceived to be the abusive opportunism of Sierra's tactic. He paid the illegal workers very little for their participation. Yet this parsimony begs the question: what could ever be an adequate exchange rate for an inscription over the body willed by another agent? Could there ever be compensation for the men's extreme vulnerability to the law? To the fact that they were risking their own place in networks and black-market forms of survival in order to legitimate and lend value to Sierra's proper name? Sierra's work, whatever its aesthetic interest may or may not be, and in full acknowledgment of its failure as a critical art practice, much less a social intervention, does raise a few urgently necessary questions about art and work in contemporaneity.

While race and ethnicity factored on a fundamental and structural level, as explored earlier, the mutually causal relationship between race and the politics of remuneration proves challenging not only because of the spectrum of ethnicities staged as "other" to white European identity, complicating through sheer heterogeneity identity itself, but also given the fact that above all other variables the problem of remuneration itself, in the form of the wage or the informal fee, is indifferent to race and ethnicity, just as it is indifferent to the social relations in which exchange is nested. This transactional indifference, ultimately, emerges as the fundamental problem against which that of racialization surfaces.

Sohn-Rethel once again offers a way to think the financial transaction that at once racializes (and genders) while maintaining a stark indifference to the particular features of labor-power. Again, the moment of exchange stands at the origin of an abstract social *synthesis* beyond the community. "The nexus of society is established by the network of exchange and nothing else."[18] Now, the way in which Sohn-Rethel derives this first principle of a social cohesion that suspends social belonging in the family, the clan, and the community summons the question of "consciousness." Oddly enough, the author's query into the limits of consciousness in relation to the necessity to labor prefigures those of discourses around performance art; consciousness is structurally, inevitably suspended at the moment of material exchange.

> In commodity exchange the action and the consciousness of people go separate ways. Only the action is abstract; the consciousness of the actors is not. The abstractness of their action is hidden to the people performing

it. The actions of exchange are reduced to strict uniformity, eliminating the differences of people, commodities, locality and date. The uniformity finds expression in the monetary function of one of the commodities acting as the common denominator to all the others. The relations of exchange transacted in a market express themselves in quantitative differences of this uniform denominator as different prices and *create a system of social communication of actions performed by individuals in complete independence of one another and oblivious to the socializing effects involved.* The pivot of this mode of socialization is the abstraction intrinsic to the action of exchange. The abstraction is the dominating form element of commodity exchange to which we given an even wider significance than Marx did, who was first to discover it.[19]

Abstraction functions at the level of a kind of habituated action that defers the specificity of the participants in the exchange. Real abstraction, then, constitutes the conditions within which an "ethics" of the human comes to be at once determined by and suspended by the market. For while agency as such is not bracketed off—if anything the illusion of free will is facilitated, even enabled, herein—the form of agency summoned in this action is not that of the personal individual but rather the space-time of the market, itself suspended over nontransactional or "normal" social interactions.[20] According to Khatib, "The abstraction belongs to the interrelationship of the exchanging agents and not to the agents themselves. For it is not the individuals who cause the social synthesis but their actions, and their actions do it in such a way that, the moment it happens, the actors know nothing of it."[21]

This impersonal "social mechanism" realizes itself as "a materialism that excludes the historical process."[22] The slip from people to things occurs at the heart of this moment of unconscious social engagement, an unconscious social synthesis: "But the essence of the postulate of equality in exchange is precisely that it cuts across the gap of experience that separates the exchangers. . . . In this way the relationship between the exchanging persons is transferred to the commodities and expressed as an equality between objects."[23] The agent, then, is the market itself. Staging indifference to any qualities outside of a vulnerability and contingency on the state's immigration law, these bodies on the (black) market demonstrate the extent to which exchange itself, rather than labor, functions as the locus of abstraction: "Abstraction does not spring from labor but from exchange as a particular mode of social interrelationship, and it is through exchange that abstraction imparts itself to labor, making it 'abstract human labor.'"[24] It is the sale and purchase of these men's time, apart from their personhood itself or that for which they are paid, that reiterates a primary abstraction. This, in turn, is marked and marked as vulnerable, now to a second order of abstraction: the law.

Sierra's work, not only in *133 Persons Paid to Have Their Hair Dyed Blonde* but across his oeuvre and in the better-known gestures in that oeuvre such as *250 cm Line Tattooed on 6 Paid People*, rests on the performance of transactional logic that, assigning a price for the labor-power and/or time of available labor-power "afforded" by lives endangered by exposure to the state apparatus, deems them at once useful, but not enough to be legally remunerated for their (surplus) labor-power.

Sierra's specific transactional logic distinguishes his artistic practice from others of his generation who address collective exertion without addressing collective labor as a technology comprising social relations. For instance, Francis Alys's 2002 artwork *When Faith Moves Mountains*, featured in his 2008 MoMA retrospective, incorporated five hundred unpaid volunteers who shoveled sand in the outskirts of Lima, Peru, in the midday sun until they collectively moved an enormous sand dune by a few inches. Both projects, Sierra's and Alys's, require the viewer to limn the dissonant relationship among meanings of the word *work*: artwork and toil. Labor in this context is especially fraught; it cannot be described by either the classic Marxian narratives of proletarianization or the terms of critique or resistance we have inherited from the socially engaged art of the present. With the obsolescence of these narratives comes the obsolescence of the regime of visibility, the conditions of social visibility, associated with them. But again, the transactional nature of Sierra's mobilization of exploitive voluntarism differs in its emphasis on the purchase of the men's task performance, or rather, passive availability to the *power of the artist's dollar to compel them to endanger themselves*.

To begin to broach this entails seeing "abstraction" as a process, an operation, and a social technology rather than a qualification of things: "The chief result is money in which abstractness assumes a separate embodiment. Then, however, the movement through which the process has been mediated vanishes in its own result, leaving no trace behind."[25] This movement itself and the transformations it effects are the "object" of inquiry.

Sierra's summoning of abstraction's pitilessness mimetically exacerbates and prefigures that to come, those cruel abstractions occurring in capitalism's racialized biopolitics that shore up value extraction by doubly devaluing some bodies over others in a way that is analogous and expands upon the historical double devaluation of women to ensure the assignation of just enough value to a highly mediated, circumscribed labor-power to keep its system operative at minimum cost, while maintaining a reserve of labor-power outside of any traditional forms of organized resistance. The totality of this new structural condition in the fragmentary composition of labor in relation to global capital is demonstrated in the artwork with greater telegraphic efficiency. Mimetic exacerbation offers a grasp of larger forms of decomposition and recomposition than can be articulated in theories of intersectionality or other social justice discourses that focus on specific forms of oppression rather than total exploitation across plural identities. Rather than focus on a particular intersection, such as North African immigration versus immigration from Turkey or the Middle East, Sierra's gesture remains capacious enough to see the total system of plural relations in a complex moving dynamic, one in which value is indifferent to particularities other than as a means of extracting labor or suspending the potential of labor-power.

Race and ethnicity played a central, pivotal role in this sadistic demonstration of the structural conditions of (abstract) everyday life yet no particular race or ethnicity became a subject of the work's content; it came to signify a *decomposition* of unified identities in a larger contemporary totality. They functioned as indices of a political economic crisis at the conjuncture of the global market and the nation-state apparatus. But this begs the question of identity and politics. We are looking, then, at an intersection, a conjuncture in which identity and a relation to economic survival come to be mutually constitutive—as determined by the state. The men deemed illegal by the state and therefore barred from access to earning a wage are then compelled to seek forms of self-support outside the law. Their contingence on a legal and juridical status barring them from legal work is in turn contingent on their social political position as migrants from elsewhere, outside the fold of Europe.

While this circuit of contingencies with relation to the law takes place outside the sphere of appearances, or outside the visitor's visual access, other forms of appearances that are presented to the viewer—dark hair dyed blonde—become an index of biopolitical abstraction, of the law as inherently arbitrary. Where, then, in this play of appearances and subject positions does "identity" factor, if at all? How might it be possible to locate the impersonal brutality and indifference to social specificity of capitalism while, in refusal of capitalism's dictates, attending to the racial and ethnic specificity of these men? How might attending to their individual historical trajectories, their stories, either illuminate or assuage the callousness of the situation made visible at the Arsenale? Would locating their identities be one way of refusing to renaturalize their precarious positions? Or would it risk the very reverse?

Black feminist scholar Kimberlé Crenshaw coined the term *intersectionality* to circumscribe the seeming contradictions that surfaced from a court case involving factory workers at General Motors (GM).[26] The car company's Black female workers initiated a labor dispute that raised the specter of social hierarchies seated in race and gender, nested within traditional labor struggles. Crenshaw inaugurated the term *intersectionality* as a way to think the conjuncture of the need for a Marxist critique alongside a robust analysis of race, and finally a feminist politics capacious enough to address both. The term has been subsequently elaborated into a kind of academic methodology despite its having originated from protests on the factory floor, a framework through which to conceptualize the confrontation and antagonism of numerous social injustices. Yet it falls under critique in turn not only for compromising the primacy of any one struggle—that of a politics of gender equity or that of the antagonism in the labor-capital dynamic—but for the way in which it unwittingly tends to a politics of particularization, fragmentation, and atomization rather than a way to recompose resistance as a class composed of myriad differences. It is unable to hold the totality of the way in which each current is at once constituted by and constitutive of capitalist social relations within any given moment of capitalism's historicity. Otherwise put, or articulated in a way that contributes to our primary thesis about the role of abstraction in the constitution of surplus-labor pools, the discourse of intersectionality cannot contain the multiplicity of contradictions that, precisely through contradiction, generate a matrix, a warp and weft of social aporias each in turn emerging from historically determined struggles (diachronically), each situated within differing subject positions (synchronically).

In "Mapping Social Reproduction Theory," Tithi Bhattacharya makes a similar point, drawn on the same apprehension that intersectionality does not adequately account for a social totality in which gender, race, and class are co-constitutive and generated by a wider logic of abstraction itself generated of the dominance of value estranged from lived experience. She argues:

> Intersectionality theory shows us a world where race, gender, and other oppressions "intersect," thereby producing a reality that is latticed—a sum total of different parts. At first glance this "whole," as an aggregate of different parts, may be the same as the Hegelian-Marxist conception of total-

ity. An elementary question about the nature of intersections, however, reveals the distinction between these two concepts. If, as intersectionality tells us, race and gender (or race and class) intersect like two streets, then surely they are two separate streets, each with its own specificities. What then is the *logic* of their intersection? I suggest that the logic and conclusions of intersectional theorists actually contradict their methodology.[27]

Recall that while visibility itself became the protagonist of *133 Persons Paid to Have Their Hair Dyed Blond*, this form of visibility highlighted above all the vulnerability of persons to a market in which they had no legal protection. As such, the market and its operations were isolated and circumscribed, shown in its most absolute and fundamental form. The piece inadvertently points out that a biopolitical state apparatus might endanger some, but in so doing it also reveals the degree to which the state apparatus must be in place to restrain the otherwise naked brutality of this market for its citizenry.

Sierra's act of visual emphasis is not synonymous with exposure or unveiling, the primary modus operandi of another (other than performance, which continues on) genre of post-minimalist art: the critique of institutions.[28] Rather, it afforded a scenario indicative of a new dynamic between labor and capital reliant on a global underclass and the creation of massive surplus populations on which the twenty-first-century global totality at once depends and occludes, a global condition unprobed by the discourse of intersectionality, which focuses on specific identities within capital rather than the systemic picture.

133 Persons framed that which the visual regime of the exhibit in 2001 both depends on and dismisses: the uneven *value* of the human. Because the work Sierra and others of his generation do is responding to a social fabric organized by forms of both transparent control and opaque disciplinary orders, that which is isolated to view is not hidden as such, as might be expected of an actually operative "civil society," any more than the "hidden abode of production" to which Marx famously refers in *Capital* is actually technically hidden.[29] It is hidden in plain sight, in the visual landscape, and yet absent in the mind of the citizen-consumer. But this absence to consciousness is precisely that which is at stake in Sohn-Rethel's account of real abstraction, happening as it does "behind the backs of men." The open secret is the asymmetrical relationship between human life and value. The social relations attendant therein, and what it means to make art in an age of austerity and restructuring in the aftermath of the Keynesian state, is finally forced into the forefront of consciousness, part of the total social "picture."[30]

My intervention here consists of the claim that the capitalist metabolic extracting value from bodies and resources, mediating it in the social and cultural field, has changed all the more to stay the same, to maintain hegemony. And Sierra's intervention affords a glimpse into a new social totality predicated on this seismic transition between global labor and global capital. The manifestation of the exhibitionary order distributing bodies, goods, and services has therefore also changed however much its basic structure remains, forged in the nineteenth-century industrial crucible. How might we trace its etiology? How do artworks clarify, if not prefigure, capital flight from core to periphery on the one hand, and the shift from surplus-value productive labor to revenues generated by the service and gig economy on the other hand? How and why have we moved from anxiety of surplus value to that of surplus populations?

Let us return once more to the scene at the Arsenale in Venice in 2001. Sierra's gesture acts like a cut in the fabric of reality. This "cut" offers a modality of analysis that is not available in the current discourses of ethical social justice. We have heard a great deal of late about art in relationship to social justice, often organized around the theme of "participation."[31] However, the social justice turn in art does not address social abstraction or a totality of social relations generated of an emergent global dynamic between labor and capital as it moves from former cores to former peripheries, requiring different forms of extraction as it goes. More specifically, this discourse—the social justice turn—does not factor the unity of labor as such, legal or illegal, into its narrative of injustice or its definition of justice. Overlooked is both the source of wealth in value-productive labor, however out of sight and mind, and the circulation of this wealth in the ever-widening labyrinth of social de- and recomposition demanded by capital as it both deracinates and reintegrates social relations globally through the totalizing operations of abstraction. The language of social justice misses social abstraction and the social technologies that both constitute and are constitutive of it: the site of exchange and the contractual (i.e., arbitrary but socially determined) act of exchange that *appears* conscious while suspending agency, much less ethics.[32]

While it literally highlighted heads and thereby the brazen ruthlessness of a market made all the more so when persons are unprotected by the state, Sierra's gesture emphasized a wider structure of habituated systemic brutality: the global exhibitionary order founded on transient bodies that are contingent on and vulnerable to abstracted social relations generated by an ever more complexly mediated liaison between capital and labor.[33] Timothy Mitchell has argued that an exhibitionary order was developed in the world's fairs of the mid- to late nineteenth century, starting with the London World's Fair of 1851, running through the Expositions Universelles in Paris in the 1860s and 1870s. He makes the case that this exhibitionary order forges the framework, template even, for numerous art world fairs and biennials in this our contemporaneity.[34] Art fairs, however much a construct of the nineteenth century, are in the contemporary globalized world located everywhere and seemingly nowhere in particular, from Venice to Gwangju to Karachi. What appeared to be about competition among nation-states articulated culturally (the London Fair, the Paris Expositions) was always structurally reticulated to the phenomenon of globalization. If anything, this un/conscious self-reflexivity of the inevitability of globalized tantalization under capitalism is inscribed in their titles: *London World's Fair*, *Exposition Universelles.*

The thematic of the World's Fair or Universal Exhibit, down to their reiterations as cornerstones of a global art world showcasing a universal art practice, begs the question of an equally global and universal underclass. Both "global turns" are made possible by capital. A global underclass, in turn, also becomes a question of surplus populations, those bodies deemed disposable because no longer structurally necessary to capitalist value production.[35] While this current text and the project from which it is drawn rely on the extant scholarly literature, and of world systems analysis, they rely above all on an etiology afforded most visibly by culture.

Sierra is not the first to take up the problem of labor from the perspective of structural necessity in which the transaction is understood to be an abstract and impersonal force rather than from the perspective of ethical social justice. While he does identify the harsh conditions of global surplus labor as symptomatic of globalization, of which the world's fairs of the nineteenth century are also exemplary historical examples, he coldly examines those conditions as features of exhibition structures now, more than a century after the inception of the international art show, in which the accelerated reach of capitalist subsumption has come to be a dialectical feature of internationalism. While his analysis of racialization and the widening expansion of surplus populations predicated on racialization certainly offers an "update," a structural analysis of the depersonalizing and dehumanizing factor of labor as it abuts art practice is not itself new. Chapter 4 explored the reification central to advanced art practices of the sixties, such as Yves Klein's living paintbrushes, which this book understands to be precursors for Sierra's attention to the global turn. But it may be helpful to turn to other thematically comparable works of previous generations of art practice in order to situate Sierra's project in relation to now canonized models of art making.

Already in 1968 in Paris, Daniel Buren had set into action the relationship between remuneration, art, and personhood. A group of sandwich men wore boards on which Buren's idiomatic white and colored stripes were painted at equally idiomatic (think: branding) 8.7 centimeter intervals. This part advertisement, part artwork unmasked commoditization of the human. Buren's clochards literalize Marx's observation that capital structurally renders subjects objects by making persons contingent on a wage relation in which they cannot afford the results of their own labor, while symmetrically making of objects subjects due to the mystification and power of the commodity fetish. Buren's men for hire performed the paradox of circulating the central and most visible social message of capital—the advertisement—while themselves remaining invisible. Although Buren was identifying something more fundamental to social relations than the role of the museum as such, namely, social abstraction founded on the sale of labor-time in parallel to Klein's gestures, his work has been understood as part of the critique of institutions in which art practices took their own institutional condition of possibility as a problem to be explored, without looking further into the degree to which those institutions rely on social abstraction while claiming to serve and represent social interests, the key dialectic of that movement. Hans Haacke also attempted to probe the relationship between museums and financial circuits in numerous pieces among his body of work, notably that in which he identified slumlords among MoMA's board members. Sierra shifts the emphasis from the institution, understood as an ideological apparatus, to a social field structured by abstract relations predicated on the exchange of labor-power, and to changes within the composition of labor pools accelerating the racialization of labor.

At around the same time as Buren's interrogation of institutional authority, a number of artists were explicitly identifying with the figure of the worker. As Julia Bryan-Wilson has shown in *Art Workers*, the rise of New Left social movements in the sixties in the United States saw a number of artists, such as Carl Andre and Robert Morris, actively conjugating work—as in art—with work, with labor-power for sale on a market.[36] These artists attempted to present the labor-capital dynamic as one in which the worker (or manager) had agency. Andre and Morris both offer a model of the artist as characterized by creative capacity, a capability itself based on a model of the subject possessed of free self-determination. Here, the artist can identify with the worker at will and electively move from the subject position of the artist to the worker and back again in a kind of free choice unconstrained by structure, history, process, or, above all, the market's categorization of persons on the basis of purported skill. Questions of identity and appropriation aside, this contradiction, or naive theater of identity, occurred at the very same moment that on the one hand theorists of culture production were questioning the category of authorship while on the other hand, theorists of labor informed by New Left inquiries into class consciousness began to posit the intellectual worker, the student or artist, as possible agents of historical change at the very moment that labor itself was losing political power. The politicization of artistic labor happened at the very moment that labor itself was undergoing seismic shifts brought about by outsourcing such that the artist was bound to identify with a vanishing subject position, literally and figuratively. Robert Morris, for instance, stated that "matter as matter rather than as symbol is a conscious political position I think, essentially Marxist."[37] Labor was being relocated in much cheaper labor pools in the Global South, from precisely those geopolitical sites from which labor might be sourced at a lower cost to capital in the interest of higher profits, precipitating the crises that in turn contributed to the immigration patterns resulting in the surplus pools available to Sierra in 2006.

Turning from the Minimalist's nostalgia for a homegrown surplus-value productive era fueled by the heroic American worker who, in turn, was offered not only a living wage but also a benefits package allowing for the daily replication of himself and that of a family, Sierra highlights the regimes of visibility and invisibility that describe precisely the historical turn to global labor pools enabling under- and unremunerated work at risk to the bearer of labor-power himself. While this turn might be generalized to situate a genre as much as an individual practice, given that "post-object art forms such as performance forecast a shift to self-performance as the evaluative prism for all labor," as Vishmidt notes, Sierra's conjugation of the current conditions of labor-power on the market under a "neoliberal" international-statist order inscribes a globalized labor market as part of the very condition for the possibility of an international art world in the twenty-first century.[38] This entwinement, a co-determination described more accurately by social reproduction theory than intersectionality, reveals the way in which each of the terms *class*, *race*, and *gender* hover in one another's blind spots, a triangulation susceptible to questions of primacy and hierarchy when in fact the terms are co-constitutive within social abstraction.

While Sierra surely emphasizes the role of race and ethnicity in a globalized order, the specificity of identity is not at stake. Instead, generalized racialization constitutive of global capital makes itself visible by the yellow highlighting to demonstrate the degree to which identity as such comes to be irrelevant to a racialized neoliberal capitalist order other than as a marker of categories separated only by the question of who can be left to die and whose lives are valuable enough to be permitted, a form of distribution answering only to the instrumental question valorization.

Sierra's gestures recognize labor as a matrix, a system, and a social technology rather than a set of individual actions or recognizable activities. This abstract social matrix produces subjectivity along the axis of disposability and value as much as it produces objects. This does not reduce the artwork to reflective illustration. If the artwork affords a flickering moment of illumination of social synthesis, it nonetheless remains impossible to render transparent in a totally reified social field in which vision itself becomes part of an equally abstracted second nature.

Conclusion

The previous seven chapters have been preoccupied with the gap between ontology—the historically contingent point of entry into which one is born—and reification under the capitalist mode of production and how the management of this gap produces subjects for on-time supply chains in the ceaseless self-replication of capital while art practices index and resist these forms of management. Refusing the primary division between intellectual and manual labor, a binary as determinative to the subject of value as gender has traditionally been, artists explore that interval both in order to pause on historical passage and transition and to suggest counter modes and transformations.[1] That purposively purposeless pause is the work of art. This, from what I have gathered from studying the history of twentieth-century abstraction across geopolitical terrain and historical moments, occurs in practices that first acknowledge their own foundational condition: they are cut from the fabric they critique and in which they are structurally implicated but on which they offer a moment of reflection only insofar as they seek to dismantle that primary reification. At their best, they offer a user's guide to forms of possible de-reified life. As the artist collective Claire Fontaine puts it in acknowledgment of this shared condition, we are all "readymade artists."[2] This is to say that the subject is subject to and of a mode of production and its concomitant social metabolic that forecloses self-transparency and creativity in any organic sense.

This book's exploration of concrete abstraction began with Seurat's *The Models* (1888) and set the painting into a provisional analogy to Marclay's *The Clock* (2010). I suggested that Seurat takes up a similar problem set more than a century earlier and in the medium of painting. I have argued that the question of aesthetic mediation, from medium to content, is a function of a more primary mediation, that of value, within the capitalist mode of production and circulation. This is not to discount historical context and attendant specificity; on the contrary, the analogy accounts for each artist's negotiation with a dominant economy and its particular quality and acceleration in the moment in which each artist found themselves working. I might have made a similar claim by turning from art practice to the discourses of art and culture in the twentieth century. Here, Clement Greenberg's writing, from "Avant-Garde and Kitsch" (1937) to "Modernist Painting" (1960), might be set into conversation with Marshall McLuhan's *Mechanical Bride*. The latter was published at a midway point between Greenberg's two most-cited essays, the first of which associated kitsch, or watered-down and *passéiste* culture, with state and market ideology against which art as an exercise in self-reflexive praxis stood firm as the first soldiers in battle, while "Modernist Painting" purports indifference to politics or ideology, replacing any preoccupation with what transpires outside the frame with exclusively that which not only remains within the frame but engages the frame itself, into a reflexive infinity, as with Frank Stella's *Black Paintings* series.[3] This latter essay is where the cliché of Greenbergian formalism comes from.

But I will leave that classical dialectic of culture and ideology to other scholars of midcentury, from Greenberg to McLuhan through Adorno and the Frankfurt School. My interest has been, rather, in the ways artists navigate and chart the as yet unformulated, as yet unrecognized real movement of history. This generous charting is articulated in their internalization of not only the thematic of labor, living and dead as congealed in the products that accelerate labor, such as machines, but above all in how the artwork engages technology, iterability, and the expanding circuits developed by capital to generate and heighten new ways to mediate that movement in subjective expression: the grapheme, the diagram, the Young-Girl, the "living paintbrush," the ready-made artist, performance, and delegated performances, all of which confront coercive and exploitive remuneration. These nodal moments take capitalist value extraction via labor-time, and the technologies enabled by the socially organized form of harvesting labor in an indifferent transactional space, as the matrix for the possibility of art. Each takes a set of external constraints and internalizes them into the fabric and operative capacity of the work itself at the level of the support. The dialectical relationship between technology and the discourse of the medium, itself an expression of the dialectical relationship between the internal dynamics of capitalist historicity and its culture industry that has run like an undercurrent throughout this book on real and aesthetic abstraction, might be a topic for someone else's book. This book has been a history of our present, the future of the avant-garde futurists, in which we have learned to be indifferently modern.[4]

I find myself tracing the prequel to McLuhan's or indeed any media theorist's understanding of the entwinement of technology and culture in art itself. What could we call the mutually constitutive relationship between that to which McLuhan's midcentury *Mechanical Bride* refers and that which Marcel Duchamp's *The Bride Stripped Bare by Her Bachelors, Even* indicates decades previous? We might imagine Duchamp's *Large Glass* as an uncanny prefiguration of the age of the internet and the modes of socialization it has enabled, with the bachelors grinding away in one visual register, the bride waiting to evanesce in her dialogue box; all etched into a medium meant to afford transparency, the very transparency summoned in classical painting and utterly foreclosed in Duchamp's delivery of the actual thing—glass. Both registers of the glass, or each area or even dialogue box, are occupied with forms that suggest mechanical part objects, as though Francis Picabia's *Jeune Fille* had "grown" up in capitalist-time, for example, updated, to be trapped forever in a glass encasing, resembling an iPhone avant la lettre. In any case, twentieth-century cultural production elaborates itself in the broad shadow of the Duchampian ready-made and its twin, Picabia's *Mechanomorph*, having but taken one step forward in considering not only the new object ontology of capitalism but indeed the new subject forged of it. That search to demarcate what might constitute a subject with agency and self-determination in a capitalist society, much less a *creative* capacity, runs the course of twentieth-century art and into that of the twenty-first.

To conclude, I will look at two instances of contemporary art, from most to least recent, that de-reify both the art object and the subject implicit in it to arrive at the horizon dialectically indicated in the eponymous passage on universal prostitution in Marx's *Economic and Philosophic Manuscripts of 1844*. I've chosen these works for how they accomplish what Anita Chari has attributed to some contemporary works of art: the capacity to de-reify the "meaning of life" insofar as life itself has come to be calcified through the commodity form that quietly and abstractly works its authority at every material level of life.[5] At times, the artwork can accomplish this delivery of perceptual illumination by aesthetically dismantling the nature of value in the social field from a materialist perspective. The artwork does this by setting into motion a series of suggestions at the level of perception that guide the viewer into ways of perceptually de-reifying the plural and myriad aspects of everyday life that appear as fragmentary and often random, or indeed oppressive and beset by scarcity.

While a market-mediated totality presents itself as atomized and as characterized by fragmentation, difference, particularity, and random order, everywhere overmanaged by forms of governmentality, the aesthetic experience affords a fleeting moment to catch a glimpse of the metabolic by which a second nature is formed, suggesting thereby a way to disassemble that second nature. As art, it does so in a way that insinuates probing the coordinates of an unconscious totality—unconscious because, as I hope to have shown, it happens "behind the back" or outside the perceptual and cognitive parameters of individual and collective consciousness.

At an exhibit at the Art Gallery at York University in April 2022, a work by Hannah Black titled *The Meaning of Life* compelled viewers to reflect on one of the most comprehensive, substantial, and overwhelming themes available to art: life's *meaning*. From the outset, the title already suggested a problem of consistency, scale, and conceptual integrity. It summoned the possibility of circumnavigating an incalculable qualitative value—meaning as such, and for life, no less—the merest conceptualization of which already demanded a notion of *totality* or a term that might serve as a synonym, given the degree to which totality as such has come to be banished from contemporary language due to its seeming affinity with totalitarianism. In other words, the title initiated a real conundrum at the level of conceptualization, one that begged the question of how this already problematic and impossible-to-figure notion—life and its meaning—might possibly be organized and delivered to apperception. It was as though the artist were arranging for an experience of impossibility verging on a cruel joke. For how might one circumscribe a question so extensive and significant yet impossible to locate without an exceptional framework at once capacious yet precise enough to broach the topic without making of it just another commercially oriented sound bite?

And aside from the problem of coherence, how might a notion as ambitious as life be addressed through an aesthetic proposition? Black's compositional approach to the thematic of life and its meaning indicates the degree to which the work of art, or at least this work that in its exemplary stance nonetheless suggests much for the capacity of *any* artwork, is uniquely poised to address an otherwise impossible totality precisely because of its inherent reflexivity and antagonism to fixed denotative referentiality. As such, it has the provisional if contingent capacity to point to that which is otherwise unknowable and certainly unformalizable.

The viewer enters the Art Gallery at York University to face an installation consisting of a large plywood wall cratered by meticulously contoured laser-cut holes. Disorientingly, the holes *depict* the particular way that glass shatters. Material and shape are perceptually and sensorially disjointed. One material (wood) mimics another (glass) in an estranging and provocative way. Black seems to be riffing on and outspeeding Picasso's optical and conceptual way of querying the boundary between real and depicted space. Peering through these purposive artful ruptures that depict shatter, however materially estranged, offers a view onto a wall on which a video of faces and voices appears. These aural expressions describe by way of fragmentary impressions the experience of rioting and looting in New York City throughout the summer of 2020 in the aftermath of the police killing of George Floyd on May 25 of that year. Police had confronted Floyd for a minor theft. The way the incident unfolded in casual brutality, which entailed a police officer bearing down with his knee on Floyd's neck until he died, revealed not only the racialization of police violence but the underlying way that racialized life is structured by forms of property, and all the more so in an economic regime in which racialized subjects are so often barred from the ownership of property.[6]

Black's holes echo the circumscribed negative space of Picabia's Young-Girl, as though to recall an entire economic and social totality elaborated around the value-productive commodity labor-power that cancels the putative social subjectivity of the labor bearer, effectively generative of a commodity in the place where the subject once stood.

In this case, too, visual access to worker-protester subjects is barred. Instead of seeing them, we now hear their voices issue from the medium of video. By contrast to the presence wrought by the audio, in the field of vision afforded by the video projection on the far side of the wooden panel, the faces from which voices issue are visually redacted. The faces are covered by an oval shape composed of depicted wood grain, the same kind of wood through which we have visual access to the video but now represented by a projection. In other words, just as wood represents glass on the material entry to the video, a projection represents wood on the projected surface. This strategy cannot help but summon the depicted wood grain of Picasso's Cubist collage, not least for how the layers of depicted material at once rhyme with and undermine the integrity of one another, generating a kind of perceptual indeterminacy that both estranges and beckons the viewer. In other words, the use of this kind of wood grain evokes the way in which art had long held presence and absence in tension, heightening both: Cubist collage's use of artificial manufactured wood grain to raise questions about the free play of the signifier, a doubling and plurality of meaning set into dialectical relation with questions of reification at the level of the structure of the interface. Collage in 1912 and video in 2022—both query the very foundations of signification, the signifier and its burden of *meaning*, but now set into relation with the problem of a racialized capitalist social field.

A similar effect of estrangement coupled with suture qualifies this politicized project; the faces are both presented and withheld. An oval-shaped faux wood grain patch covering the particular face nonetheless paradoxically presents *the* face as such, as any and every face, rendered generic by the shape. In this context, anonymity and universality almost converge in the kind of aporetic tension characteristic of the Cubist signifier. And yet, pulling and pushing against this reconstituted feeling of fugitive universality, the grain of the voice becomes all the more singular through *this* act of redaction, frustrating the viewer's access to conclusion or closure. This is to say that the audio pushes back on this strange facelessness by reintroducing the irreducible materiality and grain of the voice, a plenitude overwriting a seeming lack. Already, then, singularity and universality understood as a generic form (the oval standing in for the human face) are set into a fragile and tense relationship of co-determinacy and separation.

There's a pragmatic, and socially contingent, reason for redacting the faces. Curator Jennifer Papararo, in conversation with the artist, arrived at this particular solution to protectively cover the speakers' faces in keeping with the formal, material play mobilized by the work's atonal orchestra of material signifiers. The faces of the speakers are protected from identification, a solution that may drop off in future iterations of the piece after the statute of limitations on possible arrests has expired. However, at the level of the viewer's experience in the space of the gallery, the shielding device echoes the structural framework of the installation. It redoubles the wood panel or wall through which the image and sounds of the rioters and looters become audible and visible. A kind of flickering effect between figure and ground, absence and presence, denotation and connotation results, as well as a gradation of materials and related signifiers (the depicted wood, the real wood; the depicted shattered glass, the real "hole" in the image), generating a kind of dynamism that defamiliarizes the given, only to all the more lucidly suggest something about the nature of representability itself, including the representability of individuals in relation to the collective in a social regime that values things over people. This condition is dramatized by the oval shape as stand-in for anthros as such. The oval as a kind of generic shape to designate the human face *in general* also redoubles in the interview format afforded by video. We instinctually suture the voices to the visual component of habituated cultural vision in which torsos oriented to the frame have become typical of the interview format. This format, needless to say, asks questions about the very structure of anthros, of what and how we situate one another as speaking subjects and agents of experience.

As the voices share their exhilaration and collective trust, the viewer's sense of social risk as a manifestation of dreadful and rare courage in the face of danger begins to coalesce. The speakers are after all now shielded, but this merely heightens through negation their exposure to the violence of the state apparatus during the protests that resulted from a demand for justice as well as a demand for the *value of life*. On audio, voices relay the sensation of moving through streets together in the darkness to reclaim the commodity form and to redistribute it as a form of self-procured reparations for living in the plantation-prison-industrial complex. The material effect of these voices in the context of the gallery space and its commodity analysis of racialization is to reconnect the invisible objective abstractions that undergird "life" in its reticulation through value circulation compelled by abstractions, to a situated subjective experience in a framework that offers the viewer a chance to find those relationships in a perceptually dynamic space.

Through this process of perceptual negotiation, one recognizes a wider horizon of social relations as structured by constraints, specifically racialized capitalism, within which speech becomes both a risk and a necessity. This perceptually dawning awareness becomes more explicit when the speakers' language begins to condense around a recursive theme: the collective riot and its turn to looting. We, the viewer, come to understand that the events described take their place in the *worldwide* summer 2020 riots in the aftermath of the death of a Black man, George Floyd, at the hands of Minneapolis police. And this, too, is understood as both uniquely specific and dreadfully generic. Racialized bodies are deemed by capital to be dispensable unless pressed into the service of value production, as evidenced by the argument that the American prison-industrial complex is a continuation of the plantation system and that this underlying economic totality informs the legal, juridical, institutional, and ideological infrastructure of civil democratic *life*, a word on which the art plays.[7]

Other facets of the exhibition begin to present themselves in a similar dynamic, through the *play* of multiple material signs that coalesce as anything but play, or rather the forms of play inherent in risk. They begin to suggest the reality of the social field obfuscated by daily appearances. This "free play" accumulates to articulate the uneven value of the human in the social field in and against the sacrosanctity of the commodity. The commodity is of course *dead* labor, anonymous, socially necessary labor-time in a metabolic made possible by racialization, the place where living labor is congealed. The piece resituates this fact as the dissonant origin of a contemporary social matrix across borders. And yet the speakers sound *so alive*. They describe the sheer joy of feeling alive, indeed of coming to feel alive in the specific moment of protesting law insofar as law protects property over people. It becomes clear that insofar as law protects dead labor over living agents, smashing the law makes one feel really alive. By turns staccato and fluid, the voices convey their experience of gleaning inventory from shop displays. Relating the protests-turned-rioting-and-looting, one of the voices says: "I think you can tap into people's joy . . . tap into people's trust that are kind of revealed in those moments." What is striking is the way these voices express a spontaneous and simultaneous collectivity forged only in a moment of exceptional defiance and struggle. These subjective inscriptions are offered as fragmentary expressions of events—the riot—in resistance to circumstances that themselves offer rare perspectives into social facts. The police murder of a Black man is itself an event that dramatizes the uneven value of human life before the law forged in relation to the market and to labor-power, a body historically racialized as a source of value but not one to be remunerated or understood to have access, much less right to the social share it disproportionately enriches. Here, dispossession and marginalization are understood dialectically.

Over the course of the moments spent immersed in the multimedia ensemble that aggregates in the exhibition, despite the vitality of voices and experiences, this quality of effervescent life is at the mercy of much more highly valued forms of property, which are in turn unevenly accessible to that "life." The necropolitical aspect of the situation begins to surface with greater acuity through steps in the installation. We, the viewers, turn away from the video framed by the wood panel, only to see a shelf heaving under stacks of white T-shirts. These, in various sizes, are on offer for free.

This tactical modality of the display encourages the viewer to go ahead and take the object on the shelf. Here, the gift is posited in dialectical relation to the looted object. We are jolted into a recognition of the pivotal and arbitrary difference between the two categories of object, gifted and stolen thing, both of which in the last instance originate in labor-time, or dead labor "congealed," as Marx says, in the commodity. While this gesture of the gift, "the free giveaway," recalls Félix González-Torres's Marxian and Fanonian tactics of placing heaps of candy in the institution, it complicates that gesture by placing it into relation with the danger resulting in looting as a form of protest. The gift and theft become two sides of a relation to the object separated only by the contingency of the momentary situation. The artwork invites the viewer to perform, in a "safe space," a version of what the video interviewees relay—to take something in which the labor-time of unknown others is collected. The gesture thereby turns looting—understood as an offense to hegemonic ethics and to the labor-time inscribed in the looted object as well as the livelihoods dependent on setting it into circulation—inside out by revealing the extent to which both entail a more fundamental theft overlooked as structurally normative: that is, labor-time, the time of life as such.

That the distinction between theft and gift should be the arbitrary declaration of the institution becomes germane. Black's work qualifies both gestures—theft and gift—by setting into motion a dialectics of the gift in relation to theft as a function of the institution as an ideological state apparatus that tacitly sets race and class into categorical hierarchy under the contradictory claim of free democratic equity and citizenship. In other words, the gesture of Black's work activates the claims of the institution as a *truly* inclusive and equitable space by taking it at its word against its own historically enacted dependence on racialization and capital. "Go ahead, take the object; we are in the free space of play in which law is suspended. This is art."

The gesture also suggests that history is obfuscated by dividing and reifying racial identity and class into separate categories: white/black; gift/theft. The result is a stunning confrontation with how life as such is measured in relation to the object, the commodity. It was as though subjectivity could be mapped by race in relation to objects along the axis of gift and theft: the gift as property of the bourgeois public sphere overwriting the actual source of value, a thing sublimating social relations, and theft as a function of the street and its desublimatory brutality. But more fundamentally, the distinction is shown to be an at once petty and obscene measure of human experience in relation to commodity value insofar as this logic of value cannot be ultimately beneficial to *any* subject position (gift recipient or thief). The value-form is ultimately indifferent to human life. The social stereotypes invoked and negated by Black's gesture deliver an object lesson in the arbitrary distinctions enforced by the law and inscribed so deeply into history as to seem almost natural. As we as viewers are invited to take a shirt, we are set into relation to the looters who *risked their individual lives to take the very things in which their collective life as labor-time was already inscribed.*

Objects on offer against the aural backdrop of voices describing looting in joyous terms is a jolting reminder that the object becomes a gift in the space of the gallery only to the extent that it, as a commodity, is always already the scene of the crime insofar as profits rest on theft from the worker-subject. This is not to say that the gesture is guilt-ridden. On the contrary. The momentary pleasure in taking the T-shirt might be placed in relation to the joy of looting itself given the formality of the gallery space. This last indeterminacy among several ambiguities only makes Black's analysis more nuanced and more thrilling.

Ultimately, the centrality of the commodity object split between gift and theft is a vehicle for the question of the subject under capital. And that subject is captured in the object. Value extracted from un- or underremunerated labor-time is aggregated in objects that the worker, having produced, must purchase for self-reproduction, thereby entering twice over into a situation of subjection to the social domination that the object expresses. The object, insofar as it is defamiliarized and dismantled in the framework of noninstrumental provisional autonomy as art, frames a new cycle of a daily self-replication in which the subject becomes inscribed by a second order of social necessity, not labor-time strictly speaking but socially necessary self-replication nonetheless. This cycle, exacerbated also by racialization, operates unconsciously, outside any epistemologically accessible space—again, what Sohn-Rethel locates as "behind the backs of men."

The situated subject that Black's work evokes stands in the position of one who might decide, in the context of a simultaneous mass uprising in demand for social justice, to take back the dead labor in which the historicity of her subject position is inscribed. This primary inscription of racialized labor into dead labor is doubly violent insofar as the worker-subjects must pay for the commodity in which their under- or unremunerated labor is stored. This is to say that the work makes clear that, beneath the apparent theft of looting, the subjects have already been on the receiving end in a double theft that structures their subject position. For they must pay doubly: once through the expenditure of underremunerated labor-time and again in the risky activity of claiming or "taking."

The Meaning of Life thereby precipitates, in a kind of epiphanic jolt, the realization of the social reality of the commodity as conduit of value predicated on the *double* capture of social time as lived experience made abstract by the estranged anonymity of value-time and qualified only through lines of racialization. It teases out the recognition that waged labor finds its origins in stolen time, which redoubles in consumption in a hidden structural form. The racialized violence of value's cycle of production suddenly becomes clear as the greatest threat to "the meaning of life" as lived experience of individual and social solidarity and sovereignty. As Black's work summons discursive horizon after discursive horizon—biopolitical, economic, et cetera—the questions of racialization and the centuries of unpaid dead labor subtending the historicity of capital, inscribed in the commodity, loom large and weigh heavy as that which both determine and motivate, dialectically, collective gestures in the here and now.

Next in the labile unfolding of insights precipitated by the arterial operations of the exhibit, a flag hangs on the wall facing the video installation. Its upper left corner, where the crest would usually be, is cut out, with the hole echoing the wooden circle protecting the speakers. Once again, as with the depicted cracks of the installation and redacted faces of the video, this circular cavity might recall Picabia's paradigmatic Young-Girl expressed as negative space. Black again mobilizes a flicker effect through formal rhymes and devices, reminding us that this is one of the ways in which representations—above all of value itself—come to eclipse human life, which, dialectically, has no other way of articulating its continued existence, much less its relevance vis-à-vis value, than by smashing the commodity form.

On this flag hanging behind the T-shirts, the year, serial number, patent number, and other related data associated with the brand Chanel and its well-recognized attendant logo are projected onto the cut-out hole where the crest or logo would commonly be. Here, the insignia related to political identities and nationalities is replaced with corporate metadata. The famous Chanel logo is *represented* by its legal code because it is illegal to reproduce the iconic double-C logo. Technically speaking, this gesture might itself be misunderstood as a form of theft, for using this logo may or may not be a breach of copyright law. The work at once summons and cancels that concern by withholding the logo itself; the viewer understands that they are seeing only the data associated with the brand, given that serial and registration numbers, dates, and other abstract information, which begin to add up, stand in for the Chanel logo. The copyrighted 1925 trademark, in particular, demarcates the brand. Summoning the logo in this circuitous, because legal, way denaturalizes a piece of information fully assimilated into cultural consciousness, namely, the ubiquitous logic of property signaled by the corporate symbol.

On another level, the way that both artwork and curated exhibit maneuver around the law, be it the statute of limitations on protesters' rights or the avoidance of copyright litigation, performs a way into the dialectics of property and theft structuring the event of Floyd's murder and the protests of it. The performance of these social problems through formal play provides a key insight into how the work *as an artwork* can uniquely probe totality. It presents this totality as a matrix of social formations structured by state and market that racialize and criminalize some subject positions over others. Black's work does this for the way that signifiers set into motion by the artwork collect and settle in contingent ways.

Black's work draws these objective, empirical, and admittedly Marxist analytical concerns through elemental components shown to be the matrix of subjectivity and collectivity. That matrix is constitutive of a naturalized hostage-like situation in which life as such finds itself in a historically developed, yet by now ontologically naturalized, situation. *The Meaning of Life* makes no claim to either universalism or the particularism of identity. By contrast, the work reveals both universalism and particularism (of identity) to be subsumed into a set of social processes that configure the value of human life unevenly insofar as the value-form, represented by both money and the commodity as its mediums, are already both the results and causes of racialization and capital accumulation as twin operations, as mutually constitutive at the core of both race and capital, however much those two terms have been naturalized as discrete entities.

While Black picks up the problem of the commodity fetish once again, it is now set into relation to an everyday life revealed to be the product of racialized capital, and thereby also to activism and social struggle. And yet, far from defeatist and much less nihilist, *The Meaning of Life* delivers the joyful suggestion that life in all its vital complexity might be located in the interstices of the capitalist value-form by which it is organized and contained.

Media theorist Bernard Stiegler notes that what makes "culture" an industry—transforming it from a site of collective expressive praxis into so much static and dead labor, produced only to drive profits—is simply a certain relation to the clock, to *time*. In other words, he shifts causality from the ideology of profit to a description of experience, a phenomenology of making and of praxis. In *For a New Critique of Political Economy*, Stiegler tries to describe the peculiar modality of consciousness of the so-called creative worker in the creative culture sector, the industry that Theodor Adorno and Max Horkheimer called the *culture industry*: "The 'intermittents' (the occasional workers in theatre, film and television) ceaselessly oscillate between on the one hand the calculable employment of their noetic knowledge, this knowledge then being remunerated, that is, *traded* [*négocié*], and on the other hand the actual development of this knowledge. And it is this noeticity that the destruction of intermittence (of the 'intermittents') then eliminates and proletarianizes, that is, deskills and instrumentalizes—in order to profit the culture industries."[8]

The temporal gap, unfolding in the process of negotiating the formal demands of "the job" and the content that is to be delivered, becomes a kind of "site" of reification or negation of the living that motivates content: creativity, inspiration, and so on. Stiegler is taking a stab at describing the role of "culture" in a social field where production and consumption are co-determining, where needs are manufactured in the interest of accelerated profit maximization and management. In the era of the accelerated temporality of the algorithm, which is to say now more than ever, production and consumption are each the precondition for the other, each diminishing any interstice where that perhaps mythological and ideated purposive purposelessness of autonomous art (Kant) could take hold and in which art as something emancipated from the calculus of narrow self-interest might happen. These interstices have also been manufactured for a desired effect, which we might call the culture-effect or desired-interval-of-exception-effect: "Within the associated sociotechnical milieu, the functional opposition between production and consumption has become obsolete, and externalities must be economically *cultivated* and valorized, even though, like values, they cannot be reduced to the calculability of the economic indicators of a market economy: they require a new conception of economic value, and of its *measurement*, such that it is not reducible to *calculation*."[9]

Stiegler is expanding "value" to mean something other than the value-form (money), the symbolic measure of socially necessary labor-time. But this other, irreducible value can only be negatively indicated in the form of the language of value. It is because of the totalizing conditions of calculation and metricization of everyday life that any exception to it can only be indicated in terms of negation, or "neganthopy." It is notable that Stiegler turns to the culture sector as the locus for this observation about capitalist totality as such.

Arriving full circle to an artist with whose writing this book began, with Hito Steyerl's precise, dialectical exploration of the relationship among the production of an artwork, the historically specific conditions of labor, and the question of mediation—or rather, double mediation, first by capital and then by the technological support through which the work is presented and distributed—I will close with one of her works from 2007, titled *Lovely Andrea* (figure C.1). Commissioned by Documenta 12, at a length of twenty-eight

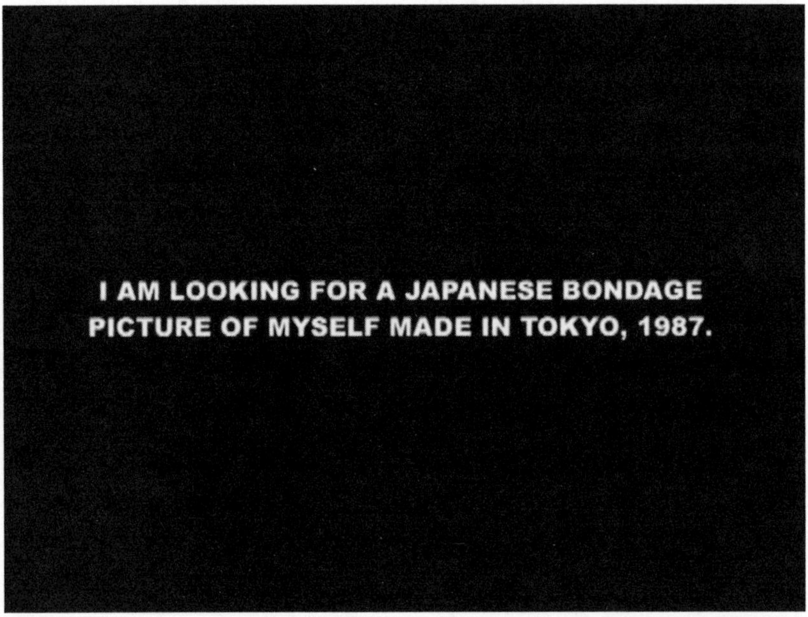

Fig. C.1. Hito Steyerl, *Lovely Andrea*, 2007. © Hito Steyerl / VG Bild-Kunst, Bonn / CARCC, Ottawa, 2024.

minutes, the video addresses traditional cultural practices transformed in modernity into anonymous disciplinary labor, ratcheted up to an art form. The plot follows the artist as she returns to Japan in 2007, twenty years after having posed as a Kinbaku or Japanese BDSM model, to locate the one picture of her that was published. The documentary emphasizes the challenge of this mission, as "not millions but billions" of images in the genre, often produced under state censorship and other social prohibitions that prevented any accurate records, make locating the picture seemingly impossible. And yet she does locate it, in a stroke of sheer "luck," as the Kinbaku model who is accompanying her says. The improbability of recognizing any one individual among the accumulated morass of production becomes one of the work's central concerns. At one point, prior to finding the picture of herself, she momentarily misrecognizes herself in another's image, only to be advised that it cannot be her as her work was unlikely to be quite so "extreme." Once she finally locates the image of herself among the millions just like it, the photographer who initially took the picture tells Steyerl that he cannot recognize her. He repeats that she has changed and that he could not possibly recall working with her from seeing her in the present. In sum, Steyerl's search for her own image offers an allegory of a self-estranged worker whose work dedifferentiates fetish-oriented eroticism from a totally administrative order, one that overwrites even her own memory and experience as much as that of others involved in its production. Her subjectivity does not seem even minimally relevant to the circulation of the image, then or now.

To add to the multiplying obstacles to self-location, the video piece moves to a discussion of its title. In 1987, Steyerl had offered a name for the woman in the picture finally identified as an image of herself: Andrea. "Andrea" is the caption to the erotic photograph of bondage. The title, then, functions as a kind of absent center, a misattributed name that refers instead to an object of the then model's respect and admiration; the viewer is instructed by Steyerl's voice-over that Andrea had been a fighter in the Partiya Karkerên Kurdistanê (PKK, Kurdistan Workers' Party), supporting Kurdish autonomy against the Turkish state, and had been murdered by the state. Her image was placed on flags and held high in public demonstrations throughout Turkey. The stories do not initially relate to one another. The adjacence is at first utterly jarring, irrelevant to the diegetic drive of the documentary. The juxtaposition of Andrea the political agent and "Andrea" the fetishized object forges a consummate dialectical image. "Andrea" and Andrea: submissive and activist; bondage model and political agent at the limit of self-preservation.

Evoking the PKK in this context raises another undercurrent, related to the documentary's exploration of the consumption of reified erotic practices objectified in glossy magazines. Initiated in 1972 in the aftermath of the state-enforced dissolution of the Turkish Marxist Leninist Party, the PKK organized not only on behalf of the autonomy of Kurdish peoples across Syrian and Turkish state lines but also to elaborate a critical feminist autonomist component. That this movement should generate one of the very few ultraleftist autonomist movements within which women participated equally informs the dialectical tension within *Lovely Andrea*.

The moment when Andrea the activist is introduced occurs as a kind of rupture in the erstwhile documentary genre, which obeys a set of constraints oriented toward delivering a sense of facticity.[10] And while the documentary opens with the disciplinary nature of Japanese bondage as a tradition originating in the artistry of war according to the tradition of the samurai, it is only in modernity that this form of warfare and art becomes a kind of popular consumable fetish. A practitioner of a highly disciplined art form is shown from the vantage of the accumulation of images in the entertainment sector of the culture industry, one file among billions of images of anonymous women, as though her mastery of this historical form were deskilled and incidental, desublimated to the point of resembling a banal (sex) crime among many recorded in a police archive and lost to memory.[11] But the film also makes references to forms of bondage in military practices across the globe. It cites the obscene and illegal humiliation of Iraqi prisoners in the US detention center in Guantánamo, among other instances.

But the ultimate momentum of the documentary consists of Steyerl's positing of this militaristic practice as fully domesticated, drawn from epic history to be subsumed into the administratively organized order of has-been fetishes. The work likens this condition of highly disciplined if seemingly deskilled and apparently anonymous labor, intended for the excitement of the fetishist consumer yet destined for the administered archive not unlike any other incidental document, to the weblike features of the rope knotted around the body in bondage. Steyerl need not have been quite so heavy-handed in her presentation of the analogy between administrative, disciplinary, and semiskilled labor and sex work. The work's success hinges on its capacity to demonstrate rather than pontificate, as when the subject of the camera's query, the artist Steyerl, cannot locate her own objectification and is no longer recognized by those who participated in that moment in which her picture suspended in a network of ropes was taken. The disidentification between the artist and lost object in the hoped-for encounter with the outmoded image performs the way the artist occupies the interstice between purposive creative agency and anonymous production, and the extent to which the condition doubles back to make the artist herself a kind of product searching for her own place in the overwhelming accumulation of interchangeable production, a kind of "ready-made" seeking to claim her own labor.

Her search through twenty years of archives, materials categorized by any number of criteria, presents the extent to which emotionally charged erotic labor, at once affective and embodied, becomes just so much data. Living labor calcified as commodity becomes part of the infrastructure, the archive. As such, it summons the question of technology in which so much reified, dead labor is embedded: "Quantification and evaluation become both essential and ordinary operations of collective life. . . . What used to get called private, intimate life, subjectivity, the body and all of living existence are now invested and colonized by capitalistic and state powers to a degree that would have appeared unthinkable and intolerable to previous generations."[12]

Steyerl above all demonstrates the degree to which the quantity enabled by technological reproducibility drains eros from pornography "like water from a sinking ship." I borrow here the structure of a phrase that Walter

Benjamin coined to describe Eugène Atget's photography. Benjamin, who writes that "Atget sucked the aura out of photography like water from a sinking ship," defines "aura" as a strange weave of time and place. Atget's extraordinary quality for Benjamin lies in avowing the qualities of the medium, namely, the fragmentary and indexical nature of photography, which afforded it the chance to jettison the baggage of painting, narrativity, and aura. Those qualities had made it but a high-end commodity for the new-fangled bourgeoisie. What made photography singularly modern was its capacity to trade auratic "presence" with truth to the timely media of capital: photography, film, anything technologically reproducible and available to the masses in the form of "simultaneous collective reception."[13]

On the other hand, Benjamin is here characteristically writing from the perspective of a messianic dialectical materialism even in the face of his advocacy of a mass political aesthetics. He balances on the fence, weighing a democratic gain in dismantling the aristocratic and bourgeois tendencies of art in the interest of a revolutionary mass subject. And even this entails a negative dimension, an undertow involving the loss of the aura, which had at times afforded exceptional experience in a totally instrumentalized set of social relations. Steyerl sucks the sexiness from pornography like water from a sinking ship. In doing so, she might rescue both. And yet this action is merely a symptom of a tendency already in motion in consumer markets where the increasing accumulation of data and wealth is reported to have an inverse effect on any experience of qualitative gratification. Steyerl is lucid, frank, and aware, which brings us closer to understanding capital but no less close to any aspect of sex other than its market saturation. Again, what is laid bare is reification itself, or the gap between experience and reification in which sex is absent.

This kind of dialectic drives *Economic and Philosophic Manuscripts of 1844*, such that each phrase builds dialectically on the previous to arrive at an attempt to describe the totality of labor relations and a path out of the reification of subjectivity by labor.

> Prostitution is only a *specific* expression of the *general* prostitution of the *labourer*, and since it is a relationship in which falls not the prostitute alone, but also the one who prostitutes—and the latter's abomination is still greater—the capitalist, etc., also comes under this head . . . so the entire world of wealth (that is, of man's objective substance) passes from the relationship of exclusive marriage with the owner of private property to a state of universal prostitution with the community. This type of

> communism—since it negates the *personality* of man in every sphere—is but the logical expression of private property, which is this negation. General *envy* constituting itself as a power is the disguise in which *greed* re-establishes itself and satisfies itself, only in *another* way. The thought of every piece of private property as such is *at least* turned against *wealthier* private property in the form of envy and the urge to reduce things to a common level, so that this envy and urge even constitute the essence of competition. Crude communism is only the culmination of this envy and of this leveling-down proceeding from the *preconceived* minimum. It has a *definite, limited* standard. How little this annulment of private property is really an appropriation is in fact proved by the abstract negation of the entire world of culture and civilization, the regression to the *unnatural* simplicity of the *poor* and crude man who has few needs and who has not only failed to go beyond private property, but has not yet even reached it.[14]

The passage is descriptive of a process that has already come to pass. It describes the existing conditions—already by 1844—of immiseration in which persons have been collectivized as general social labor-power, de-differentiated and exchanged on the labor market for a wage that barely compensates for the time spent at labor in contrast to the value to be extracted from that labor. The workers have nothing but their embodied time, calcified in first the commodity-object and ultimately in the entire matrix of the infrastructure enabling accelerated value extraction. The workers stand with nothing but their "skin in the game," facing a totality that is indifferent to their social and experiential existence. This asymmetry is allegorized in Steyerl's disciplined emotional, erotic, and difficult physical work, extracted and abstracted, lodged in a massive archive in which she cannot subjectively locate herself.

But Marx also suggests a utopian reversal of the situation—a negative dialectic—in which he imagines another situation where precisely this de-differentiated social labor that reconstitutes the subject as a function of social abstraction might open onto forms of communism simply because this abstraction draws on heretofore unseen levels of collectivization brought about by the exponentially accelerating reach of social abstraction itself. The only remaining step was to overcome the experience of seeming separation wrought by abstraction in order to seize this actual objective potential. That step remains.

As Adorno notes in a lecture on negative dialectics in November 1965, "The transition that Marx believed was just around the corner, in 1848 or thereabouts, did NOT take place. The qualitative leap that would change the world did not occur. And the proletariat failed to constitute itself as the subject-object of history, as it was supposed to according to Marx's own theory."[15] Rather than conclude that the search for social synthesis *against* the forms of abstract synthesis enforced by the labor market that reify the subject and foreclose collectivity is an obsolete question, he concludes, on the contrary, that "the failure to convert theory into practice" is the very proof that theory is more necessary than ever, in negative dialectical relation to the mistakes of the past and the potential of a meaningfully de-reified and collectivized future. This is the actuality, for Adorno, of philosophy in lived, real time, or what Marx would call the real movement of history. I cannot speak for philosophy. It is my conviction that it is the potential if not the actuality of de-reifying operations that are intrinsic to art.

Returning full circle to where this chapter began, we might reread Hito Steyerl's attention to exchangism and financial transactions as an extended commentary on modernism and the ways that aesthetic abstraction enters into dialectical relation with real abstraction. After all, if Adorno understood the work as mimetically entering the dominant structures of the time in order to dismantle and negate them from within, then this form of inscription would necessarily have to include the dominant dynamic of modernity: social abstraction and an unconscious social synthesis generated of the abstract sale of labor-time.

This brings the question back to everything that abstraction is *not*. For it might be interjected that the discussion so far has failed to take into account the main narrative about aesthetic abstraction as a process of discursive purification, and that all art since 1863 has addressed this dissolution of the plane of representation in order to critically reflect on the conditions of vision, or that the privileged objects issuing from the dissolution of painting, from Donald Judd's objects to the social turn in art, pushed for another kind of transparency, effectively updating Rodchenko for the cybernetic era. A liminal case, for instance Stella's *Black Paintings*, tested the limits of the medium by deducing line from the canvas edge and repeating it en abyme over the surface, thereby pushing surface to structure and exposing the thingness of painting. That act, characterized by words like *pushing*, *testing*, and *extrapolating*—a vocabulary derived from Greenberg's famous essay "Modernist Painting"—is one of exposure. It unveils the excesses of signification (methodological over coding) attributed to a practice, without delivering the results of the research to a particular social or political desire, as Rodchenko had done. It raises the question of what all the dismantling, exposing, and unveiling was—or is—inclined toward or disinclined from. Or perhaps that narrative rests on only one-half of the dialectic between aesthetic and real abstraction. The latter has nonetheless welled up in the repressed social unconscious, which returns again and again across modernism.

NOTES

PREFACE

1. Arrighi, *The Long Twentieth Century*.
2. Bataille, "The Language of Flowers," 11.
3. Bataille, "The Language of Flowers," 14.
4. Elson, "The Value Theory of Labour."
5. Read, *The Double Shift*, 42.

INTRODUCTION 1

1. On the index in relation to modernity, see Lütticken, *Objections*, 71. Sven Lütticken leans on Rosalind Krauss's discussion of the index in "Notes on the Index, Part I" and "Notes on the Index, Part II," in *Originality of the Avant-Garde*, 196–220. Lütticken elaborates the index as a *social* sign "par excellence" insofar as it points to its contingent source and its physical cause, necessarily embedded in the social field. The index bypasses code and offers traces, which in turn point to context. However, in a capitalist social matrix or context mediated by the opacity of the commodity and anonymous labor and by the logic of surplus extraction, the index itself is "broken," as opaque as the commodity form it points to. The "commodity is a broken index" insofar as it is an index of abstract social labor-time. The artwork operates as a secondary highly differentiated mediation of this broken already indexical mediation, offering a pause in which those pieces might be made to cohere for those who can ascertain them.

2. Krauss, *The Optical Unconscious*, 21.

3. Adorno, "Commitment," 86.

4. Greenberg stated that artists since the Impressionists remained attached to the newly proliferating bourgeoisie by "an umbilical cord of gold." Greenberg, "Avant-Garde and Kitsch," 11.

5. I owe the term *aporetic braiding* to Yve-Alain Bois's essay on Mondrian titled "New York City," in *Painting as Model*, 157–86.

6. In *The Optical Unconscious*, which could be taken as one iteration among many of the articulation of the modernist debt to a genealogy in which aesthetics

and politics are dialectically co-constitutive in their immediate separation, Krauss acknowledges her own particular debt to Fredric Jameson's *Political Unconscious*, not least for its Althusserian analysis of ideology and the resonance of that inquiry with her own turn to Jacques Lacan's theory of the unconscious. However, it does not occur to her that a tacit critique of Jameson's method emerges in her work, which will be taken up in the pages of the present book. Krauss, *The Optical Unconscious*, 21.

7. The most commonly cited articulation of the entwinement of historicity and perception is Walter Benjamin's "The Work of Art in the Age of Its Technological Reproducibility."

8. Krauss, *The Optical Unconscious*, 8.

9. For a presentation of the debates among Adorno, Lukács, and others on the entwinement of aesthetics and politics in the twentieth century, see Adorno et al. *Aesthetics and Politics*, 28–59.

10. Greenberg saw the Duchampian ready-made as too nakedly transparent to the market. He understood the ready-made to be mimicking the teleology of the market and its fascination with "the new." See Greenberg, "Necessity of 'Formalism,'" and "Counter-Avant-Garde."

11. Krauss, *The Optical Unconscious*, 2.

12. Denise Ferreira da Silva argues that the historical and temporal nature of the accumulation necessary to modern capitalism is drawn from the extraction of resources, above all coerced human labor-power. The space of commerce, and above all the Middle Passage, is irreducible to political adjudication, and yet it forms social relations everywhere globally through commercial growth. The "expropriative" appropriation of the sale of enslaved labor-power in the form of racialized persons is the very matrix of capitalism. The sea is the space that enables value to be created through enslaved labor-power while at the same time denying the site of work itself, which remains a hidden abode. Da Silva, "Unpayable Debt." See also Mawani, *Across Oceans of Law*. The notion that the sea is the place of commerce while land is the space of the state is developed effectively in Giovanni Arrighi's Marxian account of the historicity of capital accumulation. See Arrighi, *The Long Twentieth Century*.

13. Wynter, "Beyond the Categories of the Master Conception," 81–82.

14. For a sustained elaboration of Lukács's account of reification and of art as a practice of de-reification as much as of reification, see Chari, *A Political Economy of the Senses*.

15. Lütticken, *Objections*, 71. See also note 1.

16. Vishmidt, "What Do We Mean by Autonomy and Reproduction?," 35.

17. Gillick, "Abstract."

18. Toscano, "The Open Secret of Real Abstraction," 282.

19. Toscano, "The Open Secret of Real Abstraction," 282.

20. Toscano, "The Open Secret of Real Abstraction," 281.

21. For an example of his reading of art, see Althusser, "Cremonini, Painter of the Abstract," in *Lenin and Philosophy*, 230.

22. In his careful *The Capitalist Unconscious: Marx and Lacan*, Samo Tomšič argues that Marx's theory of value precedes and informs subsequent understandings of autonomy insofar as they stand in mimicry of the circuit of value production's actual autonomy from social context, its indifference to lived social relations. The autonomy of the signifier within structuralism, which is fundamental to Lacan's theory of the subject, mirrors this economic field: "Marx's analysis of the commodity form and its anticipation of the autonomy of the signifier gives way to a materialist ontology" (199). Here, discursive categories also mirror the separation and recomposition of the commodity form, especially at the level of intellectual production. For Tomšič, however, Sohn-Rethel reduces ontological categories to economic operations and is thus insufficiently dialectical. Tomšič returns to Marx's original theory of the commodity fetish to recover the dialectic constitutive of the reified subject within the codes of both capital and language. Tomšič thus reads the value-form as correlative to the symbolic. Žižek's equally Lacanian reading of the implications of Sohn-Rethel for understanding the unconscious is different. See Žižek, *The Sublime Object of Ideology*, 10–11.

23. Toscano, "The Open Secret of Real Abstraction," 284.

24. Ngai, "Visceral Abstractions."

25. Roberts, "The Commodity, the Readymade and the Value Form," in *The Intangibilities of Form*, 21–47.

26. Mitchell, "The World as Exhibition," 232–33.

27. Lütticken, *Objections*, 157.

28. Heidegger, *The Question Concerning Technology and Other Essays*, 17.

29. Sohn-Rethel, *Intellectual and Manual Labour*, 188. See also Brassier, "Wandering Abstraction"; and Sohn-Rethel, "The Formal Characteristics of Second Nature," recently translated into English by Daniel Spaulding in the inaugural issue of the web journal *Selva* and first published as "Die Formcharaktere der zweiten Nature."

30. Khatib, "'Sensuous Supra-Sensuous,'" 57.

31. Lütticken, *Objections*, 156. See also Lütticken, "Attending to Abstract Things."

32. Sami Khatib, "Marx, Real Abstraction, and the Question of Form," in Khatib et al., *Critique*, 69–92.

33. Marx, "The German Ideology."

34. Marx, "The German Ideology."

35. Marx, *Capital*, 187. Marx emphasizes the necessity of moving from abstractions (material abstractions) forming a totality to the concrete throughout both *Capital* and *Grundrisse*.

36. Marx, *Capital*, 188.

37. See Spaulding, "Value Form and Avant-Garde."

38. See Mansoor, "From Fetish to Totality."

39. Adorno, "The Concept of Intellectual Experience," in *Lectures on Negative Dialectics*, 85.

1. Steyerl, "Her Name Was Esperanza," in *Duty Free Art*, 127.

2. Steyerl, "Her Name Was Esperanza," in *Duty Free Art*, 115–33. Steyerl cites Apter, "IBB=419," 270.

3. Steyerl, "Her Name Was Esperanza," in *Duty Free Art*, 127.

4. Clark, "Olympia's Choice," 79.

5. Foster, "Mimetic," in *Bad New Days*, 63–98.

6. Lütticken, *Objections*, 71.

7. Marx, "Wages of Labor," in *Economic and Philosophic Manuscripts of 1844*.

8. Claire Fontaine, "Readymade Artist and Human Strike," in *Human Strike and the Art of Creating Freedom*, 32–49.

9. Vishmidt, *Speculation as a Mode of Production*.

10. Clark, "Olympia's Choice," 79.

11. Claire Fontaine, "Existential Metonymy and Real Abstractions," in *Human Strike and the Art of Creating Freedom*, 194; Sohn-Rethel, *Intellectual and Manual Labour*, 39.

12. Claire Fontaine, "Existential Metonymy and Real Abstractions," in *Human Strike and the Art of Creating Freedom*, 194.

13. Claire Fontaine, "Existential Metonymy and Real Abstractions," in *Human Strike and the Art of Creating Freedom*, 198.

14. Claire Fontaine, "Existential Metonymy and Real Abstractions," in *Human Strike and the Art of Creating Freedom*, 199.

15. Khatib, "'Sensuous Supra-Sensuous.'"

16. Clark, "Olympia's Choice."

17. For a definitive account of feminist art practices that address prostitution, see Wilson, *Art Labor, Sex Politics*.

18. Fraser's three entries—texts from 1985, 1992, and 2005—are available in Alberro and Stimpson, *Institutional Critique*.

19. Baker, *The Artwork Caught by the Tail*, 11. George Baker notes that he is "paraphrasing Rosalind Krauss in a different domain" when he calls the readymade *the* theoretical object of the avant-garde.

20. Greenberg, "Avant-Garde and Kitsch."

21. Marx, "Private Property and Communism," in *Economic and Philosophic Manuscripts of 1844*.

22. Marx, *Capital*, 272.

23. Marx, *Capital*, 271.

24. Marx, *Capital*, 277, 280. "The use-value which [the owner of money] gets in exchange manifests itself only in the actual utilization, in the process of consumption of labour-power" (279).

25. Marx, *Capital*, 197.

26. The way I use the term *abstraction* in this book takes on a tension latent in the Marxian usage of it. To what extent is aesthetic abstraction simply the most concrete, which is to say "realistic," way of articulating the social relations that reproduce the "abstract" processes of both value in the act of exchange and

the abstraction brought to bear by the commodity form? The problem of "real abstraction" runs through the work of any number of twentieth-century Marxists across the geopolitical spectrum, including Sohn-Rethel and Althusser. For an overview, see Toscano, "The Open Secret of Real Abstraction."

27. Lazzarato, *Experimental Politics.*

28. Postone, *Time, Labor, and Social Domination.*

29. Ngai, "Visceral Abstractions," 191–94. Through a reading of Rob Halpern's volume of poetry, *Music for Porn*, Sianne Ngai arrives at an analysis similar to what I have done of Steyerl in the present introduction—namely, that the work addresses the calcification of dead labor saturated in infrastructure yet articulated circuitously through the entanglement of promissory emotional and sexual fulfillment and the question of value. Ngai, borrowing Halpern's own language, refers to this entanglement as a "hieroglyph of value" (191). Halpern's use of catachresis to describe the abstract allegorical work of the soldier's body in *Music for Porn* helps clarify Marx's stake in his own use of catachresis to describe "value forming substance" in the value-form (192).

30. Palumbo-Mosca, "The Woman Who Painted Her Body for Artist Yves Klein" (BBC interview).

31. Irigaray, "Women on the Market," in *This Sex Which Is Not One.*

32. Gonzalez, "The Gendered Circuit."

CHAPTER ONE. GEORGES SEURAT'S MUSES, ABSTRACTED

1. For a discussion of the way in which Seurat's pointillist "dot" forged a dialogic response to and critique of the Impressionists' purportedly spontaneous paint mark in favor of a systematic, programmatic, and replicable mark or "grapheme," see Foa, *Georges Seurat*; Crary, *Suspensions of Perception*. For the most recent scholarship on Seurat's extraordinary process and the conditions of its emergence in relation to a broad spectrum of "new media" and forms of technological reproducibility specific to the mid- to late nineteenth century, see Armstrong, "Seurat's Media."

2. From Meyer Schapiro to Linda Nochlin, Norma Broude, Jonathan Crary, Eric Alliez, Carol Armstrong, and, most recently, Michelle Foa, the question of the seeming mechanistic of Seurat's "dot" has been raised only to be dismissed as reductive. However, Broude and Armstrong have located the specific print media with which Seurat seems to have been operating in tandem. See Broude, "New Light on Seurat's 'Dot.'" For Nochlin, Seurat's paintings operate allegorically, although she focuses more on the narrative depicted than on the picture's singular composition. In "Seurat's *La Grande Jatte*," Nochlin argues that modernity's promises are at once invested and negated. Seurat offers only a mosaic of boredom, of joyless leisure and torpidity, which inscribes the modern condition of anomie and alienation. For Nochlin, Seurat's work might offer an alternative to Paul Cézanne's regarding the origin of modernist painting, insofar as Seurat is resolutely reflexively located in history (e.g., time-bound signifiers,

fashion) rather than the phenomenology of perception. Seurat achieves this critique through the progressive promise of technological invention, the mechanical reiteration of the functional dot. While Félix Fénéon, who most definitively self-identified as an anarchist, supported Seurat, he was noted as having suggested that Seurat's replicable marks were monotonous and mechanical. For Nochlin, the uniformity of *La Grande Jatte*, otherwise known as *A Sunday on La Grande Jatte*, makes the slightest difference salient. As such, it articulates the way that painters, in their bid to remain timely, depended more and more on the bourgeois signifiers of exchange and circulation that inform spectacle. Finally, on the relationship between painting and capitalist clock time, see Dombrowski, *Monet's Minutes*.

3. Postone, "Abstract Labour," in *Time, Labor, and Social Domination*, 123. In *Time, Labor, and Social Domination*, a granular explication of capitalist value extraction as a function of labor-time, Postone rereads Marx against twentieth-century misreadings of capital and labor such as those that came to inform Leninist theory. He calls for a categorical reinterpretation of Marx's theory of labor in the chapter "Presuppositions of Traditional Marxism." The labor theory of value would have the artwork differentiating itself from the commodity only through an irreducible supplement signaled by autonomy, an inscription of opacity incapable of rationalization or capture by reference to necessity or chance. I thank Anita Chari for this reference.

4. I borrow the metaphor of a newly generated *anthros* from Deleuze, *Cinema 2*, 219–20, 272.

5. Crary, *Suspensions of Perception*, 165–66.

6. Crary, *Suspensions of Perception*, 165–66.

7. Argüelles, *Charles Henry*, 84.

8. Argüelles, *Charles Henry*, 84.

9. As many have argued, the noisy sphere of the market was becoming ever louder for artists in the mid- to late nineteenth century as the state apparatus that once supported artists through the official institutional system of the salon began to be replaced by a market system of galleries. See Green, "Dealing in Temperaments," 31. Nicholas Green builds on Meyer Schapiro's work on Impressionism. Schapiro, *Abstract Art*.

10. Green, "Dealing in Temperaments," 44. Green argues that this new economic field is the motor of social formations that operate seemingly independently of it. More significantly, for Green, the artwork offers the only view onto the transformations in the economic register that are illegible and inarticulable within political economic discourse.

11. Krauss, "Clock Time," repr. in *Time*, 142.

12. Krauss, "Clock Time," 214.

13. On the formal—and thereby all the more politicized—operations of "suture" in the Soviet avant-garde, ranging from photography to film, see Benjamin Buchloh's analysis of Gustave Klutcis, in *Neo-Avant-Garde and Culture Industry*.

14. Alliez, "Grey Times on *La Grande Jatte*."

15. Fry, *Seurat*.

16. Through a careful analysis of the rapid growth of private galleries through the sale of artwork independent of the state apparatus (e.g., the salon), Green, as noted earlier, makes the case that the new economic field of the mid- to late nineteenth century in Paris became the motor of social formations operating seemingly independently of, above all, aesthetic and cultural practice. Green elaborates on the case study he offers to conclude that culture affords the only way of figuring economic change that is otherwise impossible to formulate within the framework of political economy. Green, "Dealing in Temperaments," 44.

17. The theory of the simultaneous contrast of color, which Seurat believed himself to be practicing, posited that colors are not to be mixed on the canvas. Rather, their oppositional relation in accordance with the color wheel used since Johann Wolfgang von Goethe's optics produced a synthesis in the eye via a third color. This law of "the simultaneous contrast of color" cannot itself be divided from the social politics that Seurat derived from Fénéon, Peter Kropotkin, and others that sought to replace vertical hierarchy reticulated to authoritarian unity with open antagonism to arrive at social harmony on a molecular level, within the community as opposed to rule by an external sovereign. This project—namely, that of picturing a totality of social production and reception at a reflexive level—strives for a unity of economic, political, social, and aesthetic meaning. Ungersman Halprin, *Félix Fénéon*, 65–66. See also Crary's discussion of the relationship between Seurat's interest in optics and his interest in theories of egalitarian social composition, e.g., anarchism. Crary, *Suspensions of Perception*.

18. Sohn-Rethel, "The Formal Characteristics of Second Nature."

19. Sohn-Rethel, "The Formal Characteristics of Second Nature."

20. Sohn-Rethel, *Intellectual and Manual Labour*, 65.

21. Wright, "On the Origins of Abstraction."

22. On the term *petroleuse*, other than on the enormously useful and enriching eponymous press, see any bibliography on nineteenth-century French social history. These women, either mythological or factual, were understood to be the most radical wing of the Commune and were said to have occasionally set fire to the buildings where statist business was held. See Antliff, *Anarchy and Art*; Antliff, *Anarchist Modernism*; Hutton, *Neo-Impressionism and the Search for Solid Ground*; Roslak, *Neo-Impressionism and Anarchism in Fin-de-Siècle France*; Leighten, *The Liberation of Painting*; Gurianova, *The Aesthetics of Anarchy*.

23. Ungersman Halprin, *Félix Fénéon*. See also Rewald, *Seurat*; and the chapter on Knobloch in Perruchot, *La vie de Seurat*.

24. Wright, "On the Origins of Abstraction." On the Paris Commune, see Ross, *Communal Luxury*; Ross, *The Emergence of Social Space*.

25. Pollock, *The Expanding Discourse*.

26. Schapiro, *Abstract Art*, 193. See also Schapiro, *Theory and Philosophy of Art*, 194: "From the current conceptions of technology, he drew the norms of a methodological procedure in painting, bringing Impressionism up to date in light of the latest findings in science and technology." Dialectically, Schapiro reads the way that Seurat internalized disciplinary labor at the level of the grapheme or mark

itself. See also Crary, *Suspensions of Perception*. For the most recent scholarship on Seurat's extraordinary process and the conditions of its emergence in relationship to a broad spectrum of "new media" and forms of technological reproducibility specific to the mid- to late nineteenth century, see Armstrong, "Seurat's Media."

27. Baudelaire, "The Painter of Modern Life." For the best discussion of this text in the disciplinary bounds of the history of art, see Clark, "Olympia's Choice," in *The Painting of Modern Life*.

28. Baudelaire, "The Painter of Modern Life."

29. Clark, *The Painting of Modern Life*. See also Pollock, *Vision and Difference*.

30. Clark, *The Painting of Modern Life*.

31. Engels, *The Origin of the Family, Private Property and the State*.

32. Engels, *The Origin of the Family, Private Property and the State*. Engels cautions the reader that this so-called right, in his coinage "mother right," does not denote right as a modern society might legally recognize it. It means simply that lineages were traced to women as children knew who their mothers were, and mothers reciprocally recognized their children. This had nothing to do with law as such but was a symbolic form of inheritance and exchange based on birthright.

33. Engels, *The Origin of the Family, Private Property and the State*, 35.

34. Dalla Costa and James, *The Power of Women and the Subversion of the Community*, 48.

35. Gleber, *The Art of Taking a Walk*. Armstrong's *Manet Manette* carefully reconstructs the complex field of anxious contradictions around gender within capitalism in Manet's oeuvre. See, again, Pollock, *Vision and Difference*. Within the parameters of art history, Pollock, Nochlin, Armstrong, and others have posed this question through an examination of late nineteenth-century painting.

CHAPTER TWO. FRANCIS PICABIA'S REAL ABSTRACTION AND THE BEGINNINGS OF FUTURIST CYBORGS

1. Cheetham, *The Rhetoric of Purity*.

2. Marshall, *Machine Art, 1934*. Jennifer Jane Marshall traces the entry of a neoplatonic understanding of form into the Museum of Modern Art of New York's curatorial framework in part because of the architect Phillip Johnson's engagement with Platonist philosophers at Harvard and in part in synergy with curator Alfred H. Barr's hopes for a modernist conciliation with a productivist outlook. For an analysis of how this institutional and intellectual context came to influence artists throughout the mid- to late twentieth century, see also C. Jones, *Machine in the Studio*.

3. For a discussion of the term *totality* in relation to aesthetic production, see Mansoor, "From Fetish to Totality."

4. A. Jones, *Irrational Modernism*. Jones's description of Picabia's machinic form indicates the dominance of a cultural imaginary reticulated through

machinic form. However, where Jones sees an iconography, others have noted a critical analysis of the very logic of value circulation in relation to human life.

5. A. Jones, *Irrational Modernism*, 119.

6. Baker, *The Artwork Caught by the Tail*, 26.

7. Clej, "Between Dada and Marxism," 87.

8. Clej, "Between Dada and Marxism," 88. Dance historian Alina Clej notes that Tzara encountered Marxian thought early on: "Be that as it may, it appears, however, that at the age of ten Tzara knew already about profit, surplus value, capitalist exploitation, socialism, and revolution."

9. Baker, *The Artwork Caught by the Tail*, 26.

10. Baker, *The Artwork Caught by the Tale*, 24–26.

11. Marx, *Economic and Philosophic Manuscripts of 1844*.

12. In the introduction to *Grundrisse*, Marx is explicitly hostile toward the use of analogy and "aesthetic semblance," and states his aim to parse out the material and historic processes through which capital is driven by the sale of labor-power. Marx, *Grundrisse*, 83.

13. Hayles, *How We Became Posthuman*. Where Katherine Hayles explores the highly internally differentiated space-time of the digital field, which she sees as the technological mediation productive of a "post human" contemporaneity, I locate Picabia's figure as a way to explore the degree to which the "human" was already dissolved by the value-form at the moment when labor itself became fully subsumed as an abstract commodity.

14. Rancière, "The Critique of Political Economy in the *1844 Manuscripts*," in Althusser et al., *Reading Capital*, 108.

15. Sohn-Rethel, "The Formal Characteristics of Second Nature."

16. Rancière, "The Critique of Political Economy in the *1844 Manuscripts*," in Althusser et al., *Reading Capital*, 126.

17. Fer, Batchelor, and Wood, *Realism, Rationalism, Surrealism*, 108.

18. Fer, Batchelor, and Wood, *Realism, Rationalism, Surrealism*, 108. On the dominance of industrial design and commercial drawing as the matrix of the French and American avant-gardes, most notably Duchamp's practice, see Molly Nesbit's important text "The Language of Industry."

19. Nesbit, *Their Common Sense*. See also Nesbit, "The Language of Industry." For an example of how this diagrammatic operation establishes itself in twentieth-century art practices and comes to be paradigmatic in late twentieth-century art of the so-called social turn, see Mansoor, "Cristóbal Lehyt's Concrete Abstraction."

20. Foster, *Prosthetic Gods*, 148.

21. Foster, *Prosthetic Gods*, 149.

22. Poggi, preface to *Inventing Futurism*. See also Bois et al., "1909," in *Art since 1900*, 90–97.

23. Bois et al., "Formalism and Structuralism," in *Art since 1900*, 35.

24. A. Jones, *Irrational Modernism*, 115.

25. Baker, *The Artwork Caught by the Tail*, 57. See also Buck-Morss, *Dreamworld and Catastrophe*, which dissects the tension between the politics of the

Russian avant-garde and the Bolshevik vanguard. Finally, on the marriage of anarchism and communism in the context of the Soviet avant-garde, see Groys, "Installing Communism."

26. Jakobson, "Futurism," 147.

27. Jakobson, "Futurism," 147.

28. Jakobson, "Futurism," 147.

29. Bois et al., "1909," in *Art since 1900*.

30. Herf, *Reactionary Modernism*.

31. Haraway, "The Cyborg Manifesto," 9.

32. Haraway, "The Cyborg Manifesto," 9. Anja Klock also argues for a direct link from Marinetti and Italian Futurism of the 1930s to the cyber technologies of the twenty-first century. Klock, "Of Cyborg Technologies and Fascistized Mermaids." See also Alliez and Lazzarato, *Wars and Capital*.

33. For a synthesis and summary of Negri's narrative of the worker over the twentieth century, see Bellofiore, "Between Panzieri and Negri."

34. Benjamin, "The Work of Art in the Age of Its Technological Reproducibility," 101–33.

35. For a discussion of how the NEP in Soviet Russia in 1920 affected the work of the most radical faction of the Soviet avant-garde, and the ways in which some of its key figures tried to come to grips with capitalist forms of compromise, see Kiaer, *Imagine No Possessions*.

36. Recall that the commodity fetish is congealed social relations frozen in the objectification of labor-time. Recall also that for Freud it masks lack and the threat of lack with the promise of false plenitude.

37. Tronti, "Factory and Society."

38. Claire Fontaine, "Existential Metonymy and Real Abstractions," in *Human Strike and the Art of Creating Freedom*, 194.

39. Claire Fontaine, "Existential Metonymy and Real Abstractions," in *Human Strike and the Art of Creating Freedom*, 194.

40. Khatib, "'Sensuous Supra-Sensuous.'"

41. Khatib, "'Sensuous Supra-Sensuous,'" 199.

CHAPTER THREE. THE FUTURE OF THE FUTURISTS

1. Deleuze and Guattari, *A Thousand Plateaus*, 61.

2. Tiqqun, *Preliminary Materials for a Theory of the Young-Girl*, 11–14.

3. Tiqqun, *Preliminary Materials for a Theory of the Young-Girl*, 15.

4. Tiqqun, *Preliminary Materials for a Theory of the Young-Girl*, 18.

5. Tiqqun, *Preliminary Materials for a Theory of the Young-Girl*, 15.

6. Tiqqun, *Preliminary Materials for a Theory of the Young-Girl*, 16.

7. Tiqqun, *Preliminary Materials for a Theory of the Young-Girl*, 95.

8. Joselit, *Art's Properties*.

9. Sohn-Rethel, "The Formal Characteristics of Second Nature."

10. Sohn-Rethel, "The Formal Characteristics of Second Nature."

11. Rancière, “Critique and Science in Capital,” in Althusser et al., *Reading Capital*, 108.

12. Foucault, *Technologies of the Self.*

13. Morris, “Drone Warfare.”

14. “On the one hand, the value, or the past labor, which dominates living labor, is incarnated in the capitalist; on the other, instead, the labor appears as bare material labor power, as a commodity.” Marx quoted in Tronti, “Factory and Society,” 18.

15. Claire Fontaine, “Readymade Artist and Human Strike,” in *Human Strike and the Art of Creating Freedom*, 32–49.

16. Tiqqun, *Preliminary Materials for a Theory of the Young-Girl*, 112.

17. Foster uses the term *mimetic exacerbation* in *Bad New Days*. See also Sohn-Rethel, *Intellectual and Manual Labour*, 188; Brassier, “Wandering Abstraction”; and Sohn-Rethel, “The Formal Characteristics of Second Nature.”

18. Burnham, “Was Facebook an Event?,” 62, citing Tiqqun, *Preliminary Materials for a Theory of the Young-Girl*, 112.

19. Burnham, “Was Facebook an Event?,”62, citing Tiqqun, *Preliminary Materials for a Theory of the Young-Girl*, 112.

20. See Foster, *Bad New Days*, 63–98.

21. There are several texts that elaborate a timely feminist approach to communization that do not address *La Jeune Fille* or Tiqqun. Notable among them is Gonzalez, “Communization and the Abolition of Gender.” See also *Lies: A Journal of Materialist Feminism*, which is an exemplary and *original* instance of feminist engagement with crisis capitalism. In the first issue, see in particular Clementine, “Against the Couple Form”; and C. E., “Undoing Sex.”

22. Tiqqun, *The Cybernetic Hypothesis*, 107.

23. Burnham, “Was Facebook an Event?,” 63–64.

24. Toscano and Kinkle, *Cartographies of the Absolute.*

25. Marx, *Grundrisse*, 690–712.

26. *Cybernetics* has been more or less replaced in the discourse by the terms *artificial intelligence* and *machine learning*. I retain the term with reference to Tiqqun's usage of it.

27. Tiqqun, *The Cybernetic Hypothesis*, 54.

28. Tiqqun, *The Cybernetic Hypothesis*, 55–56.

29. Tiqqun, *The Cybernetic Hypothesis*, 68–69.

30. Cominotti, “Italian Design in Relation to Social and Economic Planning,” 347.

31. Cominotti, “Italian Design in Relation to Social and Economic Planning,” 347.

32. Zimmer, “Earl Moran,” 11.

33. Marx, *Grundrisse.*

34. Tiqqun, *The Cybernetic Hypothesis*, 52–53.

35. Despite its offense to some Anglophone feminist writers, Tiqqun's *Preliminary Materials for a Theory of the Young-Girl* finds its framework in the discursive

constellation set by Mariarosa Dalla Costa, Leopoldina Fortunati, Carla Lonzi, and other Marxist feminists working in Italy in the 1970s, a constellation that owed much to the critique of the socially totalizing force of productivist rationalism begun by Mario Tronti and Antonio Negri, among others. For a discussion of the expanded field of labor that subtends valorization on the factory floor and extends to the very conditions for the possibility of value (women's work), see Dalla Costa and James, *The Power of Women and the Subversion of the Community*; Fortunati, *The Arcane of Reproduction*; and Federici, *Caliban and the Witch*. See also Gonzalez, "The Gendered Circuit"; Lotringer and Marazzi, *Post-Political Politics*; and Mario Tronti's pivotal "Factory and Society."

36. Reines, "Translator's Note." Note that the author gives us what some might feel to be *too much information*. How is it that the *Jeune-Fille* makes us *emulate* her? Finally, how is it that Reines, a brilliant poet, finds the need to describe a process in which she turns her own spontaneous illness into serial sculptural objects, made of ice, no less? Isn't this already a perfect metaphor of disciplined embodied life in the late capitalist metropolis?

37. Tiqqun, *Preliminary Materials for a Theory of the Young-Girl*, 6.

38. Jameson, *Postmodernism*, 50–51. See also Jameson, *The Political Unconscious*.

39. Toscano and Kinkle, *Cartographies of the Absolute*, 7.

40. Althusser, "Cremonini, Painter of the Abstract," 45.

41. Foster, *Return of the Real*. Foster's Lacanian understanding of the real is not the same as Althusser's, however much both rely on a Lacanian account of an unrecoverable real. For Althusser, this real is always already social, political, and economic.

42. Tiqqun, *Preliminary Materials for a Theory of the Young-Girl*, 6.

43. Agamben, *Man without Content*, 40–58.

44. Agamben, *Man without Content*, 50.

45. Agamben, *Man without Content*, 50.

46. Claire Fontaine, "Readymade Artist and Human Strike," in *Human Strike and the Art of Creating Freedom*. On Duchamp in relationship to the transformed mode of object production in capital and its ramifications for the creation of the artwork, see Roberts, *The Intangibilities of Form*. See also de Duve, *The Definitely Unfinished Marcel Duchamp*.

47. Lévi-Strauss, *The Elementary Structures of Kinship*. See also Rubin, *The Traffic in Women*, 92–95; and Freud, *Totem and Taboo*.

Chapter Four. The [Young-Girl] Worker as Equipment

1. Stitch, *Yves Klein*, 174. See also Cabanas, *The Myth of Nouveau Realism*.

2. Mansoor, "Lucio Fontana and the Politics of the Gesture," in *Marshall Plan Modernism*, 69–92.

3. Mansoor, "Lucio Fontana and the Politics of the Gesture."

4. Klein, "Truth Becomes Reality."

5. Klein, "Truth Becomes Reality," 185.

6. Palumbo-Mosca, “The Woman Who Painted Her Body for Artist Yves Klein” (BBC interview).

7. Baxandall, *Painting and Experience in Fifteenth-Century Italy.*

8. Andy Warhol, interview with Benjamin H. D. Buchloh, reprinted in Michelson, *Andy Warhol*, 119–28.

9. Klein, “Chelsea Hotel Manifesto,” 4.

10. Klein, “Chelsea Hotel Manifesto,” 6.

11. Khatib, “‘Sensuous Supra-Sensuous,’” 54.

12. Khatib, “‘Sensuous Supra-Sensuous,’” 51.

13. Khatib, “‘Sensuous Supra-Sensuous,’” 50.

14. Benjamin, “The Work of Art in the Age of Its Technological Reproducibility,” 101–33.

15. For a more technical definition of subsumption as a term through which to periodize twentieth-century advanced capitalist manufacture, see “The History of Subsumption,” *Endnotes* 2 (April 2010), https://endnotes.org.uk/articles/the-history-of-subsumption.

16. Lukács, *History and Class Consciousness*, 87.

17. Marx, “Introduction,” in *Grundrisse*, 109.

18. Lazzarato, “Economic and Subjective Impoverishment under Neoliberalism,” in *Experimental Politics*, 160; Jeremy Gilbert, “Introduction,” in Lazzarato, *Experimental Politics*, xxxv.

19. Lazzarato, *Experimental Politics*, 160.

20. Klossowski, *Living Currency*, 47.

21. Klossowski, *Living Currency*, 55.

22. Daniel W. Smith, “Living Currency and Counter-Utopia,” in Klossowski, *Living Currency*, 21.

23. The best summary is in Gonzalez and Neton, “The Logic of Gender.”

24. Foucault quoted in Klossowski, *Living Currency*, 41. I excerpt a slightly longer letter.

25. Engels, *The Origin of the Family, Private Property and the State.*

26. Irigaray, “Women on the Market,” 170.

27. Irigaray, “Women on the Market,” 171.

28. Irigaray, “Women on the Market,” 171.

29. Irigaray, “Women on the Market,” 171.

30. Irigaray, “Women on the Market,” 172–73.

31. Irigaray, “Women on the Market,” 174–75.

32. Klein, “Chelsea Hotel Manifesto,” 1.

33. Klein, “Chelsea Hotel Manifesto,” 5.

34. Klein, “Chelsea Hotel Manifesto,” 5.

CHAPTER FIVE. SURPLUS BODIES

1. Dalla Costa and James, *The Power of Women and the Subversion of the Community*, 48.

2. Gonzalez, "The Gendered Circuit." See also Koshy et al., "Introduction," in *Colonial Racial Capitalism*, 1–29. The writers stress the co-constitutive nature of racialization and capital through dispossession. For a discussion of gender along similar lines of the co-constitutive historicity of cycles of capital accumulation in relation to gender, see Vishmidt and Sutherland, "(Un)making Value."

3. Foster, "Mimetic," in *Bad New Days*, 63–96.

4. For a brave and pioneering exception, see Toscano and Kinkle, *Cartographies of the Absolute*.

5. Vishmidt, *Speculation as a Mode of Production*; Leary, *Key Words*.

6. Koshy et al., *Colonial Racial Capitalism*.

7. State mediation of the labor-to-capital ratio has a long history, the task of which it is not the purpose or scope of this essay to address. One immediate example, however, might be the Canadian processing of Chinese immigration in the late nineteenth century. See Belshaw, *Colonization and Community*.

8. Foster, "Mimetic."

9. Sohn-Rethel, *Intellectual and Manual Labour*, 26–27.

10. On the origins of performance art in the context of Fluxus, Happenings, and other such postwar forms that broke with the canvas and pedestal, see Rodenbeck, *Radical Prototypes*. On performance, see also A. Jones, *Body Art*; Goldberg, *Performance Art*. On the dominance of this model of art now framed as socially engaged practice, see Bishop, *Artificial Hells*. Note that Claire Bishop in particular distinguished Sierra from among the conciliatory artists she examines in her now paradigmatic essay "Antagonism and Relational Aesthetics."

11. Rainer's letter was addressed to Abramovic's gallery, specifically to its owner, Jeffrey Deitch. Published by the Performance Club on November 11, 2011. Rainer, Douglas Crimp, and Taisha Pagget signed it. For a copy of the letter, see its republication in *Artforum*, https://www.artforum.com/news/yvonne-rainer-accuses-marina-abramovi-and-la-moca-of-exploiting-performers-198767/ (accessed July 16, 2024).

12. Vishmidt, *Speculation as a Mode of Production*, 19.

13. Vishmidt, *Speculation as a Mode of Production*, 19.

14. Vishmidt, *Speculation as a Mode of Production*, 31–32.

15. Vishmidt, *Speculation as a Mode of Production*, 28.

16. Spiegler, "When Human Beings Are the Canvas."

17. Bishop, "Antagonism and Relational Aesthetics," 71. See also Maimon, "The Third Citizen."

18. Sohn-Rethel, *Intellectual and Manual Labour*, 29. Khatib, in "'Sensuous Supra Sensuous,'" sums up Sohn-Rethel's project as follows: "Sohn-Rethel insists that commodity abstraction is real and therefore not subjective or thought-induced; thus, it is not reducible to the intellectual faculties of the Kantian transcendental subject," and yet a "*real* process of exchange" takes on the "form of *thought*, that is, an abstraction" (51). He quotes Sohn-Rethel: "Already Marx discovered a fundamental link between the form of commodity abstraction and the form of thought articulated by categories of bourgeois science: these 'are forms

of thought which are socially valid and therefore objective, for the relations of production belonging to this historically determined mode of social production, i.e. commodity production'" (51–52).

19. Khatib, "'Sensuous Supra Sensuous,'" 30, emphasis mine.

20. Khatib, "'Sensuous Supra Sensuous,'" 48.

21. Khatib, "'Sensuous Supra Sensuous,'" 45.

22. Khatib, "'Sensuous Supra Sensuous,'" 50, 71.

23. Khatib, "'Sensuous Supra Sensuous,'" 46.

24. Khatib, "'Sensuous Supra Sensuous,'" 6.

25. Khatib, "'Sensuous Supra Sensuous,'" 28.

26. Crenshaw, "Mapping the Margins." For a discussion of the way in which Crenshaw bridges a divide from discourses of oppression to exploitation, see Shaked, *The Synthetic Proposition*, 37. As Shaked notes, while Crenshaw acknowledges the need to cross among identities to adequately address economic exploitation, she remains within identity typologies rather than looking at exploitive economic structure systemically, in a Marxian register.

27. Bhattacharya, "Mapping Social Reproduction Theory," in *Social Reproduction Theory*, 17.

28. Vered Maimon has identified and examined what appears to be a paradigmatic shift in art practice, marking the transition from exposing the hidden to negotiating the open secret. She traces this in the difference between critically engaged arts associated with the critique of institutions to para-fictional practices such as that of Pierre Hueghe. See Maimon, "The Third Citizen." The question of democratic transparency and critical opacity has become something of an autonomous discourse, currently categorized as "invisibility studies." See Steiner and Veel, *Invisibility Studies*. For more on this movement in the art of the sixties and seventies in North America and Europe, known as "the critique of institutions," much of which revolved around ideology critique and the premise that the museum is an ideological state apparatus (à la Althusser), see Alberro and Stimpson, *Institutional Critique*. On the politics of exposure, see Alberro, "The Turn of the Screw."

29. Deleuze, "Post-Script on the Societies of Control."

30. Shaikh, *Capitalism*.

31. See Thompson, *Living as Form*. For a critical perspective on this phenomenon, from a leftist perspective, see Bishop, *Artificial Hells*.

32. This is the most recent in a genealogy of discourse attempting to grasp why despite a surplus of analysis about the discontents of capitalism, it is collectively replicated daily and resisted relatively little. See Tomšič, *The Capitalist Unconscious*.

33. The term *exhibitionary order* is from Timothy Mitchell, a political theorist and historian affiliated with the Department of Middle Eastern, South Asian, and African Studies at Columbia University. His paradigmatic 1989 essay, "The World as Exhibition," in which this term was coined, has become a cornerstone of art history and visual and cultural studies. A different version was published in

Preziosi, *The Art of Art History*, 409–23. See also the essay's inclusion in Mirzoeff, *The Visual Culture Reader*, 497–500.

34. Mitchell, "The World as Exhibition."

35. My project owes much to Vishmidt's, also pioneering in its sensitivity to the way in which global labor flows and the "surplus" populations generated by the capital-to-labor relation ramify in culture. Vishmidt, "Human Capital or Toxic Asset." See also Hansen, "Surplus Population, Social Reproduction and the Problem of Class Formation."

36. Bryan-Wilson, "From Artists to Art Workers," in *Art Workers*, 13–40.

37. Bryan-Wilson, "From Artists to Art Workers."

38. Vishmidt, *Speculation as a Mode of Production in Art and Capital*, 19.

CONCLUSION

1. I owe my use of the word *ontology* not to Heidegger but rather to the French-Italian Marxist Jacques Camatte. See Marxist Internet Archive, https://www.marxists.org/archive/camatte/index.htm, for a selection of Camatte's writing and his project at large.

2. The artist collective's writings have been collected on Ubu.web, http://www.ubu.com/papers/Fontaine_Readymade.pdf. See also Mansoor, *Marshal Plan Modernism*, 167–205.

3. Greenberg. "Avant-Garde and Kitsch."

4. Brassier, "Wandering Abstraction." I am grateful to have had the good fortune to discuss Sohn-Rethel's elaboration of real abstraction at the American University of Beirut, 2019.

5. Chari, *A Political Economy of the Senses*.

6. See the entirety of *Endnotes*, no. 3, "Gender, Race, Class and Other Misfortunes," September, 2013, https://endnotes.org.uk/issues/3.

7. Koshy et al., "Introduction," in *Colonial Racial Capitalism*, 1–39. The writers stress the co-constitutive nature of racialization and capital through dispossession. For a discussion of gender along similar lines of the co-constitutive historicity of cycles of capital accumulation in relation to gender, see Vishmidt and Sutherland, "(Un)making Value."

8. Stiegler, *For a New Critique of Political Economy*, 53.

9. Stiegler, *For a New Critique of Political Economy*, 51.

10. Sekula, *The Contest of Meaning*, 343–89.

11. Buchloh, "Conceptual Art 1962–1969."

12. Tiqqun, *The Cybernetic Hypothesis*, 11.

13. Benjamin, "The Work of Art in the Age of Its Technological Reproducibility," 116.

14. Marx, *Economic and Philosophic Manuscripts of 1844*.

15. Adorno, "Lecture Four: Whether Philosophy Is Possible without System," in *Lectures on Negative Dialectics*, 42–43.

BIBLIOGRAPHY

Adorno, Theodor. "Commitment." *New Left Review*, nos. 87–88 (September–December 1974): 75–89.

Adorno, Theodor. *Introduction to Sociology*. Stanford, CA: Stanford University Press, 2002.

Adorno, Theodor. *Lectures on Negative Dialectics*. Cambridge, UK: Polity Press, 2008.

Adorno, Theodor. *Negative Dialectics*. Translated by E. B. Ashton. New York: Continuum, 1973.

Adorno, Theodor, Walter Benjamin, Ernst Bloch, Bertolt Brecht, and Georg Lukács. *Aesthetics and Politics: The Key Texts of the Classic Debate within German Marxism*. London: Verso, 1977.

Agamben, Giorgio. *Man without Content*. Translated by Giorgia Albert. Stanford, CA: Stanford University Press, 1999.

Alberro, Alexander. "The Turn of the Screw: Daniel Buren, Dan Flavin, and the Sixth International Guggenheim Exhibition." *October*, no. 80 (Spring 1997): 57–84.

Alberro, Alexander, and Blake Stimpson, eds. *Institutional Critique: An Anthology of Artists' Writings*. Cambridge, MA: MIT Press, 2009.

Alliez, Eric, and Maurizio Lazzarato. *Wars and Capital*. Pasadena: Semiotext(e): 2016.

Alliez, Eric, with Jean-Clet Martin. "Grey Times on *La Grande Jatte* (The Extra-terrestrial/Seurat/The Machine-Eye)." In *The Brain-Eye: New Histories of Modern Painting*, translated by Robin Mackay, 189–252. London: Rowman and Littlefield, 2016.

Althusser, Louis. "Cremonini, Painter of the Abstract." In *Lenin and Philosophy*, translated by Ben Brewster, 229–42. New York: Monthly Review Press, 1971.

Althusser, Louis, Étienne Balibar, Roger Establet, Pierre Macherey, and Jacques Rancière. *Reading Capital: The Complete Edition*, translated by Ben Brewster and David Fernbach. London: Verso, 2015.

Antliff, Allan. *Anarchist Modernism: Art, Politics, and the First American Avant-Garde*. Chicago: University of Chicago Press, 2001.

Antliff, Allan. *Anarchy and Art: From the Paris Commune to the Fall of the Berlin Wall*. Vancouver, BC: Arsenal Pulp Press, 2007.
Apter, Andrew. "IBB=419: Nigerian Democracy and the Politics of Illusion." In *Civil Society and The Political Imaginary in Africa*, edited by John Comaroff and Jean Comaroff, 270–300. Chicago: University of Chicago Press, 1999.
Argüelles, José A. *Charles Henry and the Formation of a Psychophysical Aesthetic*. Chicago: University of Chicago Press, 1972.
Armstrong, Carol. *Manet Manette*. New Haven, CT: Yale University Press, 2002.
Armstrong, Carol. "Seurat's Media, Or a Matrix of Materialities." *Grey Room*, no. 58 (Winter 2015): 6–25.
Arrighi, Giovanni. *The Long Twentieth Century*. London: Verso, 1996.
Baker, George. *The Artwork Caught by the Tail: Francis Picabia and Dada in Paris*. Cambridge, MA: MIT Press, 2007.
Bataille, Georges. "The Language of Flowers." In *Visions of Excess: Collected Writings of Georges Bataille, 1927–1939*, edited by Allan Stoekl, 10–14. Minneapolis: University of Minnesota Press, 1985.
Bataille, Georges. *Manet*. Geneva: Skira, 1994.
Baudelaire, Charles. "The Painter of Modern Life." In *Collected Writings*, 1–35. London: Phaidon, 1995.
Baxandall, Michael. *Painting and Experience in Fifteenth-Century Italy*. New York: Oxford University Press, 1988.
Bellofiore, Riccardo. "Between Panzieri and Negri: Mario Tronti and Workerism, 1960–1970." Lecture given at the Historical Materialism conference, 2006. https://libcom.org/article/between-panzieri-and-negri-mario-tronti-and-workerism-1960s-and-1970s.
Belshaw, John Douglas. *Colonization and Community: The Vancouver Island Coalfield and the Making of the British Columbian Working Class*. Montreal: McGill-Queen's University Press, 2004.
Benjamin, Walter. "On the Concept of History." In *Walter Benjamin: Selected Writings, Volume 4, 1938–1940*, edited by Howard Eiland and Michael W. Jennings, 389–400. Cambridge, MA: Belknap Press of Harvard University Press, 2003.
Benjamin, Walter. "The Work of Art in the Age of Its Technological Reproducibility." In *Walter Benjamin: Selected Writings, Volume 3, 1935–1938*, edited by Howard Eiland and Michael W. Jennings, 101–33. Cambridge, MA: Belknap Press of Harvard University Press, 2002.
Bhattacharya, Tithi. *Social Reproduction Theory: Remapping Class*. London: Pluto, 2017.
Bishop, Claire. "Antagonism and Relational Aesthetics." *October*, no. 110 (Fall 2004): 51–79.
Bishop, Claire. *Artificial Hells: Participatory Art and the Politics of Spectatorship*. London: Verso, 2012.
Blom, Ina. "The Logic of the Trailer: Abstraction, Style and Sociality in Contemporary Art." *Texte Zur Kunst*, no. 69 (March 2008): 171–77.

Bois, Yve-Alain. *Painting as Model*. Cambridge, MA: MIT Press, 1990.

Bois, Yve-Alain, Benjamin H. D. Buchloh, David Joselit, Hal Foster, and Rosalind Krauss. *Art since 1900*. London: Thames and Hudson, 2016.

Brassier, Ray. "Wandering Abstraction." *Mute*, February 13, 2014. https://www.metamute.org/editorial/articles/wandering-abstraction.

Broude, Norma. "New Light on Seurat's 'Dot': Its Relation to Photo-Mechanical Color Printing in France in the 1880s." *Art Bulletin* 56, no. 4 (December 1974): 581–89.

Bryan-Wilson, Julia. *Art Workers: Radical Practice in the Vietnam Era*. Berkeley: University of California Press, 2009.

Buchloh, Benjamin. "Conceptual Art 1962–1969: From the Aesthetics of Administration to the Critique of Institutions." *October*, no. 55 (Winter 1990): 105–43.

Buchloh, Benjamin. *Neo-Avant-Garde and Culture Industry*. Cambridge, MA: MIT Press, 2003.

Buck-Morss, Susan. *Dreamworld and Catastrophe: The Passing of Mass Utopia in East and West*. Cambridge, MA: MIT Press, 2002.

Burnham, Clint. "Was Facebook an Event?" In *Does the Internet Have an Unconscious? Slavoj Žižek and Digital Culture*, 37–66. New York: Bloomsbury Academic, 2018.

Cabanas, Kaira M. *The Myth of Nouveau Realism*. New Haven, CT: Yale University Press, 2013.

C. E. "Undoing Sex: Against Sexual Optimism." *Lies: A Journal of Materialist Feminism* 1, no. 1 (2012): 15–43. http://www.liesjournal.net/volume1-02-undoingsex.html.

Chari, Anita. *A Political Economy of the Senses: Neoliberalism, Reification, Critique*. New York: Columbia University Press, 2015.

Cheetham, Mark. *The Rhetoric of Purity: Essentialist Theory and the Advent of Abstract Painting*. Cambridge: Cambridge University Press, 1991.

Claire Fontaine. *Human Strike and the Art of Creating Freedom*. Cambridge, MA: MIT Press, 2020.

Clark, T. J. *Farewell to an Idea*. New Haven, CT: Yale University Press, 1999.

Clark, T. J. *The Painting of Modern Life*. Princeton, NJ: Princeton University Press, 1984.

Clej, Alina. "Between Dada and Marxism: Tristan Tzara and the Politics of Position." *Cross Currents: A Yearbook of Central European Culture* 10 (1991): 85–105.

Clementine, Clémence X. "Against the Couple Form." *Lies: A Journal of Materialist Feminism* 1, no. 1 (2012): 45–54. http://www.liesjournal.net/volume1-03-againstcoupleform.html.

Cominotti, Ruggero. "Italian Design in Relation to Social and Economic Planning." In *Italy: The New Domestic Landscape; Achievements and Problems in Italian Design*, edited by Emilio Ambasz, 345–51. New York: Museum of Modern Art, 1972.

Crary, Jonathan. *Suspensions of Perception: Attention, Spectacle and Modern Culture*. Cambridge, MA: MIT Press, 1999.

Crenshaw, Kimberlé. "Mapping the Margins: Intersectionality, Identity Politics, and Violence against Women of Color." *Stanford Law Review* 43, no. 6 (July 1991): 1241–99.

Dalla Costa, Mariarosa, and Selma James. *The Power of Women and the Subversion of the Community* (1972). In *Women and the Subversion of the Community: A Mariarosa Dalla Costa Reader*, edited by Camille Barbagallo. Oakland, CA: PM Press, 2019.

da Silva, Denise Ferreira. "Unpayable Debt: Reading Scenes of Value against the Arrow of Time." In *The Documenta 14 Reader*, edited by Quinn Latimer and Adam Szymczyk. Munich: Prestel, 2017.

de Duve, Thierry, ed. *The Definitely Unfinished Marcel Duchamp*. Cambridge, MA: MIT Press, 1992.

de Duve, Thierry. "Yves Klein, or the Dead Dealer." *October*, no. 49 (Summer 1989): 72–90.

Deleuze, Gilles. *Cinema 2*. Translated by Hugh Tomlinson and Robert Galeta. Minneapolis: University of Minnesota Press, 1989.

Deleuze, Gilles. "Post-Script on the Societies of Control." *October*, no. 59 (Winter 1992): 3–7.

Deleuze, Gilles, and Félix Guattari. *A Thousand Plateaus*. Translated by Brian Massumi. Minneapolis: University of Minnesota Press, 1980.

Dickerman, Leah, and Matthew Affron. *Inventing Abstraction*. New York: Museum of Modern Art, 2012.

Dimitrakaki, Angela, and Kristen Lloyd. Introduction to *Economy: Art, Production and the Subject in the 21st Century*, 1–30. Liverpool, UK: Liverpool University Press, 2015.

Dombrowski, Andre. *Monet's Minutes: Impressionism and the Industrialization of Time*. New Haven, CT: Yale University Press, 2023.

Elson, Diane. "The Value Theory of Labour." In *Value: The Representation of Labour in Capitalism*, 115–80. London: Verso, 2015.

Engels, Friedrich. *The Origin of the Family, Private Property and the State*. New York: International Publishers, 1933.

Federici, Silvia. *Caliban and the Witch: Women, the Body and Primitive Accumulation*. Brooklyn, NY: Autonomedia, 2004.

Fer, Briony. *The Infinite Line: Remaking Art after Modernism*. New Haven, CT: Yale University Press, 2004.

Fer, Briony. *On Abstract Art*. New Haven, CT: Yale University Press, 1997.

Fer, Briony, David Batchelor, and Paul Wood. *Realism, Rationalism, Surrealism: Art between the Wars*. New Haven, CT: Yale University Press, 1993.

Fisher, Mark. *Capitalist Realism: Is There No Alternative?* London: Zero Books, 2009.

Foa, Michelle. *Georges Seurat: The Art of Vision*. New Haven, CT: Yale University Press, 2015.

Fortunati, Leopoldina. *The Arcane of Reproduction: Housework, Prostitution, Labor and Capital.* Brooklyn, NY: Autonomedia, 1996.

Foster, Hal. *Bad New Days: Art, Criticism and Emergency.* London: Verso, 2017.

Foster, Hal. *Prosthetic Gods.* Cambridge, MA: MIT Press, 2004.

Foster, Hal. *Return of the Real.* Cambridge, MA: MIT Press, 1996.

Foucault, Michel. *Technologies of the Self.* Amherst: University of Massachusetts Press, 2022.

Freud, Sigmund. *Totem and Taboo: Resemblances between the Psychic Lives of Savages and Neurotics*, translated by A. A. Brill. London: Routledge, 1919.

Fry, Roger. *Seurat.* London: Phaidon, 1972.

Giedion, Sigfried. *Mechanization Takes Command: A Contribution to Anonymous History.* 1948. Reprint, Minneapolis: University of Minnesota Press, 2013.

Gillick, Liam. "Abstract." In *Microhistorias y macromundos, Vol. 3: Abstract Possible*, edited by Maria Lind, 158–66. Mexico City: Instituto Nacional de Bellas Artes y Literatura, 2011.

Gleber, Anke. *The Art of Taking a Walk.* Princeton, NJ: Princeton University Press, 1998.

Goldberg. Roselee. *Performance Art: From Futurism to the Present.* New York: Thames and Hudson, 1979.

Gonzalez, Maya Andrea. "Communization and the Abolition of Gender." In *Communization and Its Discontents: Contestation, Critiques, Contemporary Struggles*, edited by Benjamin Noys, 219–36. New York: Minor Compositions Autonomedia, 2011.

Gonzalez, Maya Andrea. "The Gendered Circuit: Reading *The Arcane of Reproduction.*" *View Point Magazine*, September 28, 2013.

Gonzalez, Maya Andrea, and Jeanne Neton. "The Logic of Gender." *Endnotes* 3. https://endnotes.org.uk/translations/endnotes-the-logic-of-gender.

Green, Nicholas. "Dealing in Temperaments: Economic Transformations of the Artistic Field in France during the Second Half of the Nineteenth Century." In *Critical Readings in Impressionism and Post-Impressionism*, edited by Mary Tompkins Lewis, 31–47. Berkeley: University of California Press, 2007.

Greenberg, Clement. "Avant-Garde and Kitsch" (1939). In *The Collected Essays and Criticism, Volume 1: Perceptions and Judgments, 1939–1944*, edited by John O'Brian. Chicago: University of Chicago Press, 1986.

Greenberg, Clement. "Counter-Avant-Garde." *Art International* 15, no. 5 (1971).

Greenberg, Clement. "Modernist Painting" (1960). In *The Collected Essays and Criticism. Volume 4: Modernism with a Vengeance, 1957–1969*, edited by John O'Brian. Chicago: University of Chicago Press, 1993.

Greenberg, Clement. "Necessity of 'Formalism.'" *New Literary History* 3 (1971–72).

Groys, Boris. "Installing Communism." In *Aesthetic Marx*, edited by Samir Gandesha and Johan Hartle, 185–202. London: Bloomsbury, 2017.

Gurianova, Nina. *The Aesthetics of Anarchy: Art and Ideology in the Early Russian Avant-Garde.* Berkeley: University of California Press, 2012.

Hansen, Bue Rübner. "Surplus Population, Social Reproduction and the Problem of Class Formation." *Viewpoint*, October 31, 2015. https://viewpointmag.com/2015/10/31/surplus-population-social-reproduction-and-the-problem-of-class-formation/.

Haraway, Donna. "The Cyborg Manifesto." Reprinted in *Manifestly Haraway*, 8–31. Minneapolis: University of Minnesota Press, 1991 and 2016.

Hayles, N. Katherine. *How We Became Posthuman: Virtual Bodies in Cybernetics, Literature, and Informatics*. Chicago: University of Chicago Press, 1999.

Heidegger, Martin. *The Question Concerning Technology and Other Essays*. Translated by William Lovitt. New York: Garland, 1977.

Herf, Jeffrey. *Reactionary Modernism: Technology, Culture and Politics in Weimar and the Third Reich*. Cambridge: Cambridge University Press, 1986.

Hutton, John G. *Neo-Impressionism and the Search for Solid Ground: Art, Science, and Anarchism in Fin-de-Siècle France.* Baton Rouge: Louisiana State University Press, 1994.

Irigaray, Luce. "Women on the Market." In *This Sex Which Is Not One*, 170–91. Ithaca, NY: Cornell University Press, 1985.

Jakobson, Roman. "Futurism." In *My Futurist Years: Collected Essays*, translated by Stephen Rudy, edited by Bengt Jangfeldt and Stephen Rudy, 145–52. New York: Marsilio, 1992.

Jameson, Fredric. *The Political Unconscious: Narrative as a Socially Symbolic Act*. Ithaca, NY: Cornell University Press, 1981.

Jameson, Fredric. *Postmodernism, or, The Cultural Logic of Late Capitalism*. London: Verso, 1991.

Jones, Amelia. *Body Art: Performing the Subject*. Minneapolis: University of Minnesota Press, 1998.

Jones, Amelia. *Irrational Modernism: A Neurasthenic History of New York Dada*. Cambridge, MA: MIT Press, 2004.

Jones, Caroline A. *Machine in the Studio: Constructing the Postwar American Artist*. Chicago: University of Chicago Press, 1996.

Joselit, David. *Art's Properties*. Princeton, NJ: Princeton University Press, 2023.

Joselit, David. *Infinite Regress: Marcel Duchamp, 1910–1941*. Cambridge, MA: MIT Press, 1998.

Kaplan, Dana, and Eva Illouz. *What Is Sexual Capital?* Cambridge, UK: Polity, 2022.

Khatib, Sami. "'Sensuous Supra-Sensuous': The Aesthetics of Real Abstraction." In *Aesthetic Marx*, edited by Samir Gandesha and Johan Hartle, 49–72. London: Bloomsbury Press, 2017.

Khatib, Sami, Holger Kuhn, Oona Lochner, Isabel Mehl, and Beate Sontgen, eds. *Critique: The Stakes of Form*. Zurich: Diaphenes, 2020.

Kiaer, Christina. *Imagine No Possessions*. Cambridge, MA: MIT Press, 2008.

Klein, Yves. "Chelsea Hotel Manifesto." Reprinted in *Overcoming the Problematics of Art: The Writings of Yves Klein*, translated and edited by Klaus Ottmann, 193–200. Putnam, CT: Spring Publications, 2007.

Klein, Yves. "Truth Becomes Reality." Reprinted in *Overcoming the Problematics of Art: The Writings of Yves Klein*, translated and edited by Klaus Ottmann, 183–92. Putnam, CT: Spring Publications, 2007.

Klock, Anja. "Of Cyborg Technologies and Fascistized Mermaids: Giannina Censi's *Aerodanze* in 1930s Italy." *Theatre Journal* 51, no. 4 (1999): 395–415.

Klossowski, Pierre. *Living Currency*. London: Bloomsbury Academic, 2017.

Knapp, Michael, Anja Flach, and Ercan Ayboga. *Revolution in Rojova: Democratic Autonomy and Women's Liberation in Syrian Kurdistan*. Translated by Janet Biehl. London: Pluto Press, 2016.

Koshy, Susan, Lisa Marie Cacho, Jodi A. Byrd, and Brian Jordan Jefferson, eds. *Colonial Racial Capitalism*. Durham, NC: Duke University Press, 2022.

Krauss, Rosalind. "Clock Time." *October*, no. 136 (Spring 2011): 213–17. Reprinted in *Time*, edited by Amelia Groom, 142–45. Cambridge, MA: MIT Press, 2013.

Krauss, Rosalind. *The Optical Unconscious*. Cambridge, MA: MIT Press, 1993.

Krauss, Rosalind. *Originality of the Avant-Garde and Other Modernist Myths*. Cambridge, MA: MIT Press, 1985.

Lazzarato, Maurizio. *Experimental Politics: Work, Welfare, and Creativity in the Neoliberal Age*. Edited by Jeremy Gilbert. Translated by Arianna Bove et al. Cambridge, MA: MIT Press, 2017.

Leary, John Patrick. *Key Words: The New Language of Capitalism*. London: Haymarket, 2018.

Leighten, Patricia. *The Liberation of Painting: Modernism and Anarchism in Avant-Guerre Paris*. Chicago: University of Chicago Press, 2013.

Lévi-Strauss, Claude. *The Elementary Structures of Kinship*. Boston: Beacon, 1971.

Lotringer, Sylvère, and Christian Marazzi, eds. *Post-Political Politics*. Cambridge, MA: MIT Press, 2000.

Lukács, Georg. *History and Class Consciousness*. Translated by Rodney Livingstone. Cambridge, MA: MIT Press, 1971.

Lütticken, Sven. "Attending to Abstract Things." *New Left Review*, no. 54 (November–December 2008): 101–22.

Lütticken, Sven. "Living with Abstraction." *Texte Zur Kunst*, no. 69 (March 2008).

Lütticken, Sven. *Objections: Forms of Abstraction*. Vol. 1. London: Sternberg, 2022.

Maimon, Vered. "The Third Citizen: On Models of Criticality in Contemporary Artistic Practices." *October*, no. 129 (Summer 2009): 85–112.

Mansoor, Jaleh. "Cristóbal Lehyt's Concrete Abstraction: Un-Mapping the 'Global South.'" In *Cristóbal Lehyt*. New York: Americas Society, 2014. Exhibition catalog.

Mansoor, Jaleh. "From Fetish to Totality: The Work of Art in the Age of Real Abstraction." *Qui Parle* 32, no. 1 (June 2023): 245–66.

Mansoor, Jaleh. *Marshall Plan Modernism: Italian Abstraction and the Beginnings of Autonomia*. Durham, NC: Duke University Press, 2016.

Marshall, Jennifer Jane. *Machine Art, 1934*. Chicago: University of Chicago Press, 2012.

Marx, Karl. *Capital: A Critique of Political Economy.* Vol. 1. Translated by Ben Fowlkes. London: Penguin, 1976.

Marx, Karl. *Economic and Philosophic Manuscripts of 1844*. Marxists Internet Archive. https://www.marxists.org/archive/marx/works/1844/manuscripts/comm.htm.

Marx, Karl. "The German Ideology" (1845). Part 1, "Feuerbach: Opposition of Materialist and Idealist Outlook." Marxists Internet Archive. https://www.marxists.org/archive/marx/works/1845/german-ideology/ch01a.htm.

Marx, Karl. *Grundrisse: Foundations of the Critique of Political Economy*. Translated by Martin Nicolaus. London: Penguin Books in association with the *New Left Review*, 1973.

Mawani, Renisa. *Across Oceans of Law: The Komagata Garu and Jurisdiction in the Time of Empire*. Durham, NC: Duke University Press, 2018.

McLuhan, Marshall. *The Mechanical Bride: Folklore of Industrial Man*. New York: Vanguard Press, 1951.

Mercer, Kobena. *Discrepant Abstraction*. Cambridge, MA: MIT Press, 2006.

Michelson, Annette, ed. *Andy Warhol*. October Files 2. Cambridge, MA: MIT Press, 2001.

Mirowski, Philip. *Machine Dreams: Economics Becomes a Cyborg Science*. Cambridge: Cambridge University Press, 2002.

Mirzoeff, Nicholas. *The Visual Culture Reader*. 3rd ed. London: Routledge, 2013.

Mitchell, Timothy. "The World as Exhibition." *Comparative Studies in Society and History* 31, no. 2 (April 1989): 217–36.

Morgan, Lewis Henry. *Ancient Society: Or, Researches in the Lines of Human Progress from Savagery through Barbarism to Civilization*. New York: Henry Holt, 1877. Project Gutenberg, 2014, https://www.gutenberg.org/files/45950/45950-h/45950-h.htm.

Morris, Adam. "Drone Warfare: Tiqqun, the Young-Girl and the Imperialism of the Trivial." *Los Angeles Review of Books*, September 30, 2012.

Nesbit, Molly. "The Language of Industry." In The *Definitely Unfinished Marcel Duchamp*, edited by Thierry de Duve, 351–84. Cambridge, MA: MIT Press, 1992.

Nesbit, Molly. *Their Common Sense*. London: Black Dog, 2000.

Ngai, Sianne. "Visceral Abstractions." In *Theory of the Gimmick*, 174–95. Cambridge, MA: Belknap Press of Harvard University Press, 2020.

Nochlin, Linda. "Seurat's *La Grande Jatte*: An Anti-Utopian Allegory." In *The Politics of Vision: Essays on Nineteenth-Century Art and Society*, 170–93. New York: Harper and Row, 1989.

Palumbo-Mosca, Elena. "The Woman Who Painted Her Body for Artist Yves Klein." BBC Interview, October 21, 2016. https://www.bbc.com/news/entertainment-arts-37632356.

Panofsky, Erwin. *Perspective as Symbolic Form*. New York: Zone Books, 1997.

Paolucci, Paul. *Marx and the Politics of Abstraction*. Boston: Brill, 2011.

Perruchot, Henri. *La vie de Seurat*. Paris: Librarie Hachette, 1966.

Picabia, Francis. *I Am a Beautiful Monster: Poetry, Prose, Provocation*. Cambridge, MA: MIT Press, 2012.
Poggi, Christine. *Inventing Futurism: The Art and Politics of Artificial Optimism*. Princeton, NJ: Princeton University Press, 2009.
Pollock, Griselda. *The Expanding Discourse*. London: Routledge, 1992.
Pollock, Griselda. *Vision and Difference*. London: Routledge, 1998.
Postone, Moishe. *Time, Labor, and Social Domination*. Cambridge: Cambridge University Press, 1993.
Power, Nina. "She's Just Not That into You." *Radical Philosophy* 177 (January/February 2013). http://www.radicalphilosophy.com/web/rp177-shes-just-not-that-into-you.
Preziosi, Donald. *The Art of Art History: A Critical Anthology*. New York: Oxford University Press, 1998.
Rancière, Jacques. *The Politics of Aesthetics: The Distribution of the Sensible*. London: Continuum, 2005.
Read, Jason. *The Double Shift: Spinoza and Marx on the Politics of Work*. London: Verso, 2024.
Reines, Ariana. "Translator's Note." *Triple Canopy*, no. 15 (May 22, 2012). https://canopycanopycanopy.com/contents/preliminary_materials_for_a_theory_of_the_young_girl.
Rewald, John. *Seurat: A Biography*. New York: Abrams, 1990.
Roberts, John. *The Intangibilities of Form: Skill and Deskilling in Art after the Readymade*. London: Verso, 2007.
Rodenbeck, Judith. *Radical Prototypes: Allan Kaprow and the Invention of Happenings*. Cambridge, MA: MIT Press, 2014.
Roslak, Robyn. *Neo-Impressionism and Anarchism in Fin-de-Siècle France: Painting, Politics and Landscape*. London: Routledge, 2007.
Ross, Kristin. *Communal Luxury: The Political Imaginary of the Paris Commune*. London: Verso, 2015.
Ross, Kristin. *The Emergence of Social Space: Rimbaud and the Paris Commune*. London: Verso, 2008.
Rubin, Gayle. *The Traffic in Women: Notes on the Political Economy of Sex*. Durham, NC: Duke University Press, 2012.
Schapiro, Meyer. *Abstract Art*. London: Braziller, 1994.
Schapiro, Meyer. *Theory and Philosophy of Art: Style, Artist and Society*. New York: George Braziller, 1994.
Sekula, Allan. *The Contest of Meaning*. Cambridge, MA: MIT Press, 1992.
Shaikh, Anwar. *Capitalism: Competition, Conflict, Crisis*. Oxford: Oxford University Press, 2016.
Shaked, Nizan. *The Synthetic Proposition: Conceptualism and the Political Referent in Contemporary Art*. Manchester, UK: Manchester University Press, 2017.
Smith, Jason E. "Missed Encounters: *Critique de la séparation* between the Riot and the 'Young Girl.'" *Grey Room*, no. 52 (Summer 2013): 62–81.

Smith, Jason E. "Nowhere to Go: Automation Then and Now." *Third Rail*, April 2017.

Sohn-Rethel, Alfred. "Die Formcharaktere der zweiten Nature." In *Das Unvermögen der Realität: Beiträge zu einer anderen materialistischen Ästhetik*, edited by Christoph Bezzel, 185–207. Berlin: Klaus Wiesenbach, 1974.

Sohn-Rethel, Alfred. "The Formal Characteristics of Second Nature." Translated by Daniel Spaulding. *Selva*, July 20, 2019. https://selvajournal.org/the-formal-characteristics-of-second-nature/.

Sohn-Rethel, Alfred. *Intellectual and Manual Labour: A Critique of Epistemology*. London: Macmillan, 1978.

Spaulding, Daniel. "Value-Form and Avant-Garde." *Mute*, March 27, 2014. http://www.metamute.org/editorial/articles/value-form-and-avant-garde.

Spiegler, Marc. "When Human Beings Are the Canvas." *Art News*, June 2003.

Steiner, Henriette, and Kristin Veel, eds. *Invisibility Studies: Surveillance, Transparency and the Hidden in Contemporary Culture*. Bern: Peter Lang, 2015.

Steyerl, Hito. *Duty Free Art: Art in the Age of Planetary Civil War*. London: Verso, 2017.

Stiegler, Bernard. *For a New Critique of Political Economy*. Translated by Daniel Ross. Cambridge, UK: Polity, 2010.

Stitch, Sidra. *Yves Klein*. Stuttgart: Cantz Verlag, 1994.

Thompson, Nato. *Living as Form: Socially Engaged Art from 1991–2011*. Cambridge, MA: MIT Press, 2017.

Tiqqun. *The Cybernetic Hypothesis*. Cambridge, MA: MIT Press, 2020.

Tiqqun. *Preliminary Materials for a Theory of the Young-Girl*. Translated by Ariana Reines. Los Angeles: Semiotext(e), 2012.

Tomšič, Samo. *The Capitalist Unconscious: Marx and Lacan*. London: Verso, 2015.

Toscano, Alberto. "Chronicles of Insurrection: Tronti, Negri, and the Subject of Antagonism." *Cosmos and History: A Journal of Natural and Social Philosophy* 5, no. 1 (January 2009): 76–91.

Toscano, Alberto. "The Open Secret of Real Abstraction." *Rethinking Marxism* 20, no. 2 (April 2008): 273–87.

Toscano, Alberto. "The Sensuous Religion of the Multitude: Art and Abstraction in Negri." *Third Text* 23, no. 4 (July 2009): 369–82.

Toscano, Alberto, and Jeff Kinkle. *Cartographies of the Absolute*. London: Zero Books, 2015.

Tronti, Mario. "Factory and Society." In *Workers and Capital*, translated by David Broder, 12–35. London: Verso, 2019.

Ungersman Halprin, Joan. *Félix Fénéon: Aesthete and Anarchist in Fin-de-Siècle Paris*. New Haven, CT: Yale University Press, 1988.

Vishmidt, Marina. "Human Capital or Toxic Asset: After the Wage." *Mute*, January 10, 2010. http://www.metamute.org/community/your-posts/human-capital-or-toxic-asset-after-wage.

Vishmidt, Marina. *Speculation as a Mode of Production in Art and Capital*. Chicago: Haymarket Books, 2018.

Vishmidt, Marina. "What Do We Mean by Autonomy and Reproduction?" In *Reproducing Autonomy*, edited by Marina Vishmidt and Kerstin Stakemeier, 33–51. London: Mute Publishing, 2016.

Vishmidt, Marina, and Zoe Sutherland. "(Un)making Value: Reading Social Reproduction through the Question of Totality." In *Totality Inside Out: Rethinking Crisis and Conflict under Capital*, edited by Kevin Floyd, Jen Hedler Phillis, and Sarika Chandra, 67–90. New York: Fordham University Press, 2022.

Wilson, Siona. *Art Labor, Sex Politics: Feminist Effects in 1970s British Art and Performance*. Minneapolis: University of Minnesota Press, 2015.

Wright, Alastair. "On the Origins of Abstraction: Seurat and the Screening of History." *Art History*, February 2018, 72–104.

Wynter, Sylvia. "Beyond the Categories of the Master Conception: The Counter-doctrine of Jamesian Poeisis." In *C. L. R. James's Caribbean*, edited by Paget Henry and Paul Buhl, 63–91. Durham, NC: Duke University Press, 1992.

Zimmer, Daniel. "Earl Moran." *Illustration*, August 2018, 11.

Žižek, Slavoj. *The Sublime Object of Ideology*. London: Verso, 1989.

INDEX

Page numbers followed by *f* refer to figures.